Analogy as Structure and Process

HUMAN COGNITIVE PROCESSING is a forum for interdisciplinary research on the nature and organization of the cognitive systems and processes involved in speaking and understanding natural language (including sign language), and their relationship to other domains of human cognition, including general conceptual or knowledge systems and processes (the language and thought issue), and other perceptual or behavioral systems such as vision and non-verbal behavior (e.g. gesture). 'Cognition' should be taken broadly, not only including the domain of rationality, but also dimensions such as emotion and the unconscious. The series is open to any type of approach to the above questions (methodologically and theoretically) and to research from any discipline, including (but not restricted to) different branches of psychology, artificial intelligence and computer science, cognitive anthropology, linguistics, philosophy and neuroscience. It takes a special interest in research crossing the boundaries of these disciplines.

Editors

Marcelo Dascal, *Tel Aviv University*
Raymond W. Gibbs, *University of California at Santa Cruz*
Jan Nuyts, *University of Antwerp*

Editorial address
Jan Nuyts, University of Antwerp, Dept. of Linguistics (GER),
Universiteitsplein 1, B 2610 Wilrijk, Belgium.
E-mail: jan.nuyts@ua.ac.be

Editorial Advisory Board

Melissa Bowerman, *Nijmegen*; Wallace Chafe, *Santa Barbara, CA*;
Philip R. Cohen, *Portland, OR*; Antonio Damasio, *Iowa City, IA*;
Morton Ann Gernsbacher, *Madison, WI*; David McNeill, *Chicago, IL*;
Eric Pederson, *Eugene, OR*; François Recanati, *Paris*;
Sally Rice, *Edmonton, Alberta*; Benny Shanon, *Jerusalem*;
Lokendra Shastri, *Berkeley, CA*; Dan Slobin, *Berkeley, CA*;
Paul Thagard, *Waterloo, Ontario*

Volume 14

Analogy as Structure and Process: Approaches in linguistics, cognitive psychology and philosophy of science
by Esa Itkonen

Analogy as Structure and Process

Approaches in linguistics, cognitive psychology
and philosophy of science

Esa Itkonen

University of Turku

John Benjamins Publishing Company

Amsterdam / Philadelphia

Library of Congress Cataloging-in-Publication Data

Itkonen, Esa.
    Analogy as structure and process : approaches in linguistics, cognitive
        psychology and philosophy of science / Esa Itkonen.
        p.   cm. (Human Cognitive Processing, ISSN 1387–6724 ; v. 14)
    Includes bibliographical references and index.
        1. Analogy. 2. Linguistics. 3. Iconicity (Linguistics). I. Title. II.
    Series.

    P299.A48I86 2005
    410--dc22   2005049337
    ISBN 90 272 2366 1 (Hb; alk. paper)

John Benjamins Publishing Co. · P.O. Box 36224 · 1020 ME Amsterdam · The Netherlands
John Benjamins North America · P.O. Box 27519 · Philadelphia PA 19118-0519 · USA

Man kann es als einen festen Grundsatz annehmen, dass alles in einer Sprache auf Analogie beruht... (Wilhelm von Humboldt, in 1812)

Everything in language goes by analogy. (William Dwight Whitney, in 1875)

The idea that things can be ... different but the same is prerequisite to science. (Dwight Bolinger, in 1975)

Analogy-making lies at the heart of intelligence. (Douglas Hofstadter, in 1995)

Table of contents

Preface

Analogy was the mainstay of traditional linguistics. In their diachronic work, such leading representatives of Finno-Ugric linguistics as Paavo Ravila and Erkki Itkonen constantly relied on the use of analogy. Terho Itkonen, the quintessential scholar of the Finnish language, made use of and explicated analogy both in his synchronic and in his diachronic work. Thus, when analogy fell into disrepute in theoretical linguistics during the last decades of the 20th century, I knew that it was a mistake. During those dark years, Raimo Anttila was the foremost proponent of analogy in linguistics. This book is dedicated to him.

Analogy is a rich topic. Between 1990 and 2002 I have given talks on various aspects of analogy in, inter alia, Prague, Los Angeles, Turku, Sofia, Québec, Iowa City, Minneapolis, Poznan, Cologne, Paris, Budapest, Durham, Gothenburg, Berlin, Stockholm, Copenhagen, Lund, and Odense. On most occasions, there has been significant response from the audience, and I have done my best to retain it in memory.

Sections 1 and 2 of the Appendix were written by Jussi Haukioja, who also made valuable comments on the very first draft of this book. Animated discussions with Anneli Pajunen, Chris Sinha, and Jordan Zlatev have kept my interest in cognitive-linguistic questions alive. I am indebted to two anonymous referees for their thorough comments on the manuscript of this book.

Introduction

In today's cognitive science analogy has been and continues to be an object of intensive research. Until recently, the situation has been dissimilar in linguistics, due to historical circumstances that will be explored in Chapter 2. It is the purpose of this book to redress the balance.

I am convinced that analogy plays a central role in human thinking. In trying to justify my conviction, I immediately face the following problem:

> [Linguists] have not been trained as psychologists, nor do they use the experimental techniques that psycholinguists have for addressing their research problems. Given this profile, are they able to say anything interesting at all (that is, beyond speculation) about the language user's mind, or is this the province of psycholinguists? (Sandra 1998:362)

My response is to collect as much evidence as I can from a linguist's point of view and to build as plausible a case as I can both for the psychological and for the cultural reality of analogy. There surely needs to be some such thing as scientific division of labor. Thus I hope that those questions which it is not within my professional competence to answer have been or will be answered by psychologists and neurologists.

In this book analogy is treated both as structure and as process. In keeping e.g. with Miller and Johnson-Laird (1976), Sandra (1998) assumes that linguists are forced to restrict their attention to (some aspects of) structure: "As far as language processing is concerned, linguists have nothing to say" (p. 364). This notion of 'language processing' strikes me as unnecessarily narrow. Cognitive linguists routinely discuss a host of accessible-to-introspection processes (like schematization or apparent motion); and while dealing e.g. with the process of grammaticalization, diachronic linguists postulate as a matter of course such cognitive subprocesses as reanalysis and (analogical) extension. Similar remarks apply even to sentence processing proper:

> Mainstream language psychology often does not take all aspects of the dynamic nature of language use seriously... But already in the realm of syntactic structure there must be considerable room for intelligent and interactive pro-

cessing... Likewise, processing must be flexibly adaptable and adjustable...
(Nuyts 2001:19)

As a consequence, I have no inhibitions against using the notion of analogy-as-process; and this process aspect will become fully explicit in the Appendix.

In brief, analogy will be treated here as a psychologically real phenomenon which has causal efficacy both in language and in culture. It is possible, however, to use analogy merely as a descriptive device, i.e. as a means to achieve a parsimonious description of some set of data. This use of analogy has its own justification, but it is not my primary concern in this book. This phenomenon is thoroughly familiar. A description may be just a way to present the data or it may, in addition, be proposed as an hypothesis about the causal mechanism that brings the data about.

In the context of the Special Theory of Relativity, these alternative interpretations, i.e. non-causal and causal, may be illustrated as they apply to *physical reality*, in the following way:

> [S]pace and time are relatively different in moving and stationary systems, and ... both can be linked by the Lorentz transformations.   (Clark 1973:121)

> For [Einstein's] predecessors, the Lorenz transformation was merely a useful tool for linking objects in relative motion; for Einstein it was not a mathematical tool so much as a revelation about the nature itself.   (Clark 1973:120)

The distinction between non-causal and causal interpretations, as applied to *biological reality*, has been illustrated by Darwin (1998 [1859]:312–313), as follows:

> Some authors look at [the Natural System] merely as a scheme for arranging together those living objects which are most alike and for separating those which are most unlike; or as an artificial means for enunciating, as briefly as possible, general propositions ... But many naturalists think that something more is meant by the Natural System; ... I believe that something more is included; and that the propinquity of descent – the only known *cause* of the similarity of organic beings – is the bond, hidden as it is by various degrees of modification, which is partially revealed to us by our classification.
>
> (emphasis added)

The continuum from non-causal to causal interpretation, as applied to *psychological reality*, is described by Levinson (2003:177–178), as follows:

> On one interpretation, [the relative-to-absolute gradient] is simply an analytical convenience, a way of finding a common measure across tasks, populations and coding strategies. But a *more* psychological interpretation may also be in

order. One possible view would be that it represents a psychological possibility space. ... An even *stronger* psychological interpretation would be ... that both absolute and relative frames of reference are incipiently available to all subjects. (emphasis added)

For my part, I choose a strong psychological interpretation for my own examples of analogy, given e.g. in Chapter 2 (but I will mention in passing also less convincing examples of the use of analogy).

My view of language is traditional in the sense of being 'rule-based', and I treat analogy within the corresponding framework. Also the PROLOG program given in the Appendix makes use of traditional grammatical categories. A compatible but much more elaborate formalization of analogy has been given by Lepage (2003).

Over the years, Royal Skousen, e.g. in (1989), has developed a concept of linguistic analogy which, instead of being based on rules or types, is directly based on linguistic tokens; see also Skousen et al. (2002). Lavie's (2003) formalization of analogy, resulting from independent work, is to some extent similar to Skousen's. The difference between the two frameworks, i.e. rule-based vs. exemplar-based, seems fundamental, but I refrain from making any further comments on it because I am not competent to judge the technicalities of Skousen's or Lavie's model. On two or three occasions I will have reason to mention connectionism (which has clear affinities with the exemplar-based approach), but – again – I forebear to make any wide-ranging comparisons, in order not to overstep the boundaries of my competence.

Chapter 1

The concept of analogy

1.1 Analogy = Structural~functional similarity

Analogy is generally defined as 'structural similarity'. At the level of maximum generality, an analogical relationship obtains between two or more 'wholes' or 'systems' each of which has the same number of 'parts'. The relation holding between the parts of a system is that of *contiguity* (or proximity), understood in a sense wide enough to cover both physical and non-physical cases. Thus, a system is a relation of contiguity exemplified by the parts. (Of course, the common label of 'contiguity' hides huge differences between different types of systems.) The (analogical) relation holding between the systems is that of *similarity*. Because systems are relations exemplified by their parts, it follows that analogy is a *meta*relation, i.e. a relation holding between relations. In analogy, therefore, similarity is more abstract than, because building upon, contiguity. This is precisely why we speak of *structural* (rather than material) similarity. Hesse (1963:68) provides the example reproduced in Figure 1.1. The functions served by the different parts (which are left implicit by Hesse) have been added.

The hierarchical relations involved are made even more evident with the aid of a tree diagram: analogy is a two-place relation (= Sim[ilarity]) between three-place relations (= B[ird] and F[ish]); see Figure 1.2

An alternative, and typographically simpler, formulation is as follows: 'wings : lungs : feathers = fins : gills : scales'. Now, what is similar, is the *relation* between the parts of these systems. The parts themselves, e.g. feathers and scales, need not be – and are not – (materially) similar.

The relation between the parts is based on their respective *functions*; as shown by Figures 1.1–2, the functions of wings, lungs, and feathers are the same as, or similar to, those of fins, gills, and scales, respectively. It turns out that, in this particular context, the terms 'structural' and 'functional' are used nearly synonymously. 'Structural similarity' has established itself as the definition of analogy; but we have just seen that what is at issue is *functional* similarity just as well. This apparent discrepancy may be explained by recalling the general truth

	Similarity			Function
Contiguity	BIRD	FISH		
	wings	fins	→	locomotion
	lungs	gills	→	getting oxygen
	feathers	scales	→	protection

Figure 1.1 Prototypical analogy

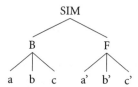

Figure 1.2 Analogy as a tree diagram

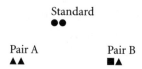

Figure 1.3 Formal analogy

that structure is based upon, or determined by, function.[1] This also explains, incidentally, why it is nearly impossible in practice to keep 'structuralism' and 'functionalism' apart.

On the other hand, it is clear that, for two systems to be analogous, it is not enough that they share a common overarching function. For instance, a man can be killed either by being hit on the head with a rock or by being put on an electric chair. But this does not mean that a rock and an electric chair are analogous 'systems'; and the reason is, simply, that their respective structures are not divisible into the same number of parts, determined by corresponding subfunctions. To be sure, it is possible to *imagine* that a rock has somehow a structure similar to the structure of an electric chair. But this would be a baseless, and therefore *bad*, analogy. And the reason would be, of course, that the function of being used as a lethal instrument is in no way inherent to a rock.

The type of structural~functional analogy represented by Figure 1.1 will be considered *prototypical* in this book. Yet, analogy is not a totally uniform notion. Consider the example given by Holyoak et al. (2001:2–3) and reproduced here in Figure 1.3.

$$\frac{10}{5} = \frac{6}{3}$$

Figure 1.4 Mathematical analogy

> The sameness that connects the standard and pair A ... does not reside in the physical forms. ... Rather, it resides in the identity of the *relation* between the two circles and the *relation* between the two triangles – 'sameness of shape', a shared relational pattern. (ibid.)[2]

This definition of analogy agrees, thus far, with what has been said above. Notice, however, that Figure 1.3 differs from Figure 1.1 insofar as geometrical shape, as such, has no function. Therefore it is advisable to assume a *continuum* that leads from structural-cum-functional analogy to purely structural (or formal) analogy, its two end-points being represented by Figures 1.1 and 1.3, respectively. For the purposes of this book, to repeat, Figure 1.1 will be taken to represent the prototypical case.

The best known example of an analogy is a mathematical equation, like the one in Figure 1.4. This equation reduces to the identity '2 = 2'. Now, examples like this have given rise to a view according to which an analogy is a *binary* and *reversible* relation that holds between two (nearly) identical entities. This notion of analogy is somewhat misleading. A typical analogy is a similarity between relations, not between entities. Therefore the above example remains a (mathematical) analogy even if we interpret the line that separates the two numbers not as a division but as an addition, namely adding together a number and its half. On this interpretation, it is still the case that the relation between the pairs of numbers is identical, but the results of the operation symbolized by the line are of course different. (Thus, this proportion is no longer an equation.) The overall relation between the two 'systems' of numbers remains analogical if we, next, add any operations to the previous one, as long as we add the same operations on both sides of the identity sign. This dispels the idea (dispelled in fact already by our 'Bird = Fish' example) that analogies have to be binary. The reversibility requirement will be examined and rejected in Sections 1.3–4.

There is a long tradition of applying the notion of analogy to *language*. According to Sapir (1921:37), new words and sentences "are being constantly created ... on the analogy of old ones", i.e. "on strictly traditional lines". He exemplifies this idea with two sentences which "fit precisely the same pattern", "differing only in their material trappings". In this case there are no specific names (like 'bird' or 'fish') for the systems, but these are made to refer to

	Similarity	
Contiguity	'The farmer kills the duckling'	'The man takes the chick'
	the farmer	the man
	kills	takes
	the duckling	the chick

Figure 1.5 Sapir's analogy

themselves (which is like replacing 'bird' by 'wings & lungs & feathers'); see Figure 1.5.

The pattern in question is *SVO*. Thus, sentences exemplifying the same pattern or construction are *analogous* to one another. Is the analogy of Figure 1.5 (meta-)analogous to the functional analogy of Figure 1.1 or to the merely-formal analogy of Figure 1.3? As might be expected, the answer to this question depends on one's overall view of language. In conformity with my own functionalist leanings, I espouse the former alternative. That is, I take the structure *SVO*, exemplified by *the farmer kills the duckling*, to have the function of expressing the content 'Agent – Action – Patient', and, in turn, I take this function to have shaped the structure *SVO*.

Just like Sapir (1921), Jespersen (1924:19) claims that the following sentences are "analogous" or "made after the same pattern": *John gave Mary an apple* and *My uncle lent the joiner five shillings*. The pattern in question is the ditransitive construction *S-V-O1-O2*. That there are indeed analogies between Sapir's as well as Jespersen's twin sentences, cannot be denied. Notice, however, that the constructions which underlie these analogies may be understood and represented in more than one way, depending on the descriptive framework that one adopts. Thus, the mere existence of analogy does not dictate how the analogous entities should be described. It might be said that in this respect analogy is *theory-neutral*.

The same notion of analogy was upheld already by de Saussure (1962 [1916]:221, 227):

> L'analogie suppose un modèle et son imitation regulière. Une forme analogique est une forme faite à l'image d'une or plusieurs autres d'après une règle déterminée. ... Toute création doit être précédée d'une comparaison inconsciente des matériaux déposés dans le trésor de la langue où les formes génératrices sont rangées selon leurs rapports syntagmatiques et associatifs [= paradigmatiques].

Of course, de Saussure had in his turn been anticipated by Paul (1975 [1880]), among many others (cf. 2.4).

Today, the notion of sentence pattern or construction is central in 'construction grammar' (cf. 2.5, C). The usefulness of this notion has been rediscovered in generativism too:

> The way the brain seems to achieve expressive variety is to store not whole sentences, but rather words and their meanings, plus *patterns* into which words can be placed ... That is, 'making sense' involves, among other things, conformity to known patterns.   (Jackendoff 1994: 12, 15)

SVO and *S-V-O1-O2* are very simple examples of a pattern or construction which (or particular instantiations of which) may serve as an (analogical) model for producing new sentences. It is also possible, however, to postulate 'constructions' of a more theoretical (and, eventually, questionable) nature. Consider the 'performative hypothesis', originally formulated by Apollonius Dyscolus in the 2nd century A.D. (cf. Itkonen 1991: 207–208). The following sentences seem dissimilar at first: *grapheis* ('you are writing'), *graphoiēs* ('may you write'), *graphe* ('write!'). However, they turn out to be structurally similar or analogous, once it is assumed that they have been derived by transformation (*metalēpsis*) from the following sentences which are structurally similar insofar as they all begin with a performative verb in the first person singular: *horizomai se graphein* ('I declare you to be writing'), *eukhomai se graphein* ('I wish for you to write'), *graphein se prostassō* ('I order you to write'). This example shows, in an anticipatory fashion, that the search for analogy is identical with the search for ('significant') *generalizations* (cf. 1.4).

The preceding examples illustrate the sense in which the notion of analogical *model* is systematically ambiguous. In its abstract sense, it may mean the structure exemplified by particular systems (e.g. the ditransitive construction *S-V-O1-O2* exemplified by Jespersen's two sentences). In its concrete sense, it may mean a particular system qua exemplification of a given structure (e.g. the sentence *John gave Mary an apple* qua exemplification of the *S-V-O1-O2* construction). I shall consider these two formulations as equivalent. They are in fact conflated e.g. in Bloomfield's (1933: 275) notion of analogy:

> A grammatical pattern (sentence-type, construction, or substitution) is often called an *analogy*. A regular analogy permits a speaker to utter speech-forms which he has not heard; we say that he utters them *on the analogy of* similar forms which he has heard.

Logically enough, Bloomfield defines 'irregular analogy' as a model with (very) few exemplifications. In quite the same way de Saussure noted, in the quotation given above, that the analogical model may be either one form or (the structure common to) several forms ("une forme faite à l'image d'*une* or *plusieurs*

Oral languages		Sign languages		Function
Noun		Nominal		Thing(-representation)
Verb	$=$	Verbal	$\rightarrow$	Action(-representation)

Figure 1.6 Analogical word-class division in sign languages and oral languages

NEG	nicht	ne-pas			-i	-nngil-	om ka
1SG: AG	ich	je	en	si-		ta-
						-ara	
3SG&N: PAT	es	le	sitä	-ki-		-in
'see'	sehe	vois	näe	-on(a)	taku-	kerek

Figure 1.7 Crosslinguistic analogy

autres"). – Notice that 'analogical model' is really a pleonasm because there can be no (structured) model which, qua model, would not be analogical.

Up to now, I have given run-of-the-mill examples of analogy. But they are just the point of departure. I intend to show – in the spirit of Humboldt's 1812 and Whitney's 1875 dictum – that analogy is *the* central concept of language and linguistics. To do so, I must now offer more imaginative examples. In doing so, I have to anticipate some points that will be discussed much more fully in the later chapters.

First, the mere fact that we speak of oral and sign *languages* shows that there is an analogy between the two types of systems of communication (cf. 2.8). The short and simple way to prove this is to show that the basic word classes serve identical functions in the auditory medium and in the visual medium. (In the present context I follow the custom of using the terms 'nominal' and 'verbal' in connection with sign languages.) Consider Figure 1.6.

Second, linguistic *typology* and universals research are based on cross-linguistic analogy. The same is true eo ipso of the possibility to *translate* from one language to another. This can be shown quite concretely by exhibiting (in Figure 1.7) the similarity between structures that serve the *common function* of expressing the meaning 'I do not see it' in German, French, Finnish, Swahili, West Greenlandic, and Wari'. The corresponding sentences are as follows: *ich sehe es nicht, je ne le vois pas, en näe sitä, sikioni, takunngilara, om ka kerek tain.* It is essential to grasp the (meta-)analogy between Figure 1.7 and Figure 1.1. It is advisable to give first the subfunctions, or the meanings-to-be-expressed.

Of course, this description cannot do justice to every detail. In particular, there is a great number of interdependencies (similar to 'discontinuous morphs') that remain unaccounted-for. For instance, there is an interdepen-

$$\frac{\text{Noun}}{\text{Verb}} = \frac{\text{Thing}}{\text{Action}}$$

Figure 1.8 Iconic analogy

dency between NEG and 'see' in *en näe* and *si-...-oni* (the corresponding affirmative forms being *näen* and *ninakiona*). At the same time, *en*, just like *si-*, is a portmanteau morph expressing both NEG and 1SG:AG, while *-ara* is a portmanteau morph expressing 1SG:AG and 3SG:PAT. There is also an interdependence between *en* and *sitä* insofar as, in Finnish, the object of a negated verb must be in the partitive case (whereas the corresponding affirmative expression is *näen sen*, with the object in the accusative case). In Wari', the marker for negation is really *om*, and *ka* is one of the five tense/mood clitics that obligatorily follow an 'operator word' like *om*. Moreover, 'see' is for simplicity interpreted here as an action (as shown by the AG vs. PAT distinction), and the tense, the mood, and the voice of the verb as well as the word order are left unaccounted-for. Nevertheless, the main point should have become clear: There is no way that we can study several languages simultaneously, unless we consider them as analogous to one another; and Figure 1.7 shows, in a preliminary fashion, how this is done. Notice also that the facts summed up by Figure 1.7 are *theory-neutral* in the sense that any typological description, regardless of its more specific formalization, has to accommodate them.

Third, the notion of *iconicity* between language and reality is identical with analogy, for the simple reason that iconicity is explicitly *defined* as 'structural similarity', which is also the definition of analogy (cf. Itkonen 1994). Therefore, it is enough to highlight part of Figure 1.6. There can be no doubt that the relation between noun and verb is similar to the relation between thing and action, which means that Figure 1.8 exemplifies the concept of analogy. (Incidentally, this analogy played a fundamental role in medieval linguistics; cf. Itkonen 1991:232–237.)

Fourth, it is natural to add that iconicity between language and reality is a special case of *analog* or *non-digital* representation. This type of representation is characteristic of so-called *mental models* in particular:

> a mental model does not have an arbitrarily chosen syntactic structure, but one that plays a direct representational role since it is analogous to the structure of the corresponding state of affairs in the world – as we perceive or conceive it.   (Johnson-Laird 1983:156)

Dennett (1991:147–149) has emphasized that the brain does not have to use the analog mode of representation. But this is just the point. It is only the more interesting to note that, as the existence of iconicity shows, language does make use of this mode of representation although there is no need for it to do so.

Fifth, it may take some mental effort to realize that the very concept of *structure*, as it applies within a single language, is based on analogy. This is illustrated e.g. by the structure of nouns or verbs in *any* language, inflectional or not. Consider the verbal inflection in Latin: *am-o* ('I love'), *ama-s* ('you-SG love'), *ama-t* ('he/she loves'), etc. Why are the grammatical meanings uniformly expressed by suffixes? Why is there not a suffixal ~ prefixal ~ infixal variation like e.g. *am-o, s-ama, a-t-ma*? This question may sound silly, but it has to be answered; and the answer is, of course, analogy: a variation like *am-o, s-ama, a-t-ma* does not exist because these units are not analogous to one another, unlike the units *am-o, ama-s, ama-t*. However, the apparent silliness of the preceding question is very significant, because it shows that analogy pervades language to such an extent that it is difficult for us to imagine a language not governed by analogy. Analogous remarks apply to a verbal paradigm in a prefixal language like Swahili: *ni-na-penda* ('I love'), *u-na-penda* ('you-SG love'), *a-na-penda* ('he/she loves'); and they also apply to a verbal paradigm in an isolating language like Yoruba: *mo fẹ́* ('I love'), *o fẹ́* ('you-SG love'), *ó fẹ́* ('he/she loves').

Of course, there are cases which contradict the general claim made in the preceding paragraph, i.e. cases of suffixal/prefixal/infixal variation within paradigms of a single language. In this respect, the structure of the Athapaskan verb is notoriously difficult (cf. Rice 2000: Ch. 2). But this forces us to specify, rather than to reject, the general claim. A genuine counter-example would be a language with a totally random formal variation or with *no* structure at all; and there certainly is no such language.

Now, we have to distinguish between different analogical levels, for instance the analogy holding between units of a single paradigm in a single language like Latin (or Swahili, or Yoruba), as opposed to the analogy holding between paradigms in different languages (as exhibited in Figure 1.7). In the former case we emphasize the *structural* aspect of the structural ~ functional similarity: in general, the members of a paradigm conform to the same type of structure (e.g. suffixal vs. prefixal). In the latter case we emphasize the *functional* aspect of the structural ~ functional similarity: both the suffixal and the prefixal means to express e.g. 1SG:AG are analogous insofar as they serve the same function. In a sense, we are moving back and forth on the functional vs. formal continuum illustrated by Figures 1.1 and 1.3. Notice, however, that

$$\frac{\text{thing-1 ('cup')}}{\text{ki-kombe}} = \frac{\text{thing-2 ('book')}}{\text{kitab-}\mathbf{u}} \rightarrow \frac{\text{thing-1 ('cup')}}{\text{ki-kombe}} = \frac{\text{thing-2 ('book')}}{\text{ki-tabu}}$$

Figure 1.9 Analogical reanalysis

the functional aspect overrides the formal one, as shown by those cases (e.g. suppletion) where the two come into conflict. We do not hesitate to set up an analogy like *I walk : I walked = I go : I went*, although it lacks formal support; and, of course, there will be pressures to bring the formal aspect of this analogy in line with its functional aspect, i.e. to replace *I went* by *I goed*.

This issue is so important that it may be good to stop for a moment and to justify the use of the same term 'analogy' in these two apparently dissimilar (= language-particular vs. cross-linguistic) cases. Consider again our prototypical analogy (Figure 1.1). Taken out of context, the scale of a fish and the feather of a bird have nothing whatever in common. It is only in the larger functional context that they can be seen as analogous. Now, I submit that exactly the same thing applies to the units *nicht, ne – pas, en, si – i, -nngil-, om ka* as expressions of negation (and, occasionally, of 1SG:AG). Moreover, it would be odd to deny that there is an analogy between typologically dissimilar (e.g. suffixal vs. pre-fixal) oral languages, given that there is no way to deny the analogy between such 'typologically' much more dissimilar languages as oral vs. sign languages (cf. Figure 1.6). Thus, the notion of cross-linguistic analogy is not in doubt.

Nor can the notion of language-particular analogy be in doubt. This point has already been established, of course (cf. Figure 1.5 and its sequel), but here I wish to give an additional example that concerns the structural type of a given language. Consider what happens when a suffixal word like the Arabic *kitab-u* ('book & Nominative') is borrowed into a prefixal language like Swahili. Here the analogical (prefixal) model is represented by a word like *ki-kombe* ('cup').

It is impossible to deny the analogical nature of this process: the word *kitab-u* is reanalyzed as *ki-tabu* on the analogy of words like *ki-kombe*; and the reanalysis becomes explicit once the plural form *vi-tabu* ('books') is formed on the analogy of plural forms like *vi-kombe* ('cups'). – The concept of (linguistic) structure is so fundamental that its analogical nature can only be explained by regarding it as "one manifestation of the *innate* faculty of analogizing" (Anttila 1989 [1972]: 103; emphasis added).

Sixth, the role of analogy in *linguistic theory* has to be mentioned. Of course, there is no hard-and-fast distinction between data and theory. Still, establishing 'clear cases' and deciding whether a certain problematical or less-than-clear case is analogous to this clear case or to that one, is a typically theoretical undertaking (cf. 2.5). The clear-case method was applied above, for instance, in establishing the analogy between Figure 1.1 (= the clear case) and Figure 1.7 (= the less-than-clear case). Sometimes the explanatory function of analogy has been denied, on the grounds that there are also 'false' analogies. It is difficult to understand how it is possible that such a claim has been seriously put forward, and that it has even found acceptance. It criticizes analogy for not being a discovery procedure for generating scientific truths. But, of course, there can be no such discovery procedure. (Notice that each and every scientific method could be 'criticized' for the same 'defect'.)

Seventh, and for the sake of completeness, the role of analogy in explaining linguistic *change* has to be mentioned in this context, even if this use of analogy is quite traditional. In general, the result of an analogical change agrees with the principle of 'one meaning – one form', or the 1M1F principle for short (cf. 2.7). Amazingly, the significance of analogical explanations has occasionally been denied, on the grounds that they are not able to *predict* the occurrence of particular linguistic changes. This is an odd criticism (and similar to the one discussed in the previous paragraph). Linguistic changes are – and are known to be – unpredictable. Therefore it is not a weakness, but a strength, of analogical accounts that they refuse to give (exact) predictions.

Eighth, in addition to language-particular and cross-linguistic analogies, there are also analogies between language and other *cognitive domains* (like visual perception, music, and logic) (cf. Chapter 3). The existence of such analogies provides important information about the 'architecture' of the mind. Notice that their existence is independent of eventual neurological confirmation or disconfirmation. To give a rough analogy, the relative similarity between German and Dutch (and the relative difference between German and Chinese) neither needs neurological confirmation nor can be refuted by apparently disconfirmatory neurological facts.

Ninth, analogy is the cornerstone of the *Weltanschauung* of each and every culture. In this context, analogy may be manifested either as a string of binary (or ternary etc.) oppositions or as an isomorphism between microcosmos (= 'man') and macrocosmos (= 'universe') or as a combination of the two. Strings of binary oppositions may be seen as (analogical) generalizations from such fundamental oppositions as 'man vs. woman' or 'day vs. night'. Strings of quaternary oppositions may be based, ultimately, on the (four) elements or cardinal points. As a particularly interesting case, it may be mentioned that, in one culture, the entire universe has been conceptualized as a string of quinary oppositions based on the phases of a prototypical love relationship (cf. 4.2).

Tenth, analogy is the driving force behind *scientific discovery*. As Willliam James put it, "geniuses are, by common consent, considered to differ from ordinary minds by an unusual development of association by similarity [elsewhere: analogy]". Thus, I cannot agree with the view of Holyoak et al. (2001:6) that "the development of large-scale theories based on analogy is a relatively rare event in science". As far as I can see, all – or nearly all – great discoveries in the history of philosophy and science are based on analogy. This claim will be supported at least by the following names: Pythagoras, Plato, Aristotle, Occam, Kepler, Descartes, Newton, Spinoza, Hobbes, Hume, Kant, Hegel, Darwin, Turing, Shannon (cf. 4.3); and others could easily be added.

In addition to pointing out the general fact that the same notion of analogy obtains e.g. in zoology, mathematics, and linguistics (cf. Figures 1.1, 1.4, 1.5), I have now enumerated ten more particular domains where the notion of analogy applies. In so doing I have made a large-scale *generalization* concerning analogies. This generalization constitutes in itself a very high-level analogy, or meta-meta- ... -meta-analogy. This serves as a first indication of the fact, to be elaborated below, that there are no a priori limits to the complexity that analogy may assume.

The notion of similarity plays a central role also in associationism and in Gestalt psychology. In these two contexts, however, similarity is an *alternative* to contiguity. In associationism, a phenomenon A calls to mind another phenomenon B, either because A and B have been contiguous, i.e. have been experienced together, or because A and B are similar (or, as it happens, because they are opposite) to each other. In Gestalt psychology, the units A, B, and C (as distinguished from some other units D, E, and F) constitute a whole either because they are contiguous or because they are similar. In these two cases, therefore, contiguity and similarity are situated 'at the same level'.

We have already seen that in analogy, by contrast, similarity is more abstract than contiguity. This can be demonstrated by constructing 'systems' whose parts are tied together not by contiguity but by concrete similarity, i.e. similarity in the sense of either associationism or Gestalt psychology. It can be maintained, for instance, that the relation (of similarity) between warm and hot is *analogous* to the relation (of similarity) between pink and red, i.e. 'warm : hot = pink : red'. Thus, contiguity is not the only relation holding between the parts of a system, although it is the most important one. To be sure, one might try to uphold the standard, contiguity-based interpretation of analogy, by claiming that warm and hot, on the one hand, and pink and red, on the other, are 'contiguous' qualities in their respective sensory domains. This ploy would not be of much use, however, because – as indicated by the quotes – this would be a *metaphor* and, thus, still a relation of similarity (cf. 1.6).

Associationism is closely connected to the concept of *induction*. As will be seen in Section 1.5, induction and analogy are dissimilar insofar as they deal, respectively, with material similarity and structural similarity. To put it roughly, while analogy compares a bird and a fish, induction compares two birds.

Analogy may be understood in the *static* sense, namely as a relation holding either between basic-level relations (which in turn hold between 'things') or between higher-level relations. Static analogy is the 'centripetal' force which keeps knowledge systems together. A knowledge system can endure in time only because its elements mutually influence or reinforce one another. This is the basic insight of structuralism, but it is also the insight that underlies Paul's (1975 [1880]) view of analogy as the force which keeps 'groups of ideas' (*Vorstellungs-gruppen*) together. (Today, connectionism has formalized Paul's basic insight.) But analogy may also be understood in the *dynamic* sense, namely as a process, or 'inference', by means of which analogy of the static type is established. The best known (even if overly restrictive) example is again the binary proportional analogy, as exemplified by an arithmetic equation: solving '10 : 5 = 6 : X' produces '10 : 5 = 6 : 3'. – The dynamic aspect of analogy will be discussed in greater detail in connection with the concept of *inference* (cf. 1.5).

It is my purpose in this book to authenticate the usefulness of analogy as a methodological tool of contemporary research. Therefore, although I shall make several references to how analogy has been defined in the past, I shall forsake to offer a systematic account of this issue. Yet, just to give an idea of the time span involved, a few words must be said about the use that Aristotle made of analogy. This may be illustrated by the following quotation:

> Likeness should be studied, first, in the case of things belonging to different genera, the formulae being 'A : B = C : D' (e.g. as knowledge stands to the object of knowledge, so is sensation related to the object of sensation), ... Practice is more specially needed in regard to terms that are far apart; for in the case of the rest, we shall be more easily able to see in one glance the points of likeness.   (*Topica* 108a, 5–15)

The notion of analogy is brought into sharper focus when metaphors based on analogy are contrasted with other types of metaphor:

> Metaphor consists in giving the thing a name that belongs to something else; the transference being either from genus to species, or from species to genus, or from species to species, or on grounds of analogy. (*De Poetica* 1457b, 5–10)

The way that Aristotle exemplifies the notion of analogy-based metaphor shows that the restrictive notion of binary proportional analogy can be traced back to him:

> Metaphor from analogy is possible whenever there are four terms so related that the second (B) is to the first (A), as the fourth (D) to the third (C); for one may then metaphorically put D in lieu of B, and B in lieu of D. ... As old age (D) is to life (C), so is evening (B) to day (A). One will accordingly describe evening (B) as the 'old age *of the day*' (D + A) ... and old age (D) as the 'evening' or 'sunset *of life*' (B + C).   (*De Poetica* 1457b, 15–25)

From today's perspective, also the other types of metaphor defined by Aristotle turn out to be analogical in character. For instance, the 'metaphor from genus to species' is represented by the case where a subordinate term is replaced by a superordinate one, like 'lying at anchor' by 'standing'. Now, it is easy to see that all particular postures which qualify as subtypes of standing do so because they are structurally similar or analogous to one another. In other words, we are dealing here with an instance of analogy-*as-generalization* (cf. 1.4). It may be added that the Latin grammarian Marcus Terentius Varro, for instance, dropped the restriction, accepted by Aristotle, that analogy should contain only four terms (cf. 2.4).

1.2 Analogy as a context-dependent phenomenon

Systems do not possess any fixed 'essences' which would determine once and for all what is or is not a possible system, or which analogies must hold between different systems. Rather, analogy is relative to the context in which it is used or, equivalently, to the point of view from which it is considered (or created). For instance, the analogy between bird and fish holds in an *anatomical* context, but in the context of *locomotion* birds are analogous to flies rather than to fish. In the same way, linguistic analogy may be exemplified not just by structurally similar sentences (cf. Figure 1.5), but also by the structural similarity between pairs (or triplets etc.) of sentences as in example (1):

$$(1) \quad \frac{\text{John ate an apple}}{\text{John ate}} = \frac{\text{John talked to Bill}}{\text{John talked}}$$

Moreover, depending on the task at hand, a given set of phenomena may be viewed either as a system of its own or as part of more and more comprehensive systems. For instance, the third declension in Latin may be viewed as a system which contains the five characteristic case-endings in singular and plural; or it may be considered, along with the other declensions, as part of the declensional system; and the declensional system may in turn be considered, together with the conjugational system, as part of the inflectional system; the inflectional system may be considered as part of Latin as a whole; Latin may be considered as part of the Italic languages, which are part of Indo-European languages, which in turn are part of the world's languages; language may be considered as part of culture, and culture as part of the reality as a whole; and this is where we have to stop.

The flexibility of analogy brings out, once again, the fact that 'contiguity' must be taken here in a quite abstract sense. It seems natural to interpret this term in such a way that the 'contiguous' parts of a system are distinct from one another. This is indeed the case with scales, fins, and gills, or with the words and constituents in a sentence like *The farmer kills the duckling*. The example of a sentence and its elliptical counterpart (*John ate an apple vs. John ate*) shows, however, that 'contiguous' parts may also overlap. (But notice that this is, to some extent, also true of feathers and wings.)

On the other hand, it must be emphasized that acknowledging the inherent context-dependence of analogy by no means entails that analogy is a 'subjective' (and therefore unreliable) notion. In practice, the contexts or points of view which have to be reckoned with are well-established or intersubjectively valid. This is illustrated by the foregoing distinctions between 'anatomy vs. locomotion' or between '3rd declension vs. declensional system vs. inflectional system (etc.)'. There is surely nothing subjective or arbitrary about the points of view exemplified by the terms of such distinctions. The non-arbitrary nature of standard analogies also gives some sort of general guarantee for their 'psychological reality' (cf. 1.7).

If analogies are considered not simultaneously but successively, then systems between which an analogy n holds at time t-1 may be 'reified', i.e. considered as objects, which means that an analogy $n + 1$ at time t-1 becomes an analogy n at time t-2; etc. To illustrate: Once the structural similarity between birds and fish has been discovered at time t-1, these two types of animal (which were considered as *relations* at t-1) may at t-2 be considered as mere *objects* which occupy 'contiguous' slots in some higher-order zoological analogy. The nature of this successive reification becomes even more evident with our example of Latin third declension. When we are considering language as part of culture, we certainly do not any longer think of the Latin third declension genitive singular marker *-is* and its relation either to the genitive plural marker *-(i)um* or to the dative singular marker *-i*, although this is where we started. We just take it for granted, having reified not just 'Latin' but also 'language'.

Or, to give another example, consider Koestler's (1967 [1964]) vast analogy between scientific discovery and humor. As he sees it, this analogy consists in the fact that in both cases two distinct conceptual frameworks are being related to each other. (But this is also where the analogy stops, because what results is in the first case a *synthesis* and in the second case, a *clash*.) Should this analogy ever be explicitly reconstructed, it might turn out to be something like a 20th-order relation. But the point is, precisely, that it has never been, and need not ever be, explicitly reconstructed. For the purposes of this analogy, entire theories are simply considered as 'objects'.[3]

1.3 A taxonomy of the relations between two analogous systems

Systems may exist already or only begin to exist, just as they can be known already or only begin to be known. It follows that the relation between any two systems that can reasonably be considered analogous may be either symmetric or asymmetric with respect to their ontological and/or epistemic status. This produces a four-way taxonomy, as shown in Figure 1.10.

These are the logical possibilities. To what extent are they actualized in fact? Our 'bird vs. fish' example illustrates Type 1 (= 'ontologically and epistemically symmetric'): birds and fish exist in the same way and are known to us equally well. Thus, the relation between the two types of animal is both ontologically and epistemically symmetric; and this relation was literally *discovered*. (There is a certain relativity of viewpoints lurking here, however. In a different environment, e.g. in a desert, fish may be both nonexistent and unknown.) – For the sake of completeness, it may be added that also two systems which neither exist nor are known would be symmetric both ontologically and epistemically; but this case can safely be ignored because there is not much that can be said about it.

Type 2 (= 'ontologically symmetric, epistemically asymmetric') represents the case where two analogous systems exist in the same way, but one of them is known later than, and with the aid of, the other. In this case, too, the analog-

		ontological	
		symmetry	asymmetry
epistemic	symmetry	1	4
	asymmetry	2	3

Figure 1.10 The taxonomy of the relations between two analogous systems

ical relation is *discovered*. The difference between Type 1 and Type 2 consists in the fact that in the former case discovery lies in the past whereas in the latter case it lies in the present or in the future. The standard illustration of the Type 2 is how the concept of *wave* has been applied in the history of science: the phenomenon of sound was really understood only when the analogy between water waves and sound waves was discovered; and the existence of light waves was discovered even later (for details, cf. Laudan 1981:127–135; Holland et al. 1986:336–342). Furthermore, the light waves turned out to be a special case of electromagnetic waves; and the analogy between all kinds of waves – from water to light – rests on the twin notions of wave length and frequency. (It is immaterial in the present context that light has turned out to possess a particle-character as well.) Now, there may be a tendency to assume that if B is discovered later than A, B must somehow be ontologically secondary vis-à-vis B. This assumption is unfounded, however. As physical phenomena, water, sound, and light, for instance, are ontologically equal. (To be sure, this presupposes that sound and light are not considered as 'secondary qualities', i.e. phenomena dependent on the human perceptual system.) Thus, their relation to one another is ontologically symmetric, even if it is epistemically asymmetric.

Type 3 (= 'ontologically and epistemically asymmetric') is exemplified by *inventions* or *creations* of any kind: first, B neither exists nor is known (to exist); next, someone invents the idea of B and then brings B into existence. It seems to be the case that B is always based on some A or other, i.e. on more primitive (analogical) models of some sort. This is shown with exceptional clarity by Gutenberg's own account of how he came to invent the printing press (cf. Koestler 1967 [1964]:121–124).[4] He knew that figures and words could be printed by means of engraving them on wood, applying thick ink on engravings, and then rubbing moist paper against them. However, this method was not suitable for mass production. On the other hand, coins were produced on a massive scale, namely by punching. But Gutenberg could not first imagine a workable synthesis of these two techniques. This happened only after he had witnessed the functioning of a wine-press: "I took part in the wine harvest. I watched the wine flowing, and going back from the effect to the cause, I studied the power of this press which nothing can resist…" – This process of invention may be reconstructed in different ways. The simple way would be to say that Gutenberg constructed in his mind an analogy between an (existent) wine-press and a (not yet existent) printing press, and thus invented the latter. In more elaborate terms, however, it could be said that the observation of a wine-press suggested to Gutenberg the analogy between engraving and punching, which then enabled him to invent the printing press as a *blend* of these two.

Type 3 may also be illustrated by various developments in the history of formal logic. At the beginning of the 50s, modal logic qua investigation of the notions of necessity and possibility was well-established, but no genuine deontic logic existed as yet. The situation changed with the publication of von Wright (1951). It was von Wright's basic insight to grasp the analogy between (existent) modal operators and (what was to be known as) deontic operators (cf. Follesdal & Hilpinen 1971:9). If the modal operators *L* and *M* are exemplified by *Lp* = 'it is necessary that p' and *Mp* = 'it is possible that p', while the deontic operators *O* and *P* are exemplified by *Op* = 'there is an obligation to do p' and *Pp* = 'there is a permission to do p', then it can be shown that the two pairs of operators behave in the same way. In particular, the basic equivalence of modal logic $Lp \equiv {\sim}M \sim p$ ('it is necessary that p iff it is not possible that not-p') has the deontic counterpart $Op \equiv {\sim}P \sim p$ ('there is an obligation to do p iff it is not permitted to do not-p'). On the other hand – as might be expected – the analogy between modal logic and deontic logic is not perfect. The tautology of modal logic $p \rightarrow Mp$ (known as 'ab esse ad posse') has no deontic analogue, like $p \rightarrow Pp$; and the iteration of operators (exemplified by *LLp*), which is permitted in most systems of modal logic, produces ill-formed deontic formulae (like *OOp*).

Furthermore, Type 3 is illustrated by the invention of many-valued logic (cf. Zinov'ev 1963:Ch. 1). Let us represent 'true' and 'false' by 1 and 0, respectively. In two-valued logic the formula $\sim p$, i.e. the negation of *p*, has the values 0 and 1 iff *p* has the values 1 and 0. The conjunction *p* & *q* has the value 0 if at least one of its conjuncts has the value 0; otherwise it has the value 1. The disjunction $p \vee q$ has the value 1 if at least one of its disjuncts has the value 1; otherwise it has the value 0. The implication $p \rightarrow q$ has the value 0 if *p* and *q* have the values 1 and 0, respectively; otherwise it has the value 1. Now, one arrives at many-valued logic in two steps: first, 0 and 1 are replaced by the *analogous* designations 'lower number' and 'higher number'; second, any numbers between 0 and 1, in addition to 0 and 1, are accepted as truth-values. If the truth-value of a formula A is expressed by /A/, then $/{\sim}A/ = 1 - /A/$. For instance, if /p/ = 0.8, then $/{\sim}p/ = 1 - 0.8 = 0.2$. The many-valued definition of conjunction is: /A & B/ = min(/A/, /B/). For instance, if /p/ = 0.8 and /q/ = 0.2, then /p & q/ = 0.2 (and, more generally, the truth-value of a conjunction is always the same as the lowest truth-value of its conjuncts). Correspondingly, /A ∨ B/ = max(/A/, /B/). For instance, if /p/ = 0.8 and /q/ = 0.2, then /p ∨ q/ = 0.8 (and, more generally, the truth-value of a disjunction is always the same as the highest truth-value of its disjuncts). The many-valued definition of implication may be less transparent: $/A \rightarrow B/ = 1$ if $/A/ \leq /B/$; and $/A \rightarrow B/ = /B/$ if $/A/ > /B/$. For instance, if $/p/ = 0.2$ and $/q/ = 0.8$, then $/p \rightarrow q/ = 1$; and if $/p/ = 0.8$ and $/q/ = 0.2$, then $/p \rightarrow q/ = 0.2$. The two parts of this definition may be explained as follows. In two-valued logic, an implication $A \rightarrow B$ has the value 1 in the three constellations $/A/ = 1$ & $/B/ = 1$, $/A/ = 0$ & $/B/ = 1$, and $/A/ = 0$ & $/B/ = 0$. This gives rise to the (analogical) many-valued *generalization*: '$A \rightarrow B$ has the value 1 whenever the value of A is the same as or lower than that of B'. On the other hand, in two-valued logic an implication $A \rightarrow B$ has the value 0 in the constellation $/A/ = 1$ & $/B/ = 0$. Again, this gives rise to the (analogical) many-valued generalization: 'whenever the value of A is higher than that of B, the value of $A \rightarrow B$ is the same as that of B'.

The invention of deontic logic and the invention of many-valued logic illustrate two distinct uses of analogy (of Type 3). Deontic logic was invented literally *on the analogy of* modal logic: first there was the system A, and then a system B, analogous to A, was invented. The case of many-valued logic is different: first there was two-valued logic, and then it was realized that it is really just a special instance of a more *general* notion, namely many-valued logic. As noted above, this generalization was achieved by replacing the two discrete numbers 1 and 0 by analogous, but more general designations 'higher number' and 'lower number'. At the same time, the discrete opposition ('either – or') was replaced by a continuum ('more or less').

It should also be noticed that there is a difference between inventing the printing press and inventing either deontic or many-valued logic, a difference which is due to the fact that in the two cases the invented entities are ontologically quite dissimilar. It seems natural to say that a system of logic begins to exist as soon as it is clearly conceived of and formalized accordingly. By contrast, there may be a considerable interval of time between conceiving of the idea of a physical artifact and bringing it into existence.

Finally, assigning the emergence of logical systems to Type 3 (= invention/creation), rather than to Type 2 (= discovery), commits one to a 'constructivist' interpretation of logic. Interestingly, this interpretation can be attacked from two opposite directions. On the one hand, on the Platonist interpretation, the founders of either deontic logic or of many-valued logic discovered a pre-existent conceptual realm. On the other hand, as far as the opposition between two-valued logic and many-valued logic is concerned, it could be claimed that it is really the latter which reveals how things are in the world as a matter of fact, given that it has given rise to *fuzzy logic*, and that the latter has proved its worth in practical applications.[5]

Formal logic has also provided the following interdisciplinary analogy of Type 3:

> the idea of a generative grammar emerged from an analogy with categorial systems in logic. The idea was to treat grammaticality [or correctness] like theoremhood in logistic systems and to treat grammatical structure like proof structure in derivations.   (Katz 1981:36)

This analogical relation is comparable to that between modal logic and deontic logic, rather than to that between two-valued logic and many-valued logic (cf. further 3.5).

Type 4 (= 'ontologically asymmetric, epistemically symmetric') represents the case where A and B are known equally well although B begins to exist later than A. This type of analogy is illustrated by the general notion of *copy*: if we have a mechanical way of producing exemplifications of A, i.e. A-1, A-2, A-3, etc., it seems natural to say that we know all of them equally well even at the moment when A-1 has been produced while A-2 and A-3 have not yet been produced. (And notice that some unforeseen event may prevent A-2 and A-3 from ever being produced.) It might also be said that while Types 1 and 2 are exemplified by *discovery* (either in the past or in the non-past), and Type 3 is exemplified by *invention* (or *creation*), Type 4 is exemplified by *imitation*.

Type 4 might conceivably be illustrated also by more outlandish cases (which again bring out the context-dependence of analogy). For Descartes, the existence of God was just as clear and distinct an idea as his own existence (based on his own self-consciousness). The same sentiment was expressed some 200 years later by James Clerk Maxwell in a letter to his wife:

> I can always have you with me in my mind – why should we not have our Lord always before us in our minds ... If we had seen Him in the flesh we should not have known Him any better, perhaps not so well.
> (quoted from Koestler 1967 [1964]:689)

It is possible that God does not exist whereas it is certain that Descartes as well as Maxwell's wife did exist. Nevertheless, Descartes claimed to know God and himself equally well while Maxwell claimed to know God and his wife equally well. Although this instance of Type 4 may seem somewhat extraordinary, it is not purely subjective, i.e. it illustrates the nature of *religious attitude*, which is certainly an intersubjective phenomenon. Moreover, that there indeed obtains a 'copying' relation between man and God, is an assumption that many are willing to assert.

Let us apply our four-way taxonomy to linguistics. The cross-linguistic analogy that underlies typological research (cf. Figure 1.7) exemplifies Type

1, with the qualification that, at the moment when they become known, newly discovered languages have the same, although less drastic, relation to better-known languages as sound waves have to water waves in Type 2. Sentence production may be thought to exemplify either Type 4 or Type 3, depending on whether it is just a matter of routine or whether it contains a 'creative' element. The latter alternative entails the possibility of linguistic change. Thus, it seems natural to view linguistic change as an exemplification of Type 3, even if the amount of 'creativity' involved in linguistic change should not be exaggerated. The difference between Types 3 and 4 turns out to be a matter of degree. On a large time scale, linguistic typology seems to combine invention/creation and discovery. First, the unconscious human mind created a set of analogous (linguistic) structures, i.e. particular languages; and then the conscious human mind discovered this analogy.

To conclude this section, a profound (and most probably, insoluble) problem surrounding the notion of analogy needs to be addressed. We might be tempted to regard analogy as purely a matter of *cognition*, and thus to identify the study of analogy as completely falling within the realm of cognitive science. But this cannot be right. The person who discovered the analogy between bird and fish was practicing zoology, not cognitive science. Similarly, those who discovered the wave-character of light were practicing physics, not cognitive science. Of course, they were *making use* of their cognitive capacities (as every human being is at any moment), but this is a different matter. It is impossible to deny that in these and similar cases the analogy is in the 'things themselves', and not only in the human mind. (It seems more appropriate to say that invention and imitation, i.e. Types 3 and 4 of our taxonomy, do fall within the realm of cognitive science.) What we have here is, of course, the perennial problem of the relation between the human mind and the mind-independent reality. As much as this problem has been debated during the last 2,500 years or so, both in the West and in the East, little genuine advance has been achieved vis-à-vis what Aristotle already said: "... but that the substrata which cause the sensation should not exist even apart from sensation is impossible" (*Metaphysica* 1010b, 30).

It goes without saying that Aristotle is here speaking about the general case, not about aberrant instances of auto-stimulation (which do occur, of course). In the Middle Ages, the Aristotelian position was reaffirmed e.g. by Boethius the Dane:

> Licet ergo res non possit intelligi praeter omnem modum intelligendi, distinguit tamen intellectus inter ipsam rem et ipsum modum intelligendi.

[= 'Although a thing cannot be understood apart from its conceptualization, the human reason nevertheless distinguishes between a thing and its conceptualization'.]   (1980 [c. 1280]; cf. Itkonen 1991:230; also p. 189–191, 213)

We must certainly admit that the Earth (= 'thing') existed already before there was anyone to conceptualize it, and in spite of the fact that, for us, the Earth is necessarily a thing-as-conceptualized, i.e. a result of our conceptualization (and verbalization). Correspondingly, claiming analogy to be *purely* a matter of cognition amounts to claiming that nothing at all exists apart from the human mind, which appears to be a somewhat quixotic position.

The remaining alternative is to assume that there is some superordinate concept equally exemplified by the human mind and the external reality. This was Peirce's view on the issue, as shown by the following remarks:

> The mind of man is adapted to the reality of being. … I hear you say: 'This smacks too much of an anthropomorphic conception.' I reply that every scientific explanation of a natural phenomenon is a hypothesis that there is something in nature to which the human reason is *analogous*; and that it really is so, all the successes of science in its applications to human conveniences are witnesses.   (quoted from Haley 1999:430, 434; emphasis added)

This analogy secures not just the possibility of science, but also the possibility of interpersonal communication. Thus, according to Haley (1999),

> [there is] one great analogy that is foundational to all forms of knowledge and communication, as far as Peirce is concerned: the great analogy between mind and nature, and hence between all (communicating) minds that are a part of nature.   (p. 433)

> In short, to whatever extent we really are capable of understanding nature, it is only because our minds are *like* nature.   (p. 435)

> Rather, as Peirce would have it, nature itself is an extension or instantiation of Mind, just as surely as the human mind is another (and inherently similar) such extension. Nature and the human mind both obey the same laws of Mind.   (p. 437)

One might question the logic according to which, if A (= mind) and B (= nature) exemplify the same structure, it is named after A, e.g. A' (= Mind), instead of choosing some neutral term.

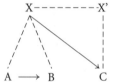

Figure 1.11 Generalizing from A to B and from B to C

1.4 Analogy as generalization

It has been customary to assume that the word 'generalization' may be used in two different senses: either 'spreading' a certain response (= acting or understanding) from A to B or extracting the invariant features common to A and B. Let us call these 'generalization-1' and 'generalization-2'. It will be seen that the concept of analogy is apt to clarify how, precisely, the two senses of 'generalization' are related.

When the functioning of analogy is discussed either in the context of the history of science or in the context of experimental psychology, most examples that are adduced illustrate Type 2 of Figure 1.10: a concrete model A helps to explain an analogous but less easily tractable phenomenon B. It is clear that this transition from A to B qualifies as a *generalization* (= generalization-1). In our example of Section 1.3 above, the notion of wave, originally related to water, was first generalized-1 to explain the phenomenon of sound, and was then further generalized-1 to explain the phenomenon of light as well. It might seem natural to present this overall process as two successive transitions: A → B → C. However, seeing A (= water) and B (= sound) as analogous means not just 'moving' from A to B but, simultaneously, assuming a structure X which, being common to both A and B, is more abstract than either one of them. (To be sure, X may have been grasped – at first – only in an implicit or confused way.) This is generalization-2. And when the notion of wave was next generalized-1 to the phenomenon of light (= C), this meant moving from X (rather than from B) to C and thus assuming – again – some more abstract structure X' shared by X and C. This is one more instance of generalization-2. Thus, instead of a simple succession A → B → C, we have the configuration given in Figure 1.11.

Up to now it has been implicitly assumed that the systems (or structures) between which an analogy holds must be situated at the same level of abstraction. The wave example shows that this need not be the case (because there is an analogy between X and C as well as between B and C). It will turn out that the concept of analogy also underlies comparing a concrete item ('token') with several abstract schemas ('types') and finding the best match (cf. 1.9).

The wave example illustrates the case where the two senses of 'generalization' are combined in a natural way: extracting the invariant structure common to A and B (= generalizing-2) makes it possible, *eo ipso*, to move from A to B (= to generalize-1). The generalization-1 based on generalization-2 may be called 'analogical extension'.

The same process may be illustrated by how Hofstadter (1995) analyzes sequences of integers; consider example (2) (from p. 58):

(2)   2,1,2,2,2,2,2,3,2,2,4,2,5,2...

Once this much has been revealed of the sequence, it has become clear that it consists of triplets of the following kind:

(3)   (212) (222) (232) (242) (252) ...

Thus, having encountered e.g. first nine integers, i.e. the three first triplets, it is easy to give the fourth triplet, which amounts to extending the analogy further or spreading the (correct) response, as shown by example (4):

(4) $\dfrac{(212)}{(222)} = \dfrac{(232)}{X}$ X = (242)

But giving precisely this answer, and not some other, presupposes that one has grasped the invariant structure (or 'template') of the sequence, namely [*2 n 2*]. Again, generalizing-1 is based on generalizing-2.

Consider a linguistic (meta-)analogue: once it has been realized that Sapir's two example sentences are analogous because they share the *SVO* structure, it is exceedingly easy to go on constructing more such sentences. Or, once the idea of ellipsis has been grasped, it is easy to produce an indefinite number of sentence pairs on the analogy of *John ate an apple* vs. *John ate*.

There is, however, an important difference between the wave example, on the one hand, and the [*2 n 2*] example or the *SVO* example, on the other. In the first case, the transition from A (= water) to B (= sound), when it happened, must have seemed to be a unique event, i.e. there was no guarantee that there would ever be an ulterior transition from B to some C (e.g. light). In the two other cases, by contrast, grasping the common structure makes it possible to produce an infinite number of new analogous items. This is the difference between discovering analogy in inanimate nature and performing analogical *actions* (cf. 1.8).

Figure 1.12 Generalizing about A and B (not from A to B, or vice versa)

A mathematical analogue to discovering analogy in inanimate nature is provided by Hofstadter (1995:195–198): What in '12344321' corresponds to '4' in '1234554321'? The answer is obviously '3', and it can be presented in the form of a binary proportion, as in example (5):

$$(5) \quad \frac{1234554321}{4} = \frac{12344321}{X} \qquad X = 3$$

What the cases discussed above have in common, is a *movement* from A to B, mediated by an abstract structure X. It is also possible, however, to make a generalization-2 about A and B without in any (obvious) sense 'moving' from A to B. This case is illustrated by our original analogy or the analogy of Type 1: grasping the structure common to birds and fish does not mean moving from the one to the other. Similarly, when Sapir's and Jespersen's sentence-pairs are understood to exemplify, respectively, the constructions *SVO* and *S-V-O1-O2*, there is no reason to speak of moving from one sentence to another. The same is true of the cross-linguistic analogy of Figure 1.7. Thus, a generalization-2 is an analogy, but there can be generalization-2 without (analogical) *extension*. This may be presented graphically as in Figure 1.12.

When in linguistics a common 'underlying' form is postulated for two or more distinct surface forms, it is typically the 'bird vs. fish' model, rather than the 'water vs. sound' model, which applies. There is one important qualification to be made, however. When less central constructions or interpretations are subsumed under the central or prototypical one, it is natural to assume that the latter has been (analogously) *extended* to them:

> Extensions from the prototype occur because of our proclivity for interpreting the new or less familiar with reference to what is already well established.
>
> (Langacker 1991a:295)

For instance, the English construction *NP-V-NP-PP* is prototypically exemplified by a transitive verb like *throw* (as in *He threw the napkin off the table*); but it may be secondarily extended so as to subsume an intransitive verb like *sneeze* (as in *He sneezed the napkin off the table*) (cf. Goldberg 1995:9–10; and here 2.5, C). Thus, whether we have generalization-2 with or without extension must be decided separately in each case.

If there is an analogical extension, or a movement, motivated by a common structure, from one system to another, it seems natural – as we just saw – to think that it has to go from more to less familiar. This is confirmed by experimental work on analogy, reviewed e.g. in Holyoak and Thagard (1995:Ch. 4–5), where it is always the case that a problem has to be solved by moving from a familiar (and readily expressible) A to a less familiar B. This assumption is not mandatory, however. Undoubtedly, the most famous scientific generalization ever achieved was Newton's insight that the same laws of inertia and gravitation govern the motion of bodies both in the heaven (= superlunary region) and on the earth (= sublunary region). This insight was *not* achieved by moving from what is familiar to what is less familiar. It was rather the opposite, namely seeing the goings-on in the heaven as what is normal and those on the earth as what is less normal. The end result was that the moon and a flying cannon ball turned out to behave *analogously*.

In linguistics, it is not uncommon that simple and frequent structures, which are in this sense 'normal', are comprehended in analogy with more complex structures, which accordingly qualify as 'less normal'. Maybe the clearest instance of this is *ellipsis*. Practically all sentences occurring in continuous speech are more or less elliptical, but they could not be adequately understood without (implicit) reference to the corresponding complete structures.

Finally, it has to be noted that the transition from two-valued to many-valued logic is also an instance of generalization: claims made about the two numbers 0 and 1 are generalized to all numbers $0 < 1$. However, this type of generalization differs from the one discussed above. Two-valued logic (just like three-valued logic) turns out to be a particular instance of many-valued logic just like light waves turned out to be a particular instance of electromagnetic waves. But water waves are not particular instances of sound waves. In the latter case, we have a transition from A to B, based on X. But in the former case we have a transition from A to X.[6]

1.5 Analogy vis-à-vis the various types of inference: Inductive, deductive, and abductive

Next, we have to clarify the relation of (dynamic) analogy to the principal types of inference. It is advisable first to discuss these *en bloc* and to turn to analogy only afterwards.

Aa & Ea
Ab
———
Eb

Figure 1.13 Inductive inference to the next case

Aa & Ea
Ab & Eb
———
$\forall x \, (Ax \rightarrow Ex)$

Figure 1.14 Inductive inference to a law

According to the received view, a deductive inference is 'non-ampliative' in the sense that the conclusion is already contained in the premises. By contrast, the conclusion of an 'ampliative' inference contains (new) information not contained in the premises. The term 'induction' is often used in the general sense of 'ampliative inference'. Nevertheless, it seems uncontroversial to say that the two principal uses of 'induction' are '(inductive) inference to *the next case*' and '(inductive) inference to *a law*'. For instance, if a child has met an individual object *a* which was an apple (= A) and turned out to be edible (= E) and if he now sees another object *b* which is an apple (= A), he will infer that it too is edible (= E). This process may be represented by means of predicate logic as in Figure 1.13.

This is clearly an instance of generalization-1, i.e. 'spreading the response' (to the next case). It does *not* involve generalization-2 (= grasping a common structure). Let us call it 'induction-1'. There is association by contiguity between *Aa* and *Ea*, and between *Ab* and *Eb*, whereas there is association by similarity between *Aa* and *Ab*, and between *Ea* and *Eb*. At the next step, having observed a couple of edible apples, the child infers the law 'All apples are edible'. This may be represented as in Figure 1.14.

Let us call this inference 'induction-2'. According to the received view, it is on the basis of induction-2 that we learn that fire is hot and water is wet and so on, or more generally, that we acquire the *lawlike* knowledge about the *observable* world.

It is reasonable to extend the notion of induction-2 so as to cover 'experimental laws' in the sense of Nagel (1961:79):

> The law that when water in an open container is heated it eventually evaporates is a law of this kind; and so is the law that lead melts at 327 C, as well

as the law that the period of a simple pendulum is proportional to the square root of its length.

Nagel expressly notes (p. 85) that experimental laws can, in principle, be asserted as 'inductive generalizations'.[7]

One may ask, with Hume, what is the *justification* for induction. For instance, what justifies us in thinking that if apples are edible today, they will be edible also tomorrow? It seems that any justification that we might want to give to induction must itself be based on induction (which has not yet been justified). Hence, we are in a logical circle. This is a genuine problem, but it need not detain us in the present context, where our concern is how people think and speak in fact. It is enough to state that in their actual thought, action, and speech people take the *general* validity of induction for granted.

Induction is an invalid form of inference: although the premises are true, the conclusion, whether a next case or a law, may be, and often is, false. Deduction is a valid form of inference: it is necessarily the case that if the premises are true, the conclusion is also true. The prototypical deductive inference is Modus Ponens (Figure 1.15).

Deduction is also involved in the received view of scientific (more precisely, 'deductive-nomological') explanation-cum-prediction, where the major premise represents a law and the minor premise represents the antecedent condition. If we assume the truth of our law '$\forall x\, (Ax \rightarrow Ex)$', i.e. 'all apples are edible', and if we find a new apple, i.e. Ac, then we can *predict* that it is edible (Figure 1.16).

First, the implication '$Ac \rightarrow Ec$' is deduced from the law (by means of Universal Instantiation), and then Modus Ponens is applied to the combination of '$Ac \rightarrow Ec$' and 'Ac'. The result is the same as in induction-1, except that this time the prediction is based on an (inductive) law.

$$\frac{p \rightarrow q}{q} \; p$$

Figure 1.15 Modus Ponens

$$\frac{\forall x\, (Ax \rightarrow Ex)}{Ec} \; Ac$$

Figure 1.16 Deductive-nomological explanation/prediction

It is important to realize that this same inference can also be interpreted as the general schema for ('deductive-nomological') *explanation* (for qualifications, see Stegmüller 1974: Ch. X). On this view, the entity c is edible *because* it is an apple, and *because* all apples are edible. This interpretation is somewhat strained, but not entirely unnatural. It works better in connection with processes (= 'Why did this entity expand?' – 'because it was a piece of metal being heated, and because all pieces of metal expand when heated'). And it works even better in connection with laws containing *theoretical* concepts (see below).

Notice that every inductive law automatically 'explains' the data on the basis of which it has been inferred. Once we have inferred '$\forall x (Ax \rightarrow Ex)$' on the basis of '$Aa \,\&\, Ea$' and '$Ab \,\&\, Eb$', we can deduce either 'Ea' or 'Eb' from '$\forall x (Ax \rightarrow Ex)$' combined with either '$Aa$' or '$Ab$'. This type of 'explanation' is rightly felt to be vacuous, but it is formally indistinguishable from genuine types of explanation, i.e. the explanation of *new* cases.

In induction-2, the premises state repeated co-occurrences of two or more observable (or 'experimental') properties and the conclusion states the lawlikeness of this type of co-occurrence. (For simplicity, I shall concentrate on the deterministic type of lawlikeness and ignore the statistical type.) Thus, the law contains the *same* observable properties that are contained in the premises. Now, this is not the only type of inference to a law. The rival notion is generally called *abduction*. It involves inferring a law which contains properties that are *different* from the observable properties contained in the premises. More precisely, (some of) the properties contained in the law are not just different observable properties, but *non-observable* properties. This is why the laws in question qualify as *theoretical* in character. Thus, this type of inference to a law is indeed distinct from induction-2.[8]

Induction and deduction, as here defined, are rather unproblematic notions. By contrast, abduction has proved to be problematic. The reason is that, unlike induction and deduction, it is a *composite* or *two-stage* process. It means finding a (tentative) *explanation* for some data; but (in this context) explanation is a *deductive* relationship. Therefore abduction means (a) *inferring* a theoretical law such that (b) the data may be *deduced* from it (plus antecedent conditions):

> What Peirce was later to call 'abduction' or 'retroduction' consists essentially in finding [= stage 1] some general hypothesis which entails [= stage 2] the known facts.   (Laudan 1981: 164)

The relationships between induction-2, deduction, and abduction may be summarized as in Figure 1.17 (with the proviso that in induction-2 'data' has

Figure 1.17 The three principal types of inference

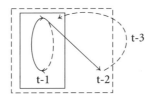

t-1: abduction t-2: deduction of new t-3: confirmation by (new
                predictions   and) true predictions

Figure 1.18 The internal structure of abduction

two parts – roughly 'cause' and 'effect' – whereas in deduction and abduction 'data' is just 'effect').

Taken in itself, abduction is an instance of *circular* thinking. The (theoretical) law which has been abduced has, as yet, no genuine support. To acquire such support, it must allow the deduction of *new* predictions about other (types of) data. Only if such predictions are made, and only if, in addition, they turn out to be *true*, has the law been (tentatively) confirmed. This is the essence of the hypothetico-deductive method (cf. Laudan 1981: 126–135). The different components of this method may be summarized as in Figure 1.18.

This brings out the inherent *ambivalence* of abduction. As the first, necessary part of the hypothetico-deductive method, it is 'good'. But if it is not followed by the deduction of new true predictions, then it turns out to be just another instance of circular thinking and, as such, it is 'bad'. This ambivalence (or the need to take the *temporal* dimension – not just t-1, but also t-2 and t-3 – into account) has hampered an adequate understanding of abduction.

The hypothetico-deductive method may be summarized as a sequence of two inferences, where (unlike in formal-logical inferences) the temporal order in which the premises are accepted is crucial. ('T' and 'O' stand for 'theory' and 'observational statement', respectively.) The first inference represents abduction while the second represents successful confirmation (see Figures 1.19 and 1.20).

$$
\begin{array}{ll}
\text{t-1} & \text{O1} \\
\text{t-2} & \text{T} \vdash \text{O1} \\
\hline
\text{t-3} & \text{T}
\end{array}
$$

Abduction of theory 'T'
(= 'T' is abduced because it entails 'O1', i.e. explains *O1*)

Figure 1.19 Abduction

$$
\begin{array}{lll}
\text{t-4} & \text{T} \vdash \text{O2} & \text{(new prediction)} \\
\text{t-5} & \text{O2} & \text{(true prediction)} \\
\hline
\text{t-6} & \text{T}
\end{array}
$$

Confirmation of theory 'T'
(= 'T' is confirmed because it produces the new true prediction 'O2')

Figure 1.20 Confirmation

The different stages of the abductive inference (Figure 1.19) are analyzed and justified by Hacking (1983:52) as follows:

> The idea is that if, confronted by some phenomenon [= *O1*], you find one explanation (perhaps with some initial plausibility) that makes sense of what is otherwise inexplicable [= 'T ⊢ O1'], then you should conclude that the explanation is probably right [= 'T'].

Within linguistics, Peirce is generally pictured as the foremost proponent of abduction. Therefore it is good to note that, according to Hacking, Peirce's attitudes on this issue underwent a gradual change: "The older he got, the more sceptical he became about [abduction], and by the end of his life he attached no weight at all to [it]." This can be explained, I think. Because of its circular character, abduction alone (Figure 1.19), i.e. as divorced from confirmation (Figure 1.20), is indeed practically worthless (or 'ambivalent', to put it more leniently). It has genuine value only when it is embedded in the larger context provided by the hypothetico-deductive method: "But the ground for believing the theory is its predictive success, and so forth [= Figure 1.20], not its explanatory power [= Figure 1.19]" (op. cit.:53).

There is one important respect in which the preceding account of abduction remains incomplete. The 'circle' of abduction (cf. Figure 1.17) is more complicated than has been indicated so far. When we first perceive the 'data' (or *O1* of Figure 1.19), it is interpreted in one way. But once we have abduced a theory which (tentatively) explains it, it is interpreted in a new and different way. In general, this aspect of abduction has not been duly acknowledged. In part at least, this results from the fact that such ways of formalization as are in current use (i.e. predicate logic or just capital letters like 'T' vs. 'O') are inadequate to express this kind of change in interpretation. Interestingly enough, this defect is easier to detect in a linguistic context where 'abduction' has generally been identified with 'reanalysis'. It is quite understandable that when some *O1* is at t-1 subjected to abduction qua reanalysis, the result which comes out at t-2 differs from what was the case at t-1. To put it briefly, the analysis of *O1* at t-1 is by definition different from its *re*analysis at t-2.[9]

Before proceeding to discuss the concept of analogy, some complementary remarks on what precedes still have to be added. The theoretical laws produced by the hypothetico-deductive method may be roughly divided into two basic types: either they deal with observable entities like planets or apples but introduce, in addition, such theoretical notions as 'inertia' and 'gravitation'; or they deal with unobservable entities (or structures) exemplifying such theoretical concepts as 'electron'. That these two cases are indeed distinct, is evident from the fact that it was possible for Newton to insist that in constructing his mechanics he was relying on ordinary induction, because he could literally *see* the phenomena he was dealing with. By contrast, no one can claim to see electrons, and therefore it is very unlikely that anyone might think to be relying on ordinary induction, when dealing with electrons. On the other hand, that Newton was *not* relying on ordinary induction, is evident from the fact that, before him, no one had been able to see what he now saw (cf. Prosch 1964:74–77). Newton's official (and influential) rejection of the hypothetico-deductive method is only the more surprising, because in his optics, for instance, he had to accept the postulation of unobservable entities (cf. Laudan 1981:96).

Laudan (1981) argues convincingly that, ever since antiquity, the self-understanding of Western natural science has been governed by a pendular movement between the two ideals of the inductive method and the hypothetico-deductive method (also called the 'method of hypothesis'). Nowadays the controversy has been settled in favor of the latter. It may be added, however, that the vacuous use of abduction remains a constant threat. Observational/intuitional data is much too easily 'explained' by theoretical concepts for which the *sole* evidence remains this very same data. Hence the need to keep emphasizing the importance of *new* (and true) predictions.

The notion of abduction given above needs to be enriched. Defined as 'explanatory insight', abduction applies equally to non-human and human phenomena. Corresponding differences in the functioning of abduction are only to be expected. Furthermore, a distinction has to be made between deductive

$$O1 \,\&\, O2$$
$$\underline{T \vdash (O1 \sim O2)}$$
$$T$$

Figure 1.21 Abductive-analogical inference

and non-deductive types of explanation. Within the philosophy of the natural sciences it is commonly assumed that explanation must be deductive in character. It is a fact, however, that practitioners of human or social sciences also make use of a non-deductive type of explanation, often called 'pattern explanation'. According to this view, a phenomenon is explained, not by subsuming it under a law, but rather showing that it fits into a more general pattern which then forms a coherent whole (cf. Itkonen 1983a: 35–38, 205–206). Abduction qua explanatory insight is compatible with both notions of explanation.[10]

Now we are finally in a position to consider analogy, as defined in Sections 1.1–4, in relation to the three principal types of inference (plus the hypothetico-deductive method). More precisely, we shall now concentrate on Types 1 and 2 of our taxonomy (cf. Figure 1.10). With this restriction, analogical thinking proceeds as follows. First, we observe two apparently unconnected phenomena (or 'systems') *O1* and *O2*. Then we realize that if a certain theory 'T' is true, then *O1* and *O2*, instead of being unconnected, are exemplifications of a common structure, which means that 'O1∼O2' is true. From this we tentatively infer that 'T' is true. As a first approximation, this can be presented as in Figure 1.21.

Next (or perhaps, simultaneously), the second premise and the conclusion are taken to constitute the premises of another inference which yields 'O1∼O2' by Modus Ponens.

It is obvious at once that the inference of Figure 1.21 exemplifies the general notion of abduction (cf. Figure 1.19). The change from 'O1&O2' to 'O1∼O2' may at first seem odd, but it in fact constitutes the merit of this formalization. That is, this formalization at least recognizes the above-mentioned *change* in interpretation which always accompanies abduction, although it still gives a rather schematic account of this change. (It is not just the relation between *O1* and *O2* but also their internal constitution which has changed.) Of course, the inference itself does not tell why the change from 'O1&O2' to 'O1∼O2' is regarded as supporting the postulation of 'T'. But this is what happens in fact: a theory which claims to establish connections is – literally – more promising than one which does not. For this, the only justification is that it is a dog/dogs & cat/cats

$$\frac{(N \rightarrow N\text{-s}) \vdash (\text{dog/dog-s} \sim \text{cat/cat-s})}{(N \rightarrow N\text{-s})}$$

Figure 1.22 Learning a grammatical rule

$$\frac{N \rightarrow N\text{-s}}{\text{horse}}$$
$$\frac{}{\text{horse-s}}$$

Figure 1.23 Applying a grammatical rule

built-in (or 'innate') feature both of ordinary thinking and of science to seek generalizations (i.e. analogies).

It was noted above that Figure 1.21 represents the *discovery* of analogy, i.e. the discovery of a structure common to two (analogous) systems. This co-incides with Types 1 and 2 of our taxonomy (cf. Figure 1.10). The Type 3, or the *invention* of analogy, could also be represented by Figure 1.21, if *O2* is interpreted, not as observed, but as *imagined* (or, perhaps, imagined to be observed).

Figures 1.14, 1.16, and 1.19 represent inductive, deductive, and abductive inferences, respectively. (Figures 1.13 and 1.15 qua representations of inductive and deductive inferences may be ignored in the present context.) Correspondingly, Figure 1.21 might be said to represent the *abductive-analogical* inference. It can be illustrated by showing, in a schematic form (cf. Figure 1.22), how a prototypical grammatical rule is learned.

First, the 'systems' *dog/dogs* (= *O1*) and *cat/cats* (= *O2*) are observed. Then follows the realization that if there is a rule like 'For all x, if x is a thing-word *N*, then the plural of x is *N-s*', then *O1* and *O2*, instead of being unconnected, are exemplifications of a common structure. This is taken to lend support to the view that there is indeed such a rule (and, simultaneously, to the view that *O1* and *O2* are indeed exemplifications of this rule). Notice that Figure 1.22 is able to express the reanalysis implicit in every abduction: what is first conceptualized as *dogs* or *cats*, is subsequently conceptualized as *dog-s* or *cat-s*.

As noted above, Figure 1.21 represents discovery and invention of analogy. However, it does not represent *application* of analogy, or Type 4 of our taxonomy (cf. Figure 1.10). In the case of the example given in Figure 1.22, this means that once the rule has been learned, it is applied to new nouns to produce new plural forms (as shown in Figure 1.23).

$$\frac{\begin{array}{l} Aa \& Ba \& Ca \& Da \\ Ab \& Bb \& Cb \end{array}}{Db}$$

Figure 1.24 Traditional 'analogical inference'

It is obvious at once that (when spelled out) Figure 1.23 exemplifies the deductive inference of Figure 1.16. Accordingly, Figure 1.23 might be said to represent the *deductive-analogical* inference. Now we see, more clearly than before, that the four types of our taxonomy are not on an equal footing. Types 1, 2, and 3 represent discovery/invention of analogy, whereas Type 4 represents the case where analogy, once it has been discovered or invented, is (merely) applied to produce new instances.

Above, the term 'analogical inference' has been given a definition that clearly differs from its traditional definition. In the philosophical literature this term typically stands for the following kind of inference: if *a* has the observable properties *A, B, C,* and *D*, and if *b* has the properties *A, B,* and *C*, then *b* has also the property *D*. This is how, for instance, Benjamin Franklin himself accounted for his discovery of the lightning rod (cf. Pera 1981:158). He listed 12 observable properties which electricity and the lightning have in common (including 'colour of light', 'crooked direction', 'swift motion', 'being conducted by metals', 'crack or noise in exploding'). In addition, electricity is attracted by points. Therefore he inferred that the lightning too is attracted by points (which means that electricity and lightning are one and the same phenomenon). – The 'analogical inference' so defined has the structure given in Figure 1.24.

It is obvious at once that this type of 'analogical inference' is an instance of induction-1 (cf. Figure 1.13). The similarities between the phenomena under investigation are observational, not structural: *a* and *b* have the *same* observational properties *A, B,* and *C*. Now, repeating the results of the preceding sections, I emphasize the non-observational or *theoretical* element in the notion of analogy. Induction deals with observable similarity whereas analogy deals with structural, non-observable similarity. Therefore the two must be kept apart. Either Franklin was dealing with observable similarities, which means that he practiced induction, not analogy; or (more likely) the phenomena he was dealing with were observationally dissimilar to the extent that in reality they were being held together by the (implicit) assumption of a common abstract structure, which means that he was practicing analogy, not induction (or 'analogical inference' in the traditional sense).

We have reached the conclusion that dynamic analogy is, primarily, a sub-type of abduction and, secondarily, a subtype of deduction. However, this conclusion may have to be qualified in the sense that every abduction is in turn more or less analogical, namely in the sense that it is necessarily based on some pre-existent model (cf. 2.7).

1.6 Analogy and metaphor; analogy and blend

After several decades of general neglect by linguists (cf. 2.2), analogy is being rediscovered by representatives of cognitive linguistics. These recent developments deserve to be commented upon.

In conformity with what has been presented in Sections 1.1–5, the discovery/invention of analogy may preliminarily be summed up as follows:

> ... an analogy is a mapping of knowledge from one domain (the base) into another (the target), which conveys that a system of relations that holds among the base objects also holds among the target objects.   (Gentner 1989:201)

It should be added that in the case of 'symmetrical' analogy (like our bird vs. fish example) the mapping may go on in both directions simultaneously (cf. Figure 1.12), which means that in this case a fixed 'base vs. target' distinction can no longer be maintained.

In the sequel Gentner (1989) offers the following example. The *problem* is the nature of heat, and the *solution* consists in the insight that 'heat flows like water', more precisely, that 'temperature difference causes heat flow just like pressure difference causes water flow'. The structural similarity between the two cases may be depicted as in Figure 1.25.

Water flow and heat flow share this higher-level structure. Because A is greater in z than in w, x flows from z to w via y. The differences obtain at lower levels: In the case of water flow, A is replaced by 'pressure' while in the case of heat flow A is replaced by 'temperature'. The objects that are substituted for x, y, z, and w differ accordingly. For instance, the source of water flow is a vessel with higher pressure while the source of heat flow is an object with higher temperature.

It is interesting (although unsurprising) to note that it is customary to conceptualize the notion of *metaphor* in exactly the same terms. For instance, Johnson (1987) and Lakoff (1987) summarize the nature of the metaphor in the abstract sentence schema TARGET IS SOURCE, and they let it be exemplified by such less abstract sentence schemas as HAPPINESS IS UP or IDEAS ARE

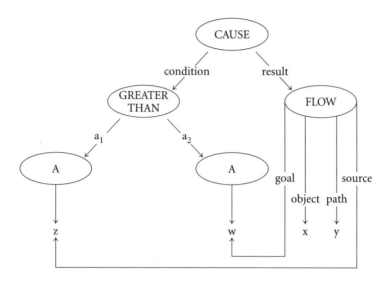

Figure 1.25 Analogy between water and heat

$$\frac{\text{one inch}}{\text{ten inches}} = \frac{\text{one second}}{\text{ten seconds}}$$
$$\cdots\cdots \qquad \cdots\cdots$$

Figure 1.26 Measures of space and time

$$\left.\begin{array}{l}\dfrac{\text{here-in-space}}{\dfrac{\text{near-in-space}}{\text{far-in-space}}}\end{array}\right\} = \left\{\begin{array}{l}\dfrac{\text{here-in-time (now)}}{\dfrac{\text{near-in-time}}{\text{far-in-time}}}\end{array}\right.$$

Figure 1.27 Distance in space as metaphor for distance in time

CONTAINERS. In these two particular examples, HAPPINESS and IDEAS are the targets, or the concepts meant to be given metaphorical expression; and UP and CONTAINER are so-called *image-schemata*, based on bodily experience, that are assumed to constitute the primary source for metaphors.[11]

To fix our ideas, let us consider in some detail a metaphor (nearly?) universally exemplified by the case systems and/or adpositional systems in the world's languages: TIME IS SPACE. It is convenient to understand this as an answer to the (implicit) question: 'What is time?' Thus, time is the target, and space is the base (or source). The target is the problem, and the base is the (tentative) solution. The solution is felt to be satisfactory to the extent that there is a structural similarity (i.e. analogy or 'mapping') between the base and the target. In the case of space and time, the structural similarity consists in that both are measurable, can be characterized in terms of 'near vs. far', etc. These similarities may be represented by means of customary proportional analogies, as in Figures 1.26 and 1.27.

To be sure, these analogies were not simply discovered. Rather, time acquired such characteristics only when, for the first time, it was explicitly compared to space. In this type of case, as Black (1962:37) put it, "the metaphor creates the similarity [rather than] formulates some similarity antecedently existing".

It is only fair to add that the creative potential of metaphor was discovered (not invented!) already by Aristotle:

> It may be that some of the terms thus related [i.e. in an analogy-based metaphor] have no special name of their own, but for all that they will be metaphorically described in just the same way. Thus, to cast forth seed-corn is called 'sowing'; but to cast forth its flame, as said of the sun, has no special name. [Assuming the standard schema of analogy A:B = C:D,] this nameless act (B), however, stands in just the same relation to its object, sunlight (A), as sowing (D) to the seed-corn (C). Hence the expression in the poet, 'sowing around a god-created *flame*'.   (*De Poetica* 1457b, 25–30)

It may be added that there is an interesting analogy between the creative notion of metaphor and the notion of (philosophical) *explication*, as envisaged by von Wright (1963:5; cf. also Itkonen 1978:208–227):

> The aim of the type of investigation, of which I am speaking, is not to 'uncover' the existing meaning (or aspect of meaning) of some word or expression, veiled as it were behind the bewildering complexities of common usage. ... [Rather,] the concept still remains to be *moulded* and therewith its logical connexions with other concepts to be *established*. The words and expressions, the use of which bewilder the philosopher, are so to speak *in search of a meaning*.

If, in moving from space to time, we do not have to do with (literal) discovery, it would seem that the only remaining alternative is invention, i.e. an analogy of Type 3, as explained in Section 1.3. It should be clear, however, that a simple dichotomy like 'discovery vs. invention' is too coarse to account for the facts involved. Although the nature of time was 'invented' with the aid of the analogy/metaphor of space, it was a *good* invention, i.e. an invention which was somehow supported by 'what time really is'. There is literally an infinite number of possible metaphors for time ('time is taste', 'time is a pair of socks', etc.), but most of them are very *bad*. In just a same way, even if a philosophical ex-

	TIME	IS	SPACE
t-1	problem	⇒	t-2 tentative solution (= implicit mapping)
		⇐	
t-3	explicit mapping (= from familiar to less familiar)		
	⇒		
t-4	confirmation of the solution		

Figure 1.28 The internal structure of metaphor

plication creates meanings, as claimed by von Wright, these have to be *good* enough to be generally *accepted* (cf. Itkonen 1983a: 132–135).

Space, in turn, is far from homogeneous, but rather contains some areas which have been understood metaphorically, i.e. in analogy to other, more primary areas. This is indicated by the fact that in the adpositional systems of most African languages (and of other languages as well) such spatial orientations as 'inside vs. outside', 'up vs. down', and 'front vs. back' are expressed by means of units referring to the *human body* (cf. Heine et al. 1991: Ch. 5).

The metaphorical process may be explicated, as in Figure 1.28, by showing the different stages that are contained in the process of answering the question 'What is time?'

Analogy-as-metaphor has a composite structure: insofar as it is a movement, at t-3, from a familiar A (= space) to a less familiar B (= time), it would seem that the difficulty lies in the problem of explicit mapping, i.e. in letting B acquire the properties of A. There was, however, a previous difficulty, namely finding out, at t-2, that it was precisely A, and not some other equally familiar phenomenon, which could solve, by implicit mapping, the problem that had been felt already earlier, i.e. at t-1. The ambivalence of the metaphorical process could be clarified by noting that the target (= B) is *temporally* primary, as shown by implicit mapping, while the source (= A) is *logically* primary, as shown by explicit mapping. And then there must be at t-4 some sort of confirmation of the proposed solution. Thus, metaphorically speaking, there are three separate 'movements' between A and B. This back-and-forth movement exemplifies the traditional notion of hermeneutic cycle (or spiral).

That space (and motion) constitute the (analogical or metaphorical) basis for abstract notions, is a very old idea. Leibniz formulated it, in 1710, as follows:

> It will ... be well to consider this analogy between sensible and non-sensible things ... as, for example, *to, with, from, before, in, outside, by, for, upon, towards* (*à, avec, de, devant, en, hors, par, pour, sur, vers*), which are all derived from place, from distance, and from motion, and afterwards transferred to ev-

ery sort of change, order, sequence, difference, agreement.

(quoted from Slagle 1975:341)

In the same vein, Karl Ferdinand Becker, a representative of 'general grammar', claimed in 1841 that non-sensible entities can only be expressed by a sort of 'translation process', namely by using words that originally refer to sensible entities (cf. Itkonen 1991:281–283).

Sometimes it seems that the concern with metaphor focuses too much on lexical semantics. Therefore it is good to remember that there exists an entire tradition of 'metaphorical grammar', which – logically enough – bases the sentence meaning on *localist* notions. A strong version of 'localism' might interpret the agent as 'source' and the patient and the recipient as, perhaps, 'primary goal' and 'secondary goal', respectively. The problem with strong localism is that there is little cross-linguistic justification for its analysis of the agent role (apart from such passive constructions where, as in Latin or German, the agent is expressed by markings for 'source', e.g. the prepositions *a(b)* or *von*). Therefore a more 'indirect' version of localist-metaphorical grammar seems called for.

According to DeLancey (1997, 2000), the two principal formal markings of the core arguments, i.e. nominative – accusative – dative and ergative – absolutive – dative, correspond, ultimately, to the semantic roles 'agent', 'theme', and 'location'. 'Agent' is (nearly) self-explanatory; and it is a non-localist notion. 'Location' subsumes such less abstract roles as 'experiencer', 'possessor', 'recipient', and 'contact-patient' (like in *He hit **the window***). 'Theme' subsumes 'change-of-state patient' (like in *He broke **the window***) as well as 'topic-of-discourse' (like the referent of the subject in ***The bank** is next to the Post Office*, where the rest of the sentence is, literally, 'location'). Now, it might seem that a sentence with a change-of-state verb (like *He broke the window*) must receive a non-localist interpretation. As DeLancey sees it, however, the state whose change is at issue is a metaphorical extension of 'location', which means that, in this instance, location is expressed by the verb, i.e. *broke*. And reversely, since there is a 'Figure vs. Ground'-type interdependence between 'theme' and 'location' (cf. ***The bank** is next to the Post Office* vs. ***The Post Office** is next to the bank*), in a sentence with a contact-verb (like *He hit the window*), where the object-noun expresses 'location', it is the verb which expresses 'theme'. (To put it roughly, it is the window where the hitting takes place, just like – more generally – it is the location where the theme is located.) – It is interesting to note that DeLancey (2000:8) explicitly recognizes the *metaphorical* nature of his proposal:

[The semantic analysis of each of the major clause types] involves a putative
localistic metaphor ... [namely] the relation between a Theme and a Location.

Heine (1997) too may be cited as a representative of 'metaphorical grammar'.
He notes (p. 31) that his "concern is exclusively with genetic motivation" of
existing constructions, which means – more specifically – that he concentrates
on the *conceptual transfer* (p. 7–8) from the earlier, and concrete, constructions
to the later, and abstract, ones. Let us illustrate this position with his analysis of *possessive* constructions (Ch. 5). He enumerates the following 'schemas'
that have served as real, historical starting-points for today's possessive constructions in different languages; X and Y stand for possessor and possessum,
respectively:

> Action Schema: X takes Y
> Location Schema: Y is at X
> Companion Schema: X is with Y
> Goal Schema: Y exists for/to X
> Topic Schema: As for X, Y exists
> Genitive Schema: X's Y exists
> Equative Schema: Y is X's (Y)

The last two schemas presuppose an antecedent coding of the possessor – possessum relation. A Source Schema – i.e. 'Y (exists) from X' – is characteristic
of attributive rather than of sentential constructions. Notice, in particular, that
Location Schema – although rather common – is nevertheless just one alternative among others. This shows that it is possible to practice 'metaphorical
grammar' without an exclusive commitment to localism.

Furthermore, it is not without interest to note in this context that in the
framework of Paul Lorenzen's (e.g. 1969) 'protophysics' (which is a general
theory of physical measurement) the central notions are defined in the order
of increasing complexity 'space > time > mass': measuring space (= geometry) presupposes nothing else; measuring time (= chronometry) presupposes
changes in some spatial relations (like changes related to the shadow of a sun-
dial, the sand in a sandglass, the swings of a pendulum, or the hands of a clock);
and measuring mass (= 'hylometry') presupposes both velocity (measured as
space-time ratios) and weight (measured by changes in spatial relations). It is
the purpose of protophysics to show how the science of physics emerges from
the everyday life (cf. Böhme 1976). In just the same way, Lorenzen's 'dialogical
logic' is meant to show how formal logic is rooted in the everyday activities of
statement and counter-statement (cf. the end of 3.5).

Even in connection with the logical reconstruction of space-time relationships, however, there remains some latitude for interpretation. *Causality*
is a spatio-temporal notion. Therefore, from the logical point of view, both
space and time could be regarded as metonymically derived from it. But one
could also set up the metonymical continuum 'space > space-time > time'. It is
well known that a series of metonymical 'micro-level' shifts may give rise to a
metaphorical 'macro-level' shift (cf. Heine et al. 1991:Ch. 4, esp. p. 114). To be
sure, the logical order need not be the same as the psychologically real order. –
While discussing metaphor, it is appropriate to mention the obvious fact that
the (contiguous) relation between the parts of a system is *metonymical.*

There is one troubling aspect in the current fascination with metaphor:
the traditional concept of *dead* metaphor seems to have been largely forgotten. However, it is true by definition that dead metaphors are *not* metaphors.
They once were, but they no longer are. Those who forget this, commit the
so-called diachronistic fallacy, like claiming that since the English word *existence* comes from the Latin verb *ex-sistere*, which means 'to stand out', the real
meaning of *existence* is still today something like 'the standing-out'.[12] Once the
diachronistic fallacy is recognized for what it is, it will also be realized that
much less of our actual thinking is metaphorical than is being claimed by afi-
cionados of metaphor. It may be added that Heine (1997), for one, is not guilty
of the diachronistic fallacy. In conformity with his goal of offering historical
(or genetic) explanations, he explicitly notes (p. 105) that it would be wrong to
assume that the real or literal meaning of a possessive construction is a locative
one, just because the latter has a long time ago given rise to the former.

The notion of metaphorical meaning presupposes the existence of non-
metaphorical or literal meaning. Sometimes the zeal to overthrow all traditional assumptions has become so intense that this simple truth has been
denied, and it has been claimed, instead, that 'all meaning is metaphorical';
but this is just muddled thinking. In addition to metaphor, there are many
other styles of speaking – including notably *sarcasm* and *irony* – which share
the feature of being more or less distanced from a default case which, in the
absence of a better term, may be called 'literal meaning'. In this crucial respect, metaphor and sarcasm are analogous (while being otherwise dissimilar).
Haiman (1998:35) makes this point very clearly in discussing the concept of
'exaggeration' (which constitutes one of the principal ways to manifest sarcasm): "the very fact of exaggeration implies the existence of an original model
whose features are to be exaggerated".

To sum up, metaphor is a subtype of analogy, or 'an analogy with added
constraints': all metaphors are analogies, but not all analogies are metaphors.[13]

For an analogy between A and B to qualify as a metaphor, it is required that A and B belong to different 'conceptual domains'. Now, this notion is irremediably vague. Birds are analogous to, but not metaphors for fish (or vice versa). Old sentences are not metaphors for new ones (and the inverse claim would not even make sense). Two-valued logic is not a metaphor for many-valued logic (and, again, the inverse claim would not make sense). Space is a metaphor for time, and money is too. But are water waves a metaphor for sound or water flows for heat? The answer depends on how one decides to define 'conceptual domain'.

Bloomfield (1933:Ch. 23) followed the Neogrammarians in considering analogical change as a principal type of linguistic change; but he restricted the notion of analogy to the binary proportional case. Those cases where no clear analogical model of the proportional type is discernible were labelled 'adaptations' by him, like the Latin *reddere* ('give back'), which was changed into *rendere* on the model of such semantically related words like *prehendere* ('take') or *vendere* ('sell'). And cases where two related structures produce a third one were called 'contaminations' or 'blends ': for instance *I am friendly with him* and *We are friends* produce the blend *I am friends with him* (p. 423).

Having accepted Bloomfield's view about the general importance of analogy, Hockett (1966:94) claimed that "analogy, blending, and editing are the basic mechanisms of the generation of speech"; and in a footnote he added that this may be true of human behavior in general. His notion of analogy is the standard one. By 'blending', he means a process where two conflicting analogies produce a new structure. For instance, a form like *swammed* may result from the following two analogies: *sigh : sighed = swim : X* and *sing : sang = swim : X*.

Bolinger (1961) examines several types of '(syntactic) blend'. His real purpose is to show that a given sentence may have two (or more) 'transformational sources' (each of which may in turn consist of more than one sentence), which makes transformational analyses of the type suggested by Lees (1960) correspondingly arbitrary. For instance, a personal construction like *John was quick* and an impersonal construction like *John's reaction was quick* produce the blend *John was quick to react* (p. 378); and there are of course analogous blends like *John was slow to react*, which means that the two models underlying the blend must possess at least some degree of abstractness. In the early days of transformational grammar, it was customary to 'explain' the ambiguity of a sentence like *Flying planes can be dangerous* by showing that it can be derived from two distinct 'deep structures'. But the case we are examining here is different. *John was quick to react* is not ambiguous. It is a blend.

The concept of 'blending' has been rediscovered in recent cognitive linguistics, where it is defined as the following type of process: a common structure (or 'generic space') is extracted from two situations (or 'spaces'), and it makes possible the creation of a fourth ('blended') situation or space which contains elements from the original two (cf. Fauconnier 2001:256–260). This process has been illustrated by means of the case in which a contemporary philosopher purports to engage in a (fictional) argument with Immanuel Kant. Certainly the most celebrated instance of blending in the history of Western thought has been the *dialectical* 'movement' from thesis A via antithesis B to synthesis C. Notice that an antithesis B is not just any antithesis but the antithesis of a thesis A, which means that A and B must share some common structure X; and the same is of course true also of the synthesis C.

In terms of the taxonomy of Section 1.3, this concept of blending is a combination of Type 2 and Type 3: once a structure common to two *analogous* systems has been *discovered*, it makes possible the *invention* of a third system. (Just remember how Gutenberg described the process of inventing the printing press.) So defined, blending – just like metaphor – turns out to be based on the more primitive notion of analogy. It is not clear, however, whether this is the sense in which Bloomfield, Hockett, and Bolinger use the term 'blend'. For them, a blend involves *two* models, whether concrete (as in Bloomfield's example *I am friends with him*) or abstract (as in Hockett's example *swammed* or in Bolinger's example *John was quick to react*). By contrast, Fauconnier's notion of blend involves only *one* (abstract) model or 'generic space', exemplified by two more concrete entities; and, based on this model, a new concrete entity is produced that combines elements from the previous two. For instance, on the basis of Sapir's analogy in Figure 1.3, we could produce the 'blend' *the farmer takes the chick* (in which *the farmer* comes from the first and *takes the chick* from the second of the two analogous sentences). So understood, 'blend' turns out to be just one exemplification of analogy among many others.

It may be added, however, that the recent notion of 'blending' has *also* been used in a different, and less constrained sense (or several such senses). For instance, when a sentence is gradually built up out of words and phrases, this process is claimed to be a succession of (non-compositional) 'blendings' (cf. Fauconnier & Turner 1996); but notice that e.g. a verb and its object do not share a common structure. (Of course, the structure of a transitive verb contains a reference to its possible object, but this is an entirely different matter.) Or, to give a more concrete example, if the meaning of *red pencil* is claimed to be a blended non-compositional integration of its constituent meanings, it is still the case that there is no structure common both to the meaning of *red* and to the meaning of *pencil*. Here 'blending' is on the verge of becoming in-distinguishable from mere *combining*. Thus, 'blending' could be a notion only contingently related to analogy, after all.[14]

1.7 Analogy and psychological reality

Analogy is not a monolithic concept. Either we may investigate analogy as it obtains in the non-human nature (cf. bird ∼ fish; water wave ∼ sound wave; superlunary region ∼ sublunary region); or we may investigate analogy as it obtains in the 'human sphere' (cf. *The farmer kills the duckling ∼ The man takes the chick; John ate an apple / John ate ∼ John talked to Bill / John talked*). In the former case there is always one analogical level more than in the latter because human thought which grasps analogy in the non-human nature must itself be in some sense analogical (and may in turn become an object of study). That there should be the same kind of relation between motion in the heavens and motion on the earth, on the one hand, and between two English sentences, on the other, may seem trivial (because, after all, the two relations are equally con-ceptualized by humans). But it may also be taken to give rise to unfathomable problems (cf. the end of 1.3).

'Human sphere' was used above as a cover term for both mental (= psycho-logical) and social phenomena. Generative linguistics has been claiming since the mid-60s that linguistics is just a subdomain of cognitive psychology. In the 70s this led to the debate about the *psychological reality* (or psychological adequacy) of linguistic descriptions.

The problem was formulated by Kac (1974: 42) as follows:

> There is a current vogue for claiming that linguistics is a psychological sci-ence. This claim, however, has puzzled some psychologists – and even a few linguists – since, for all its pretensions to psychological import, linguistics is nonetheless pursued in a way which seems to have little or nothing to do with the way in which psychological investigation is normally conducted.[15]

In other words, psychology is supposed to use the experimental method (al-though not exclusively):

> the subjects' introspections ... should, at most, serve as heuristic sources of hypotheses about cognitive processes, which should then be subjected to rigorous experimental test.   (Evans 1982: 68)

Therefore it is to be expected that a discipline like generative linguistics which claims to be part of psychology should also use this method. However, representatives of generative linguistics have consistently refused to do so. Instead, they have analyzed and continue to analyze self-invented sample sentences which their own linguistic intuition deems to be correct, which means that they fully remain within the descriptive (grammatical) tradition that has been prevalent in linguistics always and everywhere (for extensive documentation, see Itkonen 1991).

In the 70s this situation prompted two principal types of response among the critics of generative linguistics. On the one hand, those who took the commitment to psychology seriously argued that generative linguistics is methodologically unsound (cf. Botha 1971; Derwing 1973; Derwing & Harris 1975). On the other hand, others argued that what was wrong, was not the methodology of generative linguistics, or what generativists were doing (because, to repeat, it was fully in keeping with traditional linguistics), but rather their methodological self-understanding, or what they *thought* they were doing (cf. Itkonen 1974, 1975, 1978; Kac 1974; Ringen 1975; Linell 1979). For completeness, it may be added that a third position was represented by Baker and Hacker (1984), who rightly criticize generativism for mistaking linguistics for psychology (due to "a catastrophic failure to distinguish nomological investigations from normative ones" [p. 285]), but wrongly deny the viability of any type of psycholinguistics. Finally, a fourth position was represented by Katz's (1981) Platonism (cf. Itkonen 1983b).

The first of the above-mentioned positions is readily understandable, because it just claims that speculative psychology is not genuine psychology. By contrast, the second position may need some elucidation. It can be expounded in more detail as follows. *Normative* concepts like correctness/grammaticalness (or entities exemplifying such concepts) cannot be investigated by means of *observation* (which is limited to sense-perception), but have to be investigated by means of *intuition*. For instance, observation does not tell us that a given utterance is correct or incorrect. Rather, we have to know the rules (or norms) of language which this utterance either follows or fails to follow; and this kind of knowledge is called 'linguistic intuition'. Rules of language may be divided, roughly, into those for connecting forms with meanings and those for combining meaningful forms. Such rules are necessarily intersubjective or social; in Wittgenstein's terms, they are 'public' or 'open to view'. By contrast, mental structures and processes investigated by psychology (including psycholinguistics) are in general unconscious, and therefore 'hidden from view'. Social rules open to conscious intuition and unconscious individual-psychological structures-cum-processes constitute two distinct realms of phenomena which must be – and are – investigated by two distinct linguistic subdisciplines, namely 'autonomous linguistics' and 'psycholinguistics'.

These two subdisciplines do not exist side by side, as it were. Rather, autonomous linguistics is a precondition for psycholinguistics: it is possible to practice the former without having any knowledge of the latter (as was indeed the case in traditional grammar-writing), but not vice versa. It can be demonstrated quite precisely that each and every psycholinguistic experiment has been devised in light of pre-experimental and conscious (intuitive) knowledge; and this knowledge, as such, is not refuted by whatever new information may be produced by experiments. Why? – because any such new information is about a different realm of phenomena, i.e. it is not about rules (or norms) open to conscious intuition, but rather about those unconscious structures and processes that underlie such rules (cf. Itkonen 1980: 342–344).

Notice the following rough-and-ready analogy. If I measure the length of a stick and state that its length is ten inches, the notion of inch is not the result of, but is rather presupposed by, my act of measuring. In just the same way, experiments on how English relative clauses are understood presuppose the notion of English relative clause, instead of producing it. Experiments on English relative clauses cannot possibly show that there are no relative clauses in English, whereas experiments on phlogiston did show that there is no phlogiston. This type of pre-experimental intuitive knowledge of language is the subject matter of autonomous linguistics. Of course, autonomous-linguistic descriptions may suggest *hypotheses* about the unconscious psychology of language; but such hypotheses (abduced on the basis of intuitive knowledge) must be tested on the basis of *new* predictions, i.e. predictions which go beyond (conscious) intuition and are typically produced by experiments. This was the gist of the Evans-quotation above.

Often the difference between autonomous linguistics and psycholinguistics is so obvious that it would be nonsensical to deny it. For the most part, autonomous linguistics pursues the *axiomatic* ideal, which – to put it formulaically – consists in generating as much as possible (= all and only correct sentences) with as little as possible. Now, anyone even minimally acquainted with psychology knows that the (untrained) human mind does *not* operate axiomatically (= 'few non-redundant axioms, few undefined terms, few rules of inference, long derivations').[16] Montague grammar is an extreme example of an 'axiomatic', non-psychological linguistic description, i.e. a description carried out within the tradition of autonomous linguistics.

Panini's grammar constitutes a less obvious, and therefore more interesting example: "Modern linguistics acknowledges it as the most complete generative grammar of any language yet written, and continues to adopt technical ideas from it" (Kiparsky 1993:2918); and yet it makes no claim to psychological reality (cf. Itkonen 1991:5–87, esp. p. 43).[17] Thus, Panini's grammar qualifies as exemplary. But it is *not* exemplary within the tradition of psycholinguistics. Therefore it must be exemplary within some *different* tradition. The only logical alternative is the tradition of autonomous linguistics. Panini's grammar fulfills all the criteria of an 'optimal' non-psychological grammar which Katz (1981:64–73) speculated about, without being able, however, to offer any plausible examples.

It has occasionally been suggested that since the axiomatic Panini-type description is about language, but not about the psychology of language, it solves no problem. By the parity of reasoning, Euclid's axiomatics solves no problem, because it is about geometry, not about the psychology of geometry. In the late 40s and early 50s, the question of psychological reality (or psychological adequacy) had already been addressed in American structural linguistics, in terms of what came later to be known as the opposition between 'God's truth' and 'hocus-pocus'. Initially, Hockett (1966 [1948]) proposed that linguistic description could be conceptualized either as 'a game' or as 'a science'. The former is identified with mathematics; and it is further claimed that the one who regards linguistics as a game "has no criterion by which to judge the relative merits of one analysis versus another". The latter is in turn characterized as the type of analysis which does not just study a closed corpus, but is also able to "predict what *other* utterances the speakers of the language might produce". In Hockett's view, this type of analysis "parallels what goes on in the nervous system ... of a child learning his first language". It follows that, on the linguistics-as-game interpretation, "the structure of a language ... is created by the person who plays the game", whereas on the linguistics-as-science interpretation, the linguist's "purpose in analyzing a language is not to create structure, but to determine [i.e. discover] the structure actually created by the speakers of the language"; and this structure is taken to be "a state of affairs in the nervous system". With hindsight, we can say that here autonomous linguistics is being equated with *invention* and 'hocus-pocus', whereas psycholinguistics or psychologically (and even neurologically) adequate linguistics is being equated with *discovery* and 'God's truth'.[18]

The way that Hockett (1966 [1948]) characterizes the methodological options open to the linguist is illuminating but does not seem to be discriminating enough. In the present context, mathematics as the epitome of a formal discipline may profitably be replaced by axiomatic logic. Now it is clear at once that axiomatic logic is *not* just a game, without any criteria for judging the relative merits of rival descriptions. First, an axiomatic description must satisfy the twin requirements of completeness and soundness, i.e. it has to generate *all*, and *only*, valid formulae, which means that it must neither undergenerate nor overgenerate. A description which does not satisfy these requirements of 'generative adequacy' is automatically inferior to one which does. Second, there is the general requirement of *simplicity*, which means that an axiomatic description with fewer axioms and/or rules of inference and/or definitions is – ceteris paribus – automatically superior to one with more axioms etc. It is also easy to see that grammatical descriptions composed in the tradition of autonomous linguistics try to satisfy the requirement of generative adequacy while they ignore the requirement of psychological (let alone neurological) adequacy.

It follows that Hockett's overall characterization is mistaken in two respects. On the one hand, his notion of linguistics-as-game corresponds to nothing in reality; on the other, his notion of linguistics-as-science combines two distinct types of criteria, or criteria that ought to be kept apart, namely generative adequacy and psychological adequacy; and it is precisely these criteria which serve to distinguish between autonomous linguistics and psycholinguistics.

The claims I made in the preceding paragraphs may be validated as follows. At the time, Zellig Harris was the main representative of the linguistics-as-game view (cf. also Hockett 1966: 16). And yet, Harris (1961 [1949]) explicitly points out that, while linguistic description must start from a corpus of utterances, "the interest in our analysis of the corpus derives primarily from the fact that it can serve as a *predictive* sample of the language" (p. 244; emphasis added). In other words, "when a linguist offers his results as a system representing *the language as a whole*, he is *predicting* that the elements set up for his corpus will satisfy all *other* bits of talking in that language" (p. 17; emphasis added). This means that Harris' view of linguistics is based on the requirement of generative adequacy, and different descriptions are accepted or rejected depending on whether, or not, they meet this requirement. Moreover, in deciding between two generatively adequate descriptions, the criterion is the overall *simplicity*:

> The criterion [we use] … is therefore the criterion of usefulness throughout the grammar, a configurational consideration. (Harris 1966 [1946]: 146, n. 6)

> We merely select positions in which many morphemes occur, and in terms of which we get the most convenient total description. (ibid.: 150)

It is interesting to note that, at the beginning, generative linguistics repudiated the requirement of psychological adequacy and considered the requirement of generative adequacy à la Harris as fully sufficient:

> it seems to me that [any adequate notion of 'significance'] will rule out mentalism for what were essentially Bloomfield's reasons, i.e. its obscurity and inherent untestability.   (Chomsky 1975a [1955]: 86)

> The notions that enter into linguistic theory are those concerned with the physical properties of utterances, the formal arrangements of parts of utterances, ... and finally, formal properties of systems of representation and of grammars. ... We will refer to linguistic analysis carried out in these terms as 'distributional analysis'.   (ibid.: 127)

> ... the sense in which we use this term [i.e. 'distributional'] [is] borrowed from Harris.   (ibid.: 63, n. 1)

> Notice that simplicity is a *systematic* measure; the only ultimate criterion in evaluation is the simplicity of the whole system.   (Chomsky 1957: 55)

Today's cognitive linguistics has (re)rediscovered the problem of psychological reality. There are those who openly espouse the traditional intuition-based type of description: "meaning is located in conscious experience" (Talmy 2000: 5–6). Others (like Langacker) are less explicit, but still refrain from using the experimental method. And then there those who – like Derwing (1973) in his time – are of the opinion that a cognitive linguistics worthy of its name is necessarily committed to the use of the experimental method. A representative spectrum of opinions is given in Sandra & Rice (1995), Croft (1998), Sandra (1998), Tuggy (1999), and Gibbs & Matlock (1999).

As far as psychological reality is concerned, what is true of linguistic descriptions in general is also true of linguistic descriptions based on the concept of *analogy*. (Notice also that this discussion is by no means restricted to linguistics but applies with equal force to logic, mathematics, economics, etc; cf. 1.8). The ubiquity of analogy, which is both documented and explored in this book, gives some sort of prima facie guarantee of psychological reality to those analogy-based descriptions that stay 'reasonably close' to the data. It is quite clear, however, that there are also analogy-based descriptions which are not psychologically real. These may be divided into two groups: Either they are meant to be psychologically real, but – due to their overly abstract nature or excessive distance from the data – they do not achieve their purpose, which means that they are bad descriptions. Or the desideratum of psychological reality is simply irrelevant to them, which still leaves open the possibility that they may be either good or bad descriptions of their own kind. For instance, Montague grammar is based on a single construction, namely one-place function; and, applying this single construction again and again, Montague grammar manages to describe, in an approximate fashion, natural-language syntax, natural language semantics, and the isomorphic/analogical correlation between the two (cf. Itkonen 1983a: 142–152). This is an impressive achievement, which means that Montague grammar is a good 'analogical' description of the *non*-psychological type.

A strong version of (abstract) analogy-based description, i.e. the view that *all* linguistic levels are strictly analogous, has been explicitly repudiated by Hockett (1966) as psychologically inadequate. What makes the following quotation especially interesting is the fact that Hockett himself was one of the original inventors of the theory he is now criticizing:

> Stratificational theory handles the enormously complex correspondences between meaning and form by decomposing these correspondences into a succession of mappings between successive 'strata' ... This is all fine provided we regard the machinery of strata, of elements on each stratum, and of mappings from stratum to stratum as *descriptive conveniences*. ... But stratificational theory proposes that all this machinery is not only in our description but also in the language and even, in some sense, *in the speaker*. For this there is no shred of evidence, nor do I understand how there could be. And the theory reinforces our tendency of the 1940s to assume that the organization of affairs on other strata is more or less parallel [i.e. analogous] to organization on the phonological stratum. I believe this is quite impossible.   (p. 32–33)

Here, a conflict is revealed between what a theory aims at (= psychological adequacy) and what it achieves (= approximative descriptive adequacy but psychological inadequacy). This passage should give pause to those who – like J. Anderson (1992) – wish to deal with form and meaning in strictly analogous terms, at least if they also strive after psychological adequacy.

As explained in Introduction, my concern in this book is with analogy as a *psychologically real* and causally effective phenomenon. I pursued a similar research program already in Itkonen (1983a). In this book, the *causal force* that brings – inter alia – linguistic behavior about is claimed to be rationality, defined as the act of choosing (what is considered as) an adequate means to achieve the goal. It was my aim to show that one and the same notion of explanation, i.e. the so-called rational explanation (cf. 1.8), applies in such apparently disparate linguistic subdomains as pragmatics, psycholinguistics, sociolinguistics, diachronic linguistics, and universals research. In making this generalization, I was of course claiming that, in this respect, all these subdomains are analogous to each other. And since I was claiming that rationality is the causal force that brings linguistic behavior about, I was by definition also claiming psychological (or psycho-social) reality for my interpretation of the descriptions given in the above-mentioned linguistic subdomains.

The reference to linguistic typology, diachronic linguistics, and sociolinguistics entails that we need to relax the requirement that psychological reality may be achieved *only* by the use of the experimental method. This requirement is fully meaningful as long as we investigate the synchronic state of only *one* language. Within such a restricted context, a traditional linguistic description is not able to distinguish between what is purely accidental (or a 'quirk of language') and what has general psychological significance. However, ever since the linguistic typology has been placed on a secure footing, thanks to the efforts of the functionalist school, it seems possible to have access to the psychology of language without necessarily resorting to the experimental method. What occurs in (nearly) all languages must be psychologically real. Or, as was already anticipated by Boas (1964 [1911]: 21), "the occurrence of the most fundamental grammatical concepts in all languages must be considered as proof of the unity of fundamental psychological processes". As for diachronic linguistics and sociolinguistics, the nature of the data makes any experimental approach a practical impossibility. Nevertheless, psychological reality can still remain a desideratum.

Linguists may be interested to learn that representatives of other disciplines too have to wrestle with the problem of psychological reality. Cognitive anthropology is a case in point. To linguists, the following statements have a familiar ring:

> The use of parsimony provides no help in resolving the problem of psychological reality.   (Rubinstein et al. 1984: 9)

> It is clear that introspection does not offer a solution to the problem of psychological reality in cognitive analysis. ... However ... we think that introspective accounts from informants *and* from anthropologists have a large and important role to play in the study of human cognition and behavior, but as further data to be considered rather than as privileged sources of insight into the mind.   (p. 10)

It may be due to the inevitably non-experimental character of anthropological research that the authors reach the following rather gloomy conclusion:

> The best that can be said, we think, is that presented models and research techniques are inadequate for testing the psychological reality of ethnoscientific analyses.   (p. 11)

Although my concern in this book is with psychological reality, I wish to point out that linguistic description may also have other desiderata. For more than two thousand years, autonomous linguistics, epitomized by Panini, has been able to survive, while paying no, or little, attention to the notion of psychological reality (cf. Itkonen 1991). In particular, the champions of American structural linguistics did not need it:

> We can profitably discuss the intention, the form, and the history of speech ... as an institutional or cultural entity, leaving the organic and psychological mechanisms back of it as something taken for granted.   (Sapir 1921:11)

> The findings of the linguist, who studies the speech signal, will be all the more valuable for the psychologist if they are not distorted by any prepossessions about psychology.   (Bloomfield 1933:32)

Moreover, the notion of psychological reality admits of more than one interpretation. If one concentrates on describing one homogeneous language or dialect at a time, the requirement of psychological reality has a straightforward and literal meaning in this domain. But it has a different meaning in other domains. An overview of the dialects of a given language (sometimes called a 'dialect grammar'), which describes the continuous transitions from one dialect to the next, does not admit of any clear-cut individual-psychological interpretation. On a smaller scale, the same is true of the so-called 'polylectal grammars', which describe the language varieties spoken, e.g., by succeeding generations, and which include the notion of a 'creole continuum' as a special case (cf. Bailey 1973; Bickerton 1973). On a larger scale, the same is true of a 'comparative' (i.e. typological) description of structurally dissimilar languages, which can be called psychologically real only in a very indirect sense. Nor can historical reconstruction, i.e. relating the current members of a language family by means of a common protolanguage and a number of intermediate stages, be very plausibly considered as a psychological undertaking. Even those who endorse the search for psychological reality need no longer interpret it as a property of an individual mind:

> Many scholars argue that theories of cognition should stop maintaining the idea that cognitive structures are necessarily 'in the head', and acknowledge that they are dynamic systems of 'structural couplings' which model how people interact with the world and in different linguistic environments.
> (Gibbs & Matlock 1999:267)

1.8 Analogical behavior: From mechanical to creative

Norms (or rules) are necessarily norms (or rules) for *acting*. Norms of language are norms for speaking and understanding. Uttering a sentence is a typical linguistic action. Like all actions, it may be divided into several *sub*-actions, ultimately those of pronouncing particular syllables and sounds (cf. below). Therefore we must at this point consider the concept of action.

Any action exemplifies a *means – end* schema and presupposes the possibility of *choice*: given a goal, one has to choose (what one believes to be) the most adequate means to achieve it. The structure of action may be represented as in Figure 1.29.

G and *A* are mental representations of goal-states and actions, respectively. *I* and *B* represent the propositional attitudes of intending-to-achieve (or simply wanting) and believing. The schema says that if someone intends to achieve the goal *G* and believes that the action *A* (which he is capable of performing) contributes to bringing *G* about, then he must, as a matter of conceptual necessity, intend to do *A*. (This necessity is indicated by the entailment sign $\vdash$.) Thus, intention is 'transferred' from goal to action. Having this goal and this belief will then bring it about that he does *A*. The simple arrow and the double arrow stand for ordinary causation and mental causation, respectively. While *A* is a mental representation of an action, *$^{*}A$ is its spatio-temporal counterpart.

Figure 1.29 illustrates the concept of *instrumental action* (here *A). Moreover, *A is a *rational* action to the extent that it is indeed an adequate means of bringing about *G*. The *rational explanation* of an action consists in showing that the agent thought it to be an adequate means for attaining some goal (cf. Itkonen 1983a: 3.7). Or, as Newton-Smith (1981: 241) puts it:

> To explain an action as an action is to show that it is rational. This involves showing that on the basis of the goals and beliefs of the person concerned the action was the means he believed to be the most likely to achieve his goal.

It must be added, however, that also *irrational* actions can, and must, be explained on the basis of rational explanation, namely by showing how, and why, what *is* irrational in fact came to *seem* rational to the agent.

This schema applies, in principle, also to sub-actions, in which case we also have to talk about 'sub-goals' (and corresponding beliefs). As Linell (1979) and

$$\{[I{:}G \ \& \ B{:}(A \ \rightarrow \ G)] \vdash I{:}A\} \Rightarrow {}^{*}A$$

Figure 1.29 The internal structure of (rational) action

Levelt (1989) have pointed out, uttering a sentence contains several 'phonetic plans' which exemplify the general structure of action:

> A speaker's phonetic plan represents which phones go in successive timing slots. The sequence of phones in a syllable specifies the articulatory gesture to be made by the speaker *in order to* realize that syllable.
>
> (Levelt 1989: 295; emphasis added)

As the emphasized part of the quotation shows, there is a (sub)goal here, to be realized by performing an adequate (sub)action.

As far as the (rational) explanation of actions is concerned, it is irrelevant whether the goals and beliefs involved are conscious or not. This is rather obvious because e.g. phonetic plans and articulatory gestures (mentioned in the previous paragraph) are of course generally unconscious. It follows that we are committed to the concept of *unconscious rationality*, supported by a long tradition in psychology. It starts at least with William James:

> The pursuance of future ends and the choice of means for their attainment are thus the mark and criterion of the presence of mentality in a phenomenon.
>
> (quoted from Herrnstein & Boring 1965: 610)

The same tradition is being continued e.g. by Fodor (1975: 173):

> Which representation is assigned is determined by calculations which rationally subserve the utilities of the organism. There may be – perhaps there must be – some end of this hierarchy of rational decisions. But the end is not in sight. For all we know, cognition is saturated with rationality through and through.

It is quite surprising to what extent, in popular imagination, the concept of rationality is still connected to *conscious* deliberation. For more than twenty years, I have met with complete incredulity, when speaking about *unconscious* rationality. Apparently, Whitney (1979 [1875]) had encountered the same problem:

> One great reason why men are led to deny the agency of the human will in the changes of speech is that they see so clearly that it does not work consciously toward that purpose. ... There is no will to alter speech; there is only will to use speech in a way which is new; and the alteration comes of itself as a result.
>
> (p. 146–147)

In order to lay the misgivings about unconscious rationality to rest once and for all, it is good to point out that (rational) behavior amenable to rational explanation is characteristic not just of humans but also of animals, for instance *rats*:

> An *intentional* account of behavior is justified if that behavior can be shown
> to be dependent on, in the sense of being a *rational* consequence of, a set of
> beliefs and desires about the world (Dickinson 1988:310; emphasis added).
> To explain an action in terms of the agent's [e.g. rat's] beliefs and desires is
> to demonstrate that the action is *rational* with respect to the content of those
> mental states (p. 310; emphasis added). So it turns out that instrumental be-
> havior [by rats] will support an *intentional* characterization in terms of beliefs
> and desires after all. (p. 321; emphasis added)

Dennet (1991) rejects Levelt's model. To be sure, he accepts (p. 194, n. 10) the
existence of unconscious goals and beliefs just as he accepts the generally goal-
directed or purposive nature of speaking: "Human speech is purposive activity;
there are ends and means, and we somehow do a passable job of traversing the
various options" (p. 235). In his view, however, a schema like the one in Figure
1.29 is too 'bureaucratic' in its reliance on serial thinking, and he would like
to replace it by his own 'pandemonium model', in which the (verbal) action
somehow emerges out of the chaos of hundreds (if not thousands) of erratic de-
sires. But he does not even try to explain how this happens. Therefore, Levelt's
model, based on the schema of Figure 1.29, remains the only option, at least
for the time being.

Searle (1992) goes farther than Dennett (1991), in that he denies the existence of (permanently) unconscious goals and beliefs altogether. For him, the
only ontologically real levels are (potential) consciousness and neurology. The
main objection against Searle (1992) is that if rational explanations based on
unconscious goals and beliefs are taken away, there is nothing left. Rational explanations are supposed to be replaced by neurological explanations, but *we do
not have them*. We do not know whether or not we will have them in ten years
or in one hundred years. But we do know that we do not have them today.

It is useful to distinguish between *rule-governed* (or 'institutional') and *free*
actions (although this distinction may sometimes be difficult to make). In a
rule-governed action the choices have already been made for the agent, as it
were. In pronouncing a familiar word, for instance, he has in principle the
choice of *mis*pronouncing it. Or, in performing a simple arithmetic operation,
he has in principle the choice of making a deliberate mistake. In this sense,
then, even rule-governed actions remain genuine actions. In practice, however,
the agent will not make use of his freedom of choice, the reason being that –
to repeat – the well-established rules have already made the choices for him.

When there are no well-established rules, however, it seems adequate to speak of free actions. As noted above, such actions are rationally explained by the use of the schema of Figure 1.29. We must keep in mind, however, that whether or not there are in a given situation rules for acting, may be a moot point.

It follows that e.g. arithmetical operations like adding or subtracting, considered as such, do not qualify as instances of free behavior. Rather, they exemplify the notion of rule-governed (or mechanical) behavior. It is this type of behavior which lends itself most naturally to *algorithmic* description. In practice, rule-governed actions are always *subordinated* to considerations of rationality. That, at one particular moment, somebody performs this arithmetical operation and not some other, is explained by noting that he believes this action to be a means for achieving some goal that he is entertaining. In this type of context, then, one performs a rational (and free) action *by means of* performing a rule-governed action.

What is true of arithmetic, applies to language as well. If the possibility of linguistic change is excluded, i.e. if a given state of language is considered purely synchronically, it can be maintained that morpho-syntax and semantics deal with rule-governed linguistic behavior while pragmatics deals with free linguistic behavior. Accordingly, the normative concepts connected with the two domains are dissimilar, namely *correctness* and *rationality*. That these two normative dimensions, corresponding to morpho-syntax & semantics vs. pragmatics, are indeed independent of each other, can be seen from the fact that it is possible to perform rational speech acts by uttering incorrect sentences and, inversely, to perform irrational speech acts by uttering correct sentences.[19]

Computer programs for understanding and producing sentences face exactly the same problem of psychological reality as linguistic descriptions in general (cf. 1.7). The same is true of computer models designed to simulate logical behavior. At one time, it was customary to postulate the apparatus of predicate logic inside people's heads. This was wrong because several aspects of formal logic are strongly implausible from the psychological point of view, as will be argued in Section 3.5.

At first, it might seem that economic behavior is free rather than rule-governed. However, it is customary to devise algorithmic models of economic behavior, based on game and/or decision theory. This is explained by the fact that such models presuppose a strongly idealized view of reality: behavior is seen as jointly determined by the amount and the probability of the prospective gain. Thus, as a first approximation, in each different type of (economic) situation there is thought to be only one rational course of action or, equivalently, to each different type of (economic) problem there is thought to be only one correct solution. In more 'realistic' models the number of possible solutions is increased, and one from among them is chosen randomly. In real-life situations, however, such models have only limited use.

Free actions, whether of linguistic or of economic type, are governed by so-called principles of rationality. Qua normative entities, they can be observed just as little as rules of language can; and qua social or 'public' entities, their description can claim psychological reality just as much, or just as little, as linguistic descriptions of the 'autonomous' type can. Popper (1957: 157–158) made this point as follows:

> The opposite doctrine which teaches the reduction of social theories to psychology, in the same way as we try to reduce chemistry to physics, is, I believe, based on a misunderstanding. It arises from the false belief that this 'methodological psychologism' is a necessary corollary of a methodological individualism... But we can be individualists without accepting psychologism. The 'zero method' of constructing rational models is not a psychological but rather a logical method.

A distinction corresponding to that between autonomous linguistics and psycholinguistics can – and must – be made also in the domain of rational behavior, linguistic or not. Thus, Simon (1979 [1976]) and Suppes (1981) distinguish between two types of models for rational behavior, using the terminological distinctions 'substantive vs. procedural' and 'normative vs. psychological', respectively. For my part, I distinguish between 'prescriptive' and 'descriptive' rationality in Itkonen (1983a).

Hofstadter (1995: 53) too has come to see the need for a comparable distinction: "Computer chess programs *have* taught us something about how human chess-players play – namely, how they do *not* play. And much the same can be said for the vast majority of artificial-intelligence programs." He even speaks of a "surprisingly wide gulf between researchers' goals", meaning the goals of prescriptive vs. descriptive rationality. The same result, designated as the 'computational paradox', was reached already by Gardner (1985: 385):

> The paradox lies in the fact that these insights [about how people really think] came about largely through attempts to use computational models and modeling; only through scrupulous adherence to computational thinking could scientists discover the ways in which humans actually *differ* from the serial digital computer.

It is typically the case that mathematicians and computer scientists deal with prescriptive rationality, whereas psychologists and cognitive scientists deal (or at least profess to deal) with descriptive rationality.

Algorithmic descriptions have their limits. There is a general consensus that if human actions are considered in all their complexity, they cannot be predicted or formalized. In particular, this is true of artistic or scientific *creativity*. For instance, Hofstadter (1995: 177–178) claims that it is absolutely impossible to simulate scientific discoveries in the situations in which they have really happened.

Let us, in conclusion, consider the limits of instrumental action, as explicated by Figure 1.29. This figure (or any of its alternative formulations) has often been criticized for being too narrow to accommodate *instinctive* behavior or behavior driven by elementary *needs*. This criticism is, however, based on an excessively narrow concept of 'goal' (as if the achieving of goals must always be a matter of conscious and protracted deliberations about alternative means), and it loses its force once the concept of unconscious goals (and beliefs) has been accepted without reservations. The action that satisfies a need is the means to achieve the goal produced by the need.

Interestingly, the exactly opposite criticism has also been voiced, claiming that creative behavior, or more generally behavior driven by *curiosity*, cannot be adequately conceptualized in terms of instrumental action (cf. Joas 1996: 229–230). However, it does not seem far-fetched at all to view, for instance, the combination of engraving and coin-punching as a means that Gutenberg used to reach the goal of (creatively) inventing the printing press (cf. 1.3). To be sure, this interpretation presupposes that the concept of instrumental action is analogically generalized also to *intellectual* action. And of course, curiosity too may be conceptualized as a basic need, in which case the remarks made in the previous paragraph apply.

Thus, both instinctive and creative behavior may be subsumed under instrumental action. What can*not* be subsumed under it is *institutional* behavior. Berger and Luckmann (1966: 70–85) describe, in a stylized form, the 'origin of institutions'. What begins as instrumental action may, through repetition, change into habitualized action and then, by degrees, into institutional behavior. When the institution starts as an interaction between two actors A and B, the actions performed by A and B first retain their full instrumental character:

> The routinized background of A's and B's activity remains fairly accessible to deliberate intervention by A and B. ... They understand the world they themselves have made. All this changes in the process of transmission to a new generation. The objectivity of the institutional world 'thickens' and 'hardens', not only for the children, but (by a mirror effect) for the parent as well. (p. 76)

Thus, by being repeated over and over, an instrumental action may become a rule or norm. Haiman (1998: Ch. 10) describes the linguistic counterpart of this process. As was noted above, institutional or *rule-governed* actions differ from free instrumental actions in that they are beyond the scope of rational explanation.

1.9 Analogical ambiguity

If analogy-making is conceptualized as problem-solving, there may be either just one (reasonable) solution or several solutions in any given problem situation. The latter case exemplifies the notion of analogical *ambiguity*. Hofstadter (1995: 195–198) illustrates these alternatives with the following pair of examples. First, he asks the question (6):

(6)   What in '12344321' corresponds to '4' in '1234554321'?

Or, to put the problem in the form of a binary proportional analogy (7):

$$(7) \quad \frac{1234554321}{4} = \frac{12344321}{X}$$

Generally, there is no difficulty in giving the solution 'X = 3'. The very simplicity of the solution might create the impression that the role played by 4 is a uniform one. By changing the problem somewhat, however, Hofstadter manages to show that the role played by 4 consists of several components which can be teased apart. The second problem is as in (8):

$$(8) \quad \frac{1234554321}{4} = \frac{123475574321}{X}$$

This time, instead of just one solution, there are three possible solutions, namely 7, 5, or 4, each of which corresponds to a distinct criterion that could function as the basis for analogy, as enumerated in (9).

(9)   7 = 'physical neighbor of the centermost number-pair'
      5 = 'next-to-largest number in the structure'
      4 = 'numerical predecessor of the centermost number-pair'

With hindsight, it is easy to see that all these criteria were present already in the first problem, but they did not stand out because in this particular case they all produced the same result.

The 'competition model' of Bates and McWhinney (1989) has been created to deal with the same type of problem. For instance, the subject of a sentence may be characterized by word-order, agreement with the verb, or animacy. In a prototypical case, all these criteria coincide. Thus, in languages like English and Italian, the following sentences exemplify the prototypical subject: *The boy is eating the apples* and *Il ragazzo mangia i pomi* (same meaning). When the criteria no longer coincide and thus start to 'compete', languages behave differently from one another. The structurally similar sentences *The apple is eating the boy* and *Il pomo mangia il ragazzo* are understood differently, i.e. the English sentence is semantically anomalous while the Italian sentence retains the meaning 'The boy is eating the apple'. Thus, in English the word order 'wins' over animacy whereas in Italian the opposite is the case. The same is true of the sentences *The boy are hitting the girls* and *Il ragazzo colpiscono le ragazze*: The English sentence is understood as an ungrammatical expression with the meaning 'The boy is hitting the girls', whereas the Italian sentence is perfectly grammatical and expresses the meaning 'The girls are hitting the boy'. Thus, in English the word order 'wins' over agreement, whereas in Italian the opposite is the case. Bates and McWhinney (1989: 46–47) are able to show that English is nearly unique among the world's languages in attaching an (almost) exclusive importance to word order. Even an isolating language of a rather pure type like Chinese differs from English in preferring, in case of a conflict, animacy over word order.

It may be good to add an example of phonological competition, mentioned by Bates and McWhinney on p. 52. Should a written nonsense word like *mave* be pronounced /mæv/ or /meɪv/? There are obvious (analogical) models for both choices, i.e. either *have* or *cave, save, mane* etc. The situation could be represented as in Figure 1.30.

The fact that only one word (= *have*) supports the /Cæv/ model is counterbalanced by its great frequency. This situation has an analogue in the theory of linguistic change. The form of a single word which is either exceptionally frequent or exceptionally significant may constitute a model after which the forms of semantically related words are reshaped.

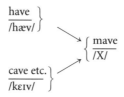

Figure 1.30 An exemplification of the competition model

The similarity between the two above-mentioned cases of 'competition' may not be obvious at once. In the phonological example, we have two concrete models competing with each other. What would be the corresponding models e.g. in the case of *The apple is eating the boy*? On the one hand, there should be a model which has already won the competition, i.e. a model which illustrates the all-importance of word order in English; on the other, there should be a model which has lost the competition, i.e. a model which shows that it *could* have been possible to give up the SVO order, if the agent – patient relation is semantically transparent enough. Now, a sentence type which emphasizes the crucial importance of word order in English is exemplified e.g. by *John loves Mary*, which can be interpreted in one way only although both agreement and animacy would allow two interpretations. On the other hand, precisely because English is a uniquely rigid *SVO* language, it is not easy to find unaffected examples of cancelling the importance of word order. The closest things that come to mind are sentences like *John I like* or the semigrammatical *Sad am I* (which occurs in the song 'Yesterday').

Jackendoff (1987) has outlined an apparatus, called 'preference rules system', for describing analogical ambiguity or, in his words, for describing the choice between competing interpretations. (Interestingly, he seems unaware of the connection with analogy). To start with, he illustrates his point (p. 144–145) by showing how the two gestalt-psychological notions of proximity (= contiguity) and similarity may be used to form groups among distinct configurations of circles. Four distinct cases may now be distinguished: (a) proximity and similarity coincide; (b) proximity wins; (c) similarity wins; (d) proximity and similarity counter-balance each other (= ambiguity). These cases may be illustrated by means of Figures 1.31–34.

From the analogical point of view, it could be said that each figure is first compared both to a 'proximity model' and to a 'similarity model' and is then

Figure 1.31 Proximity = similarity

Figure 1.32 Proximity > similarity

Figure 1.33 Proximity < similarity

Figure 1.34 Proximity or similarity?

interpreted in accordance with the model that it happens to be analogous to. That this view indeed captures Jackendoff's intent, can be seen from how he applies the 'preference rules' idea to the description of word meanings: "... a [TYPE] concept may be mentally filled out by a system of conditions working together as a preference rule system... its decompositional properties make possible a computational *comparison* of the [TYPE] with novel [TOKENS]" (p. 146; emphasis added). As a result of the comparison, the different 'things' (= tokens) are assigned to that type which they are the most similar (= analogous) to. This idea is, to repeat, captured by my account of the proximity/similarity example. Jackendoff is surely right to claim that "once the basic nature of preference rule systems has been isolated, it is possible to recognize them everywhere in psychology" (p. 145). However, the real meaning of this claim becomes clear only once the connection with analogy has been grasped, because analogy is indeed a pervasive 'horizontal' capacity which cuts through all cognitive domains (cf. Chapter 3).

Just like Jackendoff (1987), Johnson (1987) and Lakoff (1987) are committed to the idea that processes of comparison or matching are all the time going on between abstract and concrete entities. Let us assume that thinking indeed proceeds on the basis of metaphorical exploitation of image-schemata. This means, then, that at each moment we have to entertain several candidate schemata in light of which we might interpret whatever we are experiencing or thinking; and we must choose the one which offers the best fit, i.e. the highest degree of structural similarity. Is love (in this particular context) a path, or a force, or a container? Or should we perhaps coin some new metaphor like LOVE IS MONEY? – This last question brings up the issue of *bad* analogies (or metaphors). Many examples of bad or at least questionable analogies will be discussed in Chapter 4.

Hofstadter (2001:504) reaffirms the interpretation given above: "The process of inexact matching between prior categories and new things being perceived (whether those 'things' are physical objects or bite-size events or grand sagas) is analogy-making par excellence. How could anyone deny this?"

1.10 The limits of analogy

At this point, it may have come to look like analogy is an all-encompassing phenomenon. Therefore it is good to delineate its limits, or to show what it is *not*.

Analogy must (ultimately) rest on something non-analogical; otherwise there would be infinite regress. Just like metaphorical meanings presuppose the existence of non-metaphorical ones, so analogies between observable phenomena presuppose the existence of non-analogical observation (and thus, by implication, the corresponding set of basic observational categories). There is, in principle, an analogy between one bird and one fish, but not between two birds, because in the latter case the similarity is material, not structural. (As expected, there has to be a grey area between material and structural, as e.g. in comparing a sparrow and an ostrich.) Thus, phenomena related by similarity associations fall outside of analogy. This applies also to association by contiguity. For instance, it is clear that there is no reason why a part should be analogous to the whole of which it is a part. It follows that the notion of *hierarchy*, exemplified for instance by tree diagrams, is independent of the notion of analogy.[20]

Induction, being based on associations by contiguity and similarity, is non-analogical (cf. Figures 1.13 and 1.14); so is deduction, for different reasons (cf. Figures 1.15 and 1.16). The same is true of testing, i.e. falsification (which is deductive) and confirmation (which is non-deductive) (cf. Figure 1.18). Experimentation and measurement, as part of the testing of theories, are non-analogical too. Furthermore, any type of combination (illustrated by the use of logical connectives) or elaboration (illustrated by quantification) is non-analogical in itself. However, insofar as any of the processes mentioned here are viewed from the perspective of *learning*, analogy comes into picture, because all learning is based on previous experience, more precisely on a structural similarity between what has been experienced in the past and what is being experienced in the present. Again, to avoid infinite regress, learning must have a non-analogical starting point.

Moreover, it seems clear today that at least some *social* concepts (like 'person', 'dominance, or 'request') are innate. Therefore, not all non-concrete thinking can be seen as metaphorical extension of physical or 'embodied' image-schemata. (Remember too that dead metaphors have, by definition, ceased to be metaphors.) There also seem to be irreducible 'leaps' in the emergence of abstract thinking. Most obviously, there is the leap from 'is' to 'ought'. This is valid both in an *ethical* and in an *institutional* sense. It seems incontestable that ethical principles like 'be fair!' or 'do to others what you wish to be done to yourself!' can be neither reduced to nor derived from actual behavior. The same is true of well-established institutional *norms*, most notably norms (or rules) of *language*. The existence of such 'leaps' can be interpreted as pointing to the innateness of *normativity*.

As has been repeated several times, analogy consists in finding a common structure that underlies apparently disparate phenomena. Any (sub-)processes that may be involved in this overall process – like abstraction, idealization, and generalization – are thus part of analogy. This just goes to show that all theoretical thinking is imbued with analogy. As Hofstadter (1995:63) aptly put it, "analogy-making lies at the heart of intelligence".

Now, the reverse is also the case: lack of intelligence is often equivalent to lack of analogy-making, i.e. either to the inability to grasp the right analogy or to the inclination to construct a wrong analogy. However, just as in connection with 'good' thinking above, it is not the case that 'bad' thinking could be exhaustively explicated in terms of analogy. For instance, such fallacies as contradiction, circularity, or infinite regress have in themselves nothing to do with (lack of) analogy.

The validity of the preceding account may be tested by comparing it to what Polya (1973 [1945]) has to say about the nature of scientific (more precisely, mathematical) invention/discovery. He claims (p. 130) to be dealing with "mental operations typically useful with solving problems". The bulk of his text (pp. 37–232) is divided into nearly 70 sections, only one of which bears the title 'analogy'. Prima facie, this might seem to indicate that analogy is not so important, after all.

On closer inspection, however, this impression disappears. Polya repeatedly singles out the four operations of 'analogy', 'generalization', 'specialization', and 'mathematical induction'. Now, the second and the third operations result from analogy by either deleting or adding attributes, respectively; and the fourth is related to 'generalization'. Moreover, the titles of some sections are obvious reformulations of analogy, like 'Do you know a related problem?', 'Have you seen it before?', 'Here is a problem related to yours and solved before'. In other sections, the connection with analogy becomes evident upon reading. 'Auxiliary elements' means elements that have to be added to achieve the analogy between old and new. 'Bright idea' means finding the 'essential connection', i.e. the analogy between old and new (as, to use Aristotle's example, in perceiving that "the varying aspects of the moon are like the various aspects of a ball which is illuminated from one side so that one half of it is shiny and the other half dark", p. 59). 'Can you use the result?' asks whether you can extend the solution to new analogous problems. 'Variation of the problem' means changing the problem in imagination until the right analogy is found. And so on.

Several sections repeat, under new titles, what has been said before. Some sections (like 'Modern heuristics' and 'Subconscious work') apply to scientific discovery/invention as a whole. There are also sections which do not deal with specific mental operations at all, but rather with some related aspects, like 'Figures', 'Pedantry and mastery', 'Terms, old and new'. Some sections merely add relevant quotations, like 'Bolzano', 'Descartes', 'Leibniz', 'Pappus'. It seems that only the sections on logical techniques (like 'Reductio ad absurdum') as well as those on 'Decomposing and recombining' and 'Separat[ing] the various parts of the condition' deal with mental operations which are clearly non-analogical in nature. This is only to be expected in view of the non-analogical nature of deduction, on the one hand, and of the part – whole relationship, on the other, as discussed above. (To be sure, it is possible to see a connection between 'Decomposing and recombining' and 'Variation of the problem', of which the latter – as we have seen – is closely related to analogy.)

Although Polya professes to be interested only in discovery/invention, he in fact also considers the situation *after* the discoveries or inventions have been made. This is one more valuable aspect of his discussion:

> Even fairly good students, when they have obtained the solution of the problem and written down neatly the argument, shut their books and look for something else. Doing so, they miss an important and instructive phase of the work. By looking back at the completed solution, by reconsidering and reexamining the result and the path that led to it, they could *consolidate* their knowledge and develop their ability to solve problems.
>
> (p. 14; emphasis added)

Just like discovery/invention corresponds to my notion of 'dynamic analogy', the aspect of 'consolidation' that Polya is talking about here corresponds to my notion of 'static analogy' (cf. 1.1). Once a generalization about A and B has been made, it has to be kept in mind; and it is the same thing, namely the analogy between A and B, that makes possible the one and the other.

In sum, Polya (1973 [1945]) confirms the central role of analogy in intellectual life, but also shows that analogy does not explain everything. It is obvious that if a theory explains literally *everything*, then it has no value. A weaker version of this criticism is to say that a theory 'explains too much'. Now, this type of criticism must be treated with caution. It is easy to imagine that Newton's mechanics may initially have *appeared* to explain 'too much', because it purported to explain (in the domain of mechanical behavior) everything that goes on both on the earth and in the heavens. But then it turned out that, instead of explaining too much, it achieved a generalization that was significant enough. If one has misgivings about what appears to be the excessive explanatory power of analogy, one might do well to envisage the possibility of a meta-analogy between Newtonian mechanics and analogy.

CHAPTER 2

Analogy inside linguistics

2.1 General remarks

The role of analogy is so obvious in closed systems like phonology and (inflectional) morphology that it cannot be sensibly denied. Therefore, when dealing with these linguistic 'levels' in Sections 2.3 and 2.4, I shall merely present the theory-neutral analogical foundation on which more specific phonological and morphological theories have to be erected. By contrast, the functioning of analogy in syntax and in (sentence-level) semantics has sometimes been contested, which means that these subdomains will be given a more extensive and more argumentative treatment in Sections 2.5 and 2.6. In diachronic linguistics, explanation-by-analogy has always been taken for granted (in deeds if not in words), as will be shown in Section 2.7; and the concept of grammaticalization will be singled out for a more detailed discussion. Given the basic analogy between speech and signing, particular spoken languages may manifest this analogy to different degrees, as shown in Section 2.8. First of all, however, we have to dispatch in Section 2.2 a set of objections to the effect that analogy is a somehow misconceived notion.

2.2 Objections against the concept of analogy

The notion of analogy played a central role in traditional linguistics, in particular in the following three domains. In diachronic linguistics the ('material') principle of sound change was counter-balanced by the ('spiritual') principle of analogy. In developmental psycholinguistics the child was assumed to abstract a common pattern from utterances it had heard and thus to form new expressions on the analogy of old ones. In synchronic linguistics, analogy was taken to be the centripetal force which keeps paradigms (of sounds, of lexical and grammatical morphemes, and of sentence structures) together and, as such, constitutes the very basis of speaking and understanding (for documentation, see Itkonen 1991: 199–200, 287–290, 299–304). In more recent times, generativism has been known for its hostility towards analogy. Therefore we must find out whether this attitude is justified or not.

It is interesting to note that in his dissertation Chomsky (1975a [1955]: 131) still subscribed to the traditional view:

> A primary motivation for this study is the remarkable ability of any speaker of a language to produce utterances which are new both to him and to other speakers, but which are immediately recognizable as sentences of the language. We would like to reconstruct this ability within linguistic theory by developing a method of analysis that will enable us to *abstract from a corpus of sentences a certain structural pattern, and to construct, from the old materials, new sentences conforming to this pattern*, just as the speaker does.   (emphasis added)[1]

We have distinguished here between analogy and induction (cf. 1.5). Traditionally, however, the two have been lumped together. Therefore it is noteworthy that in a paper presented in 1958, Chomsky (1964a: 181) asserted, in consonance with the preceding quotation, that "when we learn our native language we make some very complicated inductions".

This attitude soon came to change. Chomsky (1957) had claimed that there was no discovery procedure for grammars, i.e. no method for deriving grammars from linguistic data; and because any such method has to be analogical (or 'inductive') in character, it followed (or seemed to follow) that there was no use for analogy (or 'induction') in linguistics. This change of mind was insofar gradual as Chomsky (1964b: 59) still admitted that analogy might be acceptable in the explanation of linguistic change; but even this concession was soon withdrawn by generative-minded practitioners of diachronic linguistics (for documentation, see Anttila 1977a). The general anti-analogical position was formulated in Chomsky (1965: 47–59), and it has been more recently restated as follows:

> It seems that there is little hope in accounting for our [linguistic] knowledge in terms of such ideas as analogy, induction, association, reliable procedures, good reasons, and justification in any generally useful sense.
> (Chomsky 1986: 12; repeated quasi verbatim on p. 55 and 222)

Chomsky's argument 'no discovery procedure, no analogy' was accepted, with few exceptions (e.g. Householder 1971; Anttila 1989 [1972]; Derwing 1973), and still today it provides the basic rationale for the entire generative enterprise. The innateness hypothesis is supported by the 'poverty of the stimulus' argument: the data encountered by the child is too limited to constitute an adequate basis for making such *analogical* generalizations as might underlie the comprehension and the production of complex sentences; therefore the child must be aided by innate linguistic knowledge. Similarly, the modularity hypothesis maintains that the mind is divided into a central system, governed by *analogy*, and a set of informationally encapsulated modules: the former, being impervious to scientific treatment, constitutes a 'mystery', whereas the latter, being more tractable, constitute a 'problem' for the study of language (see Fodor 1983, esp. p. 107). – The problem of modularity will be addressed in Chapter 3.

With the benefit of hindsight one cannot help wondering why the 'no discovery procedure, no analogy' argument was accepted nearly universally, because it is clearly less than cogent. It contains at least the following six shortcomings.

First, it is just wrong to argue that since there is no discovery procedure, there is no analogy. The premise is simply false. As Derwing (1973:60–61) already pointed out, on Chomsky's own terms there *must* be a discovery procedure for (mental) grammars. The language-acquisition device (or any of its more recent terminological equivalents) is claimed to take the ('limited', 'impoverished') linguistic data as the input and to *mechanically* produce the mental grammar as the output, which is synonymous with saying that it is a discovery procedure. At present, of course, nobody has been able to describe this discovery procedure in detail (mainly because it would require taking the non-linguistic context into account to a much higher degree than has seemed practicable). But this just shows that important descriptive work remains to be done.

Second, in Chomsky's formulations the lack of discovery procedures and the consequent need for innateness coincides with the denial that there can be any *simple* (or 'elementary') methods of analogy or induction involved in language-acquisition and/or in sentence production and understanding. But why should they be simple? The complexity of the innate universal grammar whose existence generativists have been willing to postulate is not limited in advance in any way. Therefore it would be inconsistent to impose such a priori limitations upon any innate analogical/inductive capacities that we may have reason to postulate. In this context one should recall Chomsky's own reference to "very complicated inductions" in his 1958 lecture (cf. above).

Third, the rationale for generative grammar was originally claimed to consist in its capacity to account for the "fundamental fact about the normal use of language, namely the speaker's ability to produce and understand instantly new sentences" (Chomsky 1965:57–58; see also the citation from Chomsky 1975a [1955] above). This ability was called *creativity*:

> The most striking aspect of linguistic competence is what we may call the 'creativity of language', that is, the speaker's ability to produce new sentences, sentences that are immediately understood by other speakers although they bear no *physical resemblance* to sentences which are 'familiar'.
>
> (Chomsky 1966: 4; emphasis added)

Creativity was in turn identified with *recursivity*: "recursive rules ... provide the basis for the creative aspect of language use" (Chomsky 1967: 7, also 1965: 8). Now, two mistakes have been lumped together here. On the one hand, it is being claimed that generative grammar should provide a model for performance (= sentence production and understanding), but this was *not* really Chomsky's position (cf. below). On the other, it was soon admitted that recursivity has nothing to do with creativity: "What I have elsewhere called the 'creative aspect of language use' [cannot] be identified with the recursive property of grammars. [My f]ailure to keep these very different concepts separate has led to much confusion" (Chomsky 1975b: 230, n. 11). "What I have elsewhere called the 'creative aspect of language use' remains ... a mystery to us" (p. 138).

Curiously enough, Chomsky's recantation on 'creativity' seems to have gone unnoticed, witness Jackendoff's more recent statement: "The fundamental motivation behind generative syntax is of course [sic] the creativity of language" (1992: 23). Therefore it must be stated with as much clarity as possible that creativity is *not* the fundamental motivation behind generative syntax. The most that can be said is that generative syntax accounts for the *innovative* aspect of language. However, being innovative in this sense simply consists in the capacity to form new (and meaningful) combinations of old sentence structures and lexical units. In fact, Jackendoff (1994: 12) has come to espouse this traditional view when he notes that "expressive capacity" is achieved by mentally storing "words and their meanings, plus the *patterns* into which words can be placed". Now this capacity is of course indistinguishable from the traditional *analogical* capacity, as defined e.g. by Bloomfield (1933) and – following him – by Hockett (1966). This is a sobering thought. There is no reason to speak of the 'creativity of syntax'. But if one cannot bear to give up this expression, one should at least realize that Bloomfield's and Hockett's view of syntax is just as 'creative' as Chomsky's.

Fourth, the traditional view was that novel sentences are never completely novel, precisely because they are constructed 'on the analogy of old ones'. By this was simply meant that even if a new sentence happens to contain new lexical morphemes, it has to exemplify one or another familiar sentence *pattern* (and, by the same token, has to contain familiar *grammatical* morphemes). But now Chomsky (e.g. 1968:10) was claiming that the speaker-hearer was able to produce and understand *completely novel* sentences, i.e. "sentences not even similar in pattern to sentences heard in the past"; and this was apparently taken to show that analogy is not enough.

What we have here is an interesting inference from a true premise to a false conclusion. On those rare occasions where Chomsky cared to define 'complete novelty', he defined it as the lack of any *physical* similarity or resemblance (cf. the quotation from Chomsky 1966:4, above; also Chomsky 1965:58). Indeed, there is no physical similarity e.g. between Sapir's two analogous sentences (cf. Figure 1.5). But from this unquestionable fact Chomsky (1968:10) wrongly inferred that "the number of *patterns* underlying our normal use of language is orders of magnitude greater than the number of seconds in a lifetime" (emphasis added). As implausible as it may sound, sentence patterns and individual sentences are being conflated here; and individual sentences are assumed to be 'completely novel' vis-à-vis one another if they just are non-identical. This is shown by the fact that, having presented sentences like 'It is difficult for him to understand this lecture' and 'He read the book that interested the boy', Chomsky (1968:42) goes on to claim that these sentences "are as 'unfamiliar' as the vast majority of those that we encounter in daily life". But surely, because of the familiarity of the patterns that they exemplify, these sentences are as familiar as any sentences can possibly be. Incidentally, the same argument is used e.g. by Postal (1968:267): a sentence A is defined to be completely novel vis-à-vis another sentence B if only B is not exactly identical with, or a repetition of, B.

These simple issues have been misunderstood for so long that some additional clarification is called for. Analogy has always been defined as *structural* similarity, and not as *material* or *physical* similarity (cf. 1.1). Therefore it is wrong to redefine analogy as physical similarity. It is true of course that the ability to produce and understand new sentences cannot be accounted for in terms of physical similarity. But this fact has no bearing at all on the viability of the notion of analogy.

Fifth, producing and understanding (new) sentences are clearly *processes*, i.e. they belong to the linguistic *performance*. At least since Chomsky (1965) it was abundantly clear that generative grammar concerns itself with competence, not with performance. Competence was said to 'underlie' (p. 4), or be 'incorporated in' (p. 9), performance, a claim which is later repeated for 'I-language' in Chomsky (1986:25, 1992:2). But the words 'underlie' and 'incorporate' do not possess any clear meanings here. Under the normal interpretation, if A is incorporated in B, the model of B literally contains the model of A. The suggestion, however, is rejected that the hypotheses about I-language need to be in any way constrained by facts of performance, which means that I-language (formerly 'competence') retains an autonomous status. This is well illustrated e.g. by Berwick and Weinberg (1984), who, although anxious to vindicate the Chomskyan line of thinking, do *not* incorporate a generative grammar in their parser (as was noted also by Nuyts 1992: 131). For them, it is sufficient that the grammar be 'compatible' with the parser. From the psychological point of view, however, the possession and use of language can be exhaustively described in terms of production, understanding, and storage (where, N.B., hypotheses about storage are constrained by evidence from producing and understanding.) In all this there is no place and no need for competence (or I-language), as was already pointed out by Steinberg (1970). In actual fact, 'competence' (or 'I-language') is a name given to the result of describing sentences which the grammarian's (conscious) linguistic intuition deems to be either correct or incorrect; and therefore the conclusion seems inevitable that 'competence' (or 'I-language') is just a misleading designation for the subject matter of traditional autonomous linguistics.[2] – The most important point in the present context is, however, that unlike the notion of competence, the notion of dynamic analogy captures precisely that *process* aspect which underlies the "fundamental fact about the normal use of language", i.e. the ability to produce and understand new sentences. (This is why Bloomfield and Hockett assigned such a central role to analogy.)

Sixth, Chomsky presented his audience with a choice: either to offer some explicitly analogical account or to accept his own anti-analogical account:

> We can give substance to the proposal by explaining 'analogy' in terms of I-language, a system of rules and principles that assigns representations of form and meaning to linguistic expressions, but no other way to do so has been proposed; and with this necessary revision in the proposal, it becomes clear that 'analogy' is simply an inappropriate concept in the first place.
>
> (Chomsky 1986: 32)

Thus, in Chomsky's view, the only way to account for analogy is to show that it is "an inappropriate concept in the first place". But the argument should really be turned around. Dynamic analogy (involved in sentence production and understanding) is a process; the Chomskyan grammar is a description of competence, and therefore a description of structure, not of process; therefore the Chomskyan grammar is an inappropriate account of analogy in the first place.

This point needs to be further clarified. What we have here is a choice between describing a certain phenomenon either in terms of process or in terms of structure. It is self-evident, however, that 'process' really means '*structure-and*-process' (because processes, rather than taking place in a vacuum, must have something, i.e. structures, which they apply to). Thus, we have a choice between a complex account (= structure-and-process) and a simple account (= structure). The phenomenon to be described matches the complex account, but not the simple account: sentence production and understanding consist of (structures-and-)processes, not of mere structures. When spelled out, Chomsky's 'proposal' amounts to the incongruous proposal to think of processes as if they were not processes, but structures (= 'representations of form and meaning'). When this is clearly understood, Chomsky's proposal loses whatever plausibility it may have seemed to possess.

To sum up, even if there were no explicit processual account of analogy (as involved in sentence production and understanding), it would still be impossible to accept Chomsky-type structural descriptions as an account of (dynamic) analogy, because – conceptually – they are of the *wrong type*. The important point is, however, that a processual account of (syntactic) analogy will be first outlined here in Section 2.3, B and then actually given in the Appendix. Thus, it is no longer true that "no other way to explain analogy has been proposed", as Chomsky put it in the above quotation. Of course, the account of (dynamic) analogy that will be given here is far from definitive. But at least it is of the *right type*, i.e. it is a description of (structure-and-)*process*, and not just of structure.

Some of the points that I made above are dealt with in greater detail by Nuyts (1992) in Chapter 2 (= 'Linguistic knowledge and language use: Chomsky revisited'), even if analogy is not his primary concern. Nuyts (2001: 16–17) further points out that the process aspect is absent not just from the tree diagrams of generative linguistics, but also from the pictorial diagrams of cognitive linguistics (which, to be sure, are meant to be complemented by such introspection-based processes as 'apparent motion' and 'windowing of attention').

In the remainder of this section I shall make a few additional remarks. The misgivings about analogy have sometimes been expressed by claiming that "analogy is too powerful". According to Kiparsky (1974:259), for instance, the general concept of analogy allows the following proportional opposition: 'ear: hear = eye: *heye'; and since there is no such verb as to *heye* (meaning 'to see') in English, Kiparsky takes the general concept of analogy to be refuted.

This argument is less than cogent because it amounts to claiming that analogy is a meaningful concept only if all possible analogies are actual analogies. Such a position rules out the very notion of *false* analogy. Therefore, it does not make sense. It could be argued, just as well, that the following example (1) refutes the concept of analogy:

$$(1) \quad \frac{\text{I walked}}{\text{I walked the dog}} = \frac{\text{I slept}}{\text{*I slept the dog}}$$

However, rather than refuting the concept of analogy, what this example actually shows is that it is not reasonable to apply analogy in total disregard of the facts. It is a fact about English that *to walk* has both an intransitive and a transitive reading whereas *to sleep* has only an intransitive reading. It would not be reasonable to try to describe these verbs without taking this fact into account. In just the same way, it is a fact about English that there is no prefix /h-/ which could turn a noun into a corresponding verb (à la *eye* → *heye*). – Let us consider one more example, i.e. (2):

$$(2) \quad \frac{\text{John painted the house}}{\text{John painted the house red}} = \frac{\text{John saw the house}}{\text{*John saw the house red}}$$

Does this example refute analogy, by showing that it is 'too powerful'? Of course not, and the reason why it does not is the same as above. It does not make sense to try to describe the English verbs *to paint* and *to see*, while ignoring their semantics, or the fact they are semantically dissimilar: the former is a resultative verb whereas the latter is not.[3] Science seeks generalizations, and there is no (theoretical) generalization without analogy (cf. 1.4). It goes without saying that not every imaginable generalization is a true one. (Otherwise science would not be needed at all.) It would be unreasonable to take this to mean that we have to give up the search for true generalizations and, with it, the use of analogy.

In his criticism of analogy, Kiparsky (1975) is willing to accept opposite strategies as long as they suit his purpose: either analogy is wrong, which means that it is dispensable; or analogy is right, which means that it tries to capture the same thing which is captured by rules of generative grammar, which means – once again – that analogy is dispensable. Let us spell this out. On the one hand, according to Kiparsky, the unsophisticated concept of analogy predicts that "speakers should form the plural of *dog* sometimes with [-s] on the analogy of *cats*, sometimes with [-z] on the analogy of *birds*, and sometimes with [-ɪz] on the analogy of *fishes*, depending maybe on which sort of plural happened to precede in the context" (p. 188). These predictions are obviously false, which means that unsophisticated analogy is dispensable. On the other hand, still according to Kiparsky, it is possible to envisage a sophisticated concept of analogy which is context-sensitive, takes distinctive features into account, etc. However, "generative phonology argues that at the point at which the analogies begin to make the right generalizations, they are indistinguishable from [generative] rules" (p. 189). Thus, sophisticated analogy is dispensable.

Again, the argument is less than cogent. Even if, on Kiparsky's own terms, sophisticated phonological analogy and generative phonology as practiced in the mid-70s are "indistinguishable", we still have a choice between the two. I submit that the choice is obvious. Choosing the former alternative involves revealing the interesting connections that phonology has with other linguistic levels (cf. Ch. 2), with non-linguistic cognition (cf. Ch. 3), and with human culture in general (cf. Ch. 4). As for choosing the latter alternative, nobody remembers any more what, exactly, it involves (quite apart from the fact that it would entail considering phonology as a self-contained domain without any interesting connections to anything that might exist outside of it).

Diachronic linguistics contains its own version of the anti-analogical argument. The use of analogy to explain language change has been repudiated on the putative grounds that analogy is unable to *predict* when, and in which specific way, linguistic changes are going to take place. This too is a less than cogent argument. It has always been known that linguistic changes are in principle unpredictable, which means that the corresponding explanations must be *post hoc* or *a posteriori*:

> Our tracing of the etymology of a word is the following-up of a series of acts of name-making, consisting chiefly in the new applications of old material. And every one of those acts was one of choice, involving the free working of the human will, only under the government, as always and everywhere, of conditions and motives... [W]e can only deal with the case *a posteriori*, reasoning back toward the mental condition from the act in which it is manifested.
> (Whitney 1979 [1875]: 143–144; similarly Itkonen 1981, 1982a, 1984)

No theory can predict linguistic changes. If an analogy-based theory claimed to be able to predict linguistic changes, it would rightly be treated with suspicion (for more discussion, cf. Becker 1990: 15–28).

It was mentioned in Section 1.6 that there is renewed interest in analogy within the school of cognitive linguistics. This interest, however, has a curiously ahistorical character. On the basis of Fauconnier (2001), for instance, one might easily think that there was no analogy in linguistics before 1980. This may in turn create the impression that the generative objections against the 'old' concept of analogy were justified, and that what is now being proposed is a completely 'new' concept of analogy, untainted by the flaws of the old one. As I have tried to prove in what precedes, such an impression would be mistaken.

p	t	k
b	d	g
m	n	ŋ
f	s	χ

Figure 2.1 Phonological system

Both Lepage (2003) and Lavie (2003) contain a wealth of useful information concerning the vicissitudes that the notion of analogy has undergone in the course of its history.

2.3 Phonology

It is a general truth that units in a well-structured system are defined, or constituted, by their mutual similarities and differences. Therefore it is logical enough that Trubetzkoy, the founder of structuralist phonology, recognized analogy (under the name of 'proportional opposition') as the centripetal force which keeps (phonological) systems together (cf. Trubetzkoy 1958 [1939]: 60–66). Consider the simple system given in Figure 2.1.

In this type of system the phoneme /k/ is defined by four distinctive features, which are elicited by contrasting /k/ with its closest neighbours: it is a voiceless (as opposed to /g/), non-nasal (as opposed to /ŋ/), and velar (as opposed to /t/) occlusive (as opposed to /χ/). Phonological oppositions of this type are called *proportional*. They may be made more explicit by showing the precise place of /k/ in each of the four 'chains' of proportional oppositions (3–6):

(3)   voiceless   p:b = t:d = k:g

(4)   non-nasal   p:m = t:n = k:ŋ

(5)   velar   p:t:k = b:d:g = m:n:ŋ = f:s:χ

(6)   occlusive   p:f = t:s = k:χ

Thus, the distinctive features of /k/ are identical with the *differences* between /k/ and its neighbours. 'Difference' between *X* and *Y* is just another term for the *relation* between *X* and *Y*. Now, as can be seen from (3)–(6), the differences/relations between /k/ and its neighbors are the *same* as the differences/relations between other pairs (or triplets) of phonemes in each of the four chains of oppositions. Hence, by definition, there is an *analogy* between these pairs (or triplets).

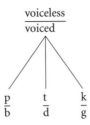

Figure 2.2 Phonological analogy as a tree diagram

The contrary of a proportional opposition is an *isolated* opposition, like that between /k/ and /s/ in our system. Isolated oppositions do not recur in the system. In other words, they contribute nothing to the coherence of the system. This is just another way of saying that their contraries, i.e. proportional oppositions, *are* crucial to the coherence of the system.

Any meaningful opposition between *A* and *B* is based on some 'deeper' similarity between *A* and *B*, which constitutes their basis of comparison (*Vergleichsgrundlage* or *tertium comparationis*). For instance, the opposition between /k/ and /g/ is based on the fact that they both are non-nasal velar occlusives. If there is no similarity, there is no opposition either (as, to use Trubetzkoy's own example on p. 60, there is none between a bottle of ink and the freedom of will). Differences in the constitution of the basis of comparison give rise to additional pairs of opposition (like 'one-dimensional' vs. 'many-dimensional' and 'privative' vs. 'equipollent'). However, as far as the idea of *structured system* is concerned, they are secondary vis-à-vis the notion of proportional opposition. – The analogical basis of phoneme analysis has been further elaborated on by Householder (1971: 65–67).

Our discussion of phoneme analysis may be related to the discussion of the preceding chapter as follows. Each of the pairs *p:b*, *t:d*, and *k:g* constitutes a 'minisystem' with two parts. The minisystems are analogous to each other because they are structurally similar or exemplify a common structure, shown in Figure 2.2.

As a consequence, *t:d* and *k:g* are comparable (or meta-analogous) to 'feathers : lungs : wings' and 'scales : gills : fins', respectively, or to *The farmer : kills : the duckling* and *The man : takes : the chick*, respectively; and 'voiceless : voiced' is comparable, in the latter case, to *SVO* (cf. Figures 1.2 and 1.4).

It is a very old idea that a unit is what other units are *not*: as Spinoza put it, "omnis determinatio est negatio". Saussure took this idea literally and claimed that in a system there are nothing but differences, which means that structural units are defined *purely* negatively. This is a logical impossibility (cf. Itkonen 1991:298–299). Trubetzkoy points out (p. 60), more reasonably, that units of a system may sometimes receive a purely negative definition.

Trubetzkoy also notes explicitly (p. 81) that the principles introduced by him apply to any systems of opposition, and not only to phonological systems. This is the program for general ('semiotic') structuralism.

2.4 Morphology

Next, let us move from phonology to morphology. The Roman grammarian and polymath Marcus Terentius Varro (116–127 B.C.) understood analogy (= *analogia*) as a general organizing principle, illustrated e.g. by the proportion 'daughter : mother = son : father'. According to Varro, the same principle recurs both in arithmetic and in language. Consider the constellation of numbers in Figure 2.3.

There is a parallelism (or more technically, a meta-analogy) between Figure 2.3 and the constellation of inflected words in Figure 2.4.

Varro presents the declensional system of Latin in the form of a matrix such that the cases are placed on horizontal lines while the genders (and the numbers) are placed on vertical lines. Only part of the paradigm of the adjective *albus* ('white') is given explicitly. On the one hand, the relation between *albus* and *alba* is the same as that between *albo* and *albae*, just like 1 : 10 = 2 : 20. On the other hand, the relation between *albus* and *albo* is the same as that between *alba* and *albae*, just like 1 : 2 = 10 : 20.

1	2	4
10	20	40
100	200	400

Figure 2.3 Basis for mathematical analogy

CASE GENDER	NOM	DAT	GEN
MASC	albus	albo	albi
FEM	alba	albae	albae
NEUTER	album	albo	albi

Figure 2.4 Basis for morphological analogy

The examples given above illustrate Varro's notion of 'disjoined analogy'. His notion of 'conjoined analogy' is illustrated by the three incompletive tenses, i.e. imperfect, present, and simple future, in (7):

$$(7) \quad \frac{\text{legebam ('I was reading')}}{\text{lego ('I am reading')}} = \frac{\text{lego ('I am reading')}}{\text{legam ('I will be reading')}}$$

In other words, the relation of past to present is the same as the relation of present to future. Furthermore, the incompletive tenses stand in an analogical relation to the completive ones, namely pluperfect, perfect, and future perfect (with the respective meanings 'I had read', 'I have read', 'I will have read'), as shown by the ternary analogy (8).

(8)   legebam : lego : legam = legeram : legi : legero

Thus, all the facts can be summarized in the second-level analogy (9):

$$(9) \quad \left\{ \frac{\text{Imperfect}}{\text{Present}} = \frac{\text{Present}}{\text{I Future}} \right\} = \left\{ \frac{\text{Pluperfect}}{\text{Perfect}} = \frac{\text{Perfect}}{\text{II Future}} \right\}$$

The Alexandrian grammarian Aristarchos and his followers are mentioned by Varro as practitioners of this type of (proportional) analogy in linguistic analysis (cf. Varro 1938:X, 37–52). The question as to whether language is regular ('analogical') or irregular ('anomalous') provides the larger background for the preceding discussion. For instance, Varro was well aware that derivation is less regular than inflection (cf. Itkonen 1991:194–200).

Varro's tradition was continued by Paul (1975 [1880], esp. Ch. 5). He regards language as a system of 'groups of ideas' (*Vorstellungsgruppen*) which are mutually related, by associations of varying strength, on the basis of similarities of form and/or meaning. More precisely, he distinguishes between 'material groups' (*stoffliche Gruppen*) and 'formal groups' (*formale Gruppen*), exemplified, for instance, by all cases of a single (singular) noun and by all (singular) nouns inflected in a single case, respectively. For instance, the Latin noun *hortus* ('garden') inflected in (the singular of) the five cases constitutes a material group, whereas all nouns inflected e.g. in the dative singular constitute a formal group. These nouns exemplify the different declensions, of which only the first three are mentioned by Paul (p. 107) (= *mensae, rosae* ...; *horto, anno* ...; *paci, nocti* ...). Following Anttila (1977a:25–32), the interrelations of material and formal groups may be depicted as in Figure 2.5.

The interaction of material and formal groups produces the following proportional analogies: *mensa : mensam : mensae : mensae : mensā = hortus : hortum : horti : horto : horto = pax : pacem : pacis : paci : pace.*

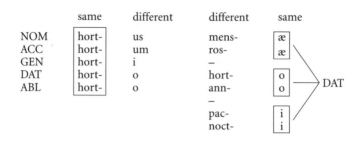

Figure 2.5 Material group and formal group according to Hermann Paul

The notion of 'formal group' needs to be made more precise because it co-incides with the notion of 'grammatical meaning'. In the Latin grammar it is standardly assumed that a finite verb expresses five distinct grammatical mean-ings. For instance, the word-form *amo* ('I love') is active, indicative, present, 1. person, singular. Just like the distinctive features of /k/ in phonological analy-sis (cf. above), these separate meanings are elicited by contrasting *amo* with its closest neighbours in the morphological system: *amo* vs. *amor* = active vs. pas-sive; *amo* vs. *amem* = indicative vs. subjunctive; *amo* vs. *amabam* = present vs. imperfect; *amo* vs. *amamus* = singular vs. plural; *amo* vs. *amas* = 1 vs. 2 person. In the 'core' system of Latin finite verbs (excluding the imperative forms), there are two voices, two moods, six or four tenses (in indicative and in subjunctive, respectively), two numbers, and three persons, which means that (ignoring al-lomorphic variation) there are 120 finite verb forms. They constitute a system which is organized, and held together, by the following analogical relationships.

Active vs. passive: There are ten chains of proportional oppositions, corre-sponding to the six tenses of indicative and the four tenses of subjunctive, and starting with indicative present, or (10):

(10)   amo : amas : amat : amamus : amatis : amant = amor : amaris : amatur : amamur : amamini : amantur; etc.

Indicative vs. subjunctive: There are eight chains of proportional oppositions, corresponding to the four common tenses of these two moods, both in active and in passive, and starting with indicative present, or (11):

(11)   amo : amas : amat : amamus : amatis : amant = amem : ames : amet : amemus : ametis : ament; etc.

Tense: This can no longer be represented by a single *set* of opposition chains, but must rather be represented by several *blocks* of such sets. For instance, 'present' is contrasted with five other tenses (two of which are not shared by the

Present		Imperfect	etc.
amo : amas : ...	=	amabam : amabas : ...	
amem : ames : ...	=	amarem : amares : ...	
amor : amaris : ...	=	amabar : amabaris : ...	
amer : ameris : ...	=	amarer : amareris : ...	

Figure 2.6 A fragment of the Latin tense system

subjunctive). Thus, 'present' is constituted by four chains (= active & indicative, active & subjunctive, passive & indicative, passive & subjunctive), which are first contrasted *en bloc* with the corresponding four chains constituting the imperfect, and then likewise for the other tenses; see Figure 2.6.

Singular vs. plural: Because this opposition occurs in every voice, mood, and tense, there are twenty chains of oppositions (twelve in indicative and eight in subjunctive), starting with active, indicative, present, or (12):

(12)   amo : amas : amat = amamus : amatis : amant; etc.

1 vs. 2 vs. 3 person: Because this threefold opposition too occurs in every voice, mood, and tense, there are here too twenty chains of oppositions, starting with active, indicative, present, or (13):

(13)   amo : amamus = amas : amatis = amat : amant; etc.

It should be possible to summarize all this data in some more conspicuous way. Consider how the functioning of two or more variables is represented in sociology. For simplicity, let us deal with binary variables only (cf. Boudon 1974). The cases from two (= *A* and *B*) to five variables (*A*, *B*, *C*, *D*, and *E*) are handled as in Figures 2.7–10.

Because every Latin verb-form expresses five grammatical meanings and thus participates in five distinct paradigms simultaneously, it is the case with five variables, depicted in Figure 2.10, that applies to the Latin conjugation. Of course, the number of the values varies depending on the variable. The variables 'voice', 'mood', and 'number' have two values while 'person' has three values. The variable 'tense' is more complicated because the number of its values is dependent on the variable 'mood': there are six values in the indicative and four in the subjunctive. There are many possible ways to represent the functioning of five variables, but here the traditional format will be chosen. For reasons of space, 'tense' is exemplified only by two values, namely 'present' and 'imperfect'; see Figure 2.11.

It is the purpose of this formalization to bring out the fact that each verb-form is – literally – an *intersection* of five distinct paradigms, each of which

	A	Ā
B	–	–
B̄	–	–

Figure 2.7 Two variables

	C		C̄	
	A	Ā	A	Ā
B	–	–	–	–
B̄	–	–	–	–

Figure 2.8 Three variables

		C		C̄	
		A	Ā	A	Ā
D	B	–	–	–	–
	B̄	–	–	–	–
D̄	B	–	–	–	–
	B̄	–	–	–	–

Figure 2.9 Four variables

		E				Ē			
		C		C̄		C		C̄	
		A	Ā	A	Ā	A	Ā	A	Ā
D	B	–	–	–	–	–	–	–	–
	B̄	–	–	–	–	–	–	–	–
D̄	B	–	–	–	–	–	–	–	–
	B̄	–	–	–	–	–	–	–	–

Figure 2.10 Five variables

has its own analogical relations. For this purpose, the present formalization is good enough, but it is not the ideal one. Ideally, a given verb-form should be *surrounded* by its closest neigbours, i.e. the closeness of association should be iconically reflected as spatial closeness. Consider the form *amabat* (= Act. Ind. Imperf. 3SG). It should be surrounded by such forms as *amabatur* (= same, except in voice), *amaret* (= same, except in mood), *amat* & *amavit* & *amaverat* & *amabit* & *amaverit* (= same, except in tense), *amas* & *amo* (= same, except in person), *amabant* (= same, except in number). To some extent, the above

			PRES		
		ACT		PASS	
		IND	SUBJ	IND	SUBJ
	1.	amo	amem	amor	amer
SG	2.	amas	ames	amaris	ameris
	3.	amat	amet	amatur	ametur
	1.	amamus	amemus	amamur	amemur
PL	2.	amatis	ametis	amamini	amemini
	3.	amant	ament	amantur	amentur

			IMPERF		
		ACT		PASS	
		IND	SUBJ	IND	SUBJ
	1.	amabam	amarem	amabar	amarer
SG	2.	amabas	amares	amabaris	amareris
	3.	amabat	amaret	amabatur	amaretur
	1.	amabamus	amaremus	amabamur	amaremur
PL	2.	amabatis	amaretis	amabamini	amaremini
	3.	amabant	amarent	amabantur	amarentur

Figure 2.11 The five grammatical meanings (= 'variables') of the Latin verb system

formalization fulfils the requirement of spatial closeness, but not quite. In a *n*-dimensional hyperspace this could be achieved.

In the spirit of Paul and Anttila, Bybee (1985: Ch. 3) points out that there are varying 'relations of power' between the units of a paradigm. First, some units, often marked by zero expression, are 'basic' with respect to others. In the Latin verb, it seems natural to take either *amo* or *amat* as basic (even if neither of them is strictly speaking a zero form; cf. below). Second, some (groups of) units are more closely related and thus constitute sub-wholes within the verbal system. Thus, as Varro already realized (cf. above), the incompletive and the completive tenses constitute two large sub-wholes. The former contains the imperfect (*amabam*, etc.), the present (*amo*, etc.), and the future (*amabo*, etc.) in active and passive indicative. The latter contains the pluperfect (*amaveram*, etc.), the perfect (*amavi*, etc.), and the future perfect (*amavero*, etc.) in the two voices of indicative. In the two sybsystems the basic forms are the present and the perfect, respectively.

Whatever else the inflectional morphology of a given language may be, it is certainly a system held together by crisscrossing analogies like those described above. Otherwise, it would be simply impossible to learn and memorize such huge amounts of data. Besides, if there are more moods, more voices, and distinct subject – object markings for all combinations of persons in the transitive verb, the complexity of data increases accordingly. In Cayuga, for instance, there are some 120 personal prefixes (= subject – object markings) to be learned (cf. Sasse 1988). In the verbal system of West Greenlandic, with seven moods and both intransitive and transitive inflection, there are in principle more than 240 affirmative personal endings; and this number becomes even greater when distinct negative endings are taken into account (cf. Fortescue 1984).

The use of analogy does not entail any particular conception of morpheme, or of morphological analysis. Bybee (1985:77–78) opts for the Word-and-Paradigm model. In the same vein, Bauer (1992:152) notes that the Word-and-Paradigm model, which is adequate for languages with a complex (inflectional) morphology, is based on the fact that units of a given paradigm are *contrasted* with one another:

> In WP morphology ... the word-form is derived by a number of processes or operations which apply to the lexeme. ... The linguist as analyst can deduce what these processes are by consideration of the entire paradigm in which the lexeme appears, and by contrasting the word-forms which appear in that paradigm. In this way syntax and morphology are kept clearly distinct, which is not necessarily the case in a system which takes the morpheme as its basic unit.

The same lesson can be learned from the way that S. Anderson (1992:Ch. 3) justifies the use of the WP model and, with it, the distinction between syntax and morphology. The traditional 'concatenating' morphology is faced with a set of well-known problems posed e.g. by 'replacive' morphs, 'subtractive' morphs, and zero morphs. As Anderson points out, the grammatical meaning 'past' implicit in *sang* is really expressed by the *relation* between *sing* and *sang*; and, we may add, this relation is of course *analogous* to that between the more transparent (= concatenating) forms *walk* and *walk-ed*. Similarly, in Russian the genitive plural of feminine nouns is expressed by deleting the final *-a* of the nominative singular, which again can be grasped only as a relation, e.g. *molecula : molecul*, analogous to the relation *atom : atom-ov*.

Finally, consider once again the case of the Latin verb-form *am-o* ('I love'). It expresses five grammatical meanings, but it seems equally awkward to say that they are all expressed just by *-o* and to say that some of them (in particular, the meaning 'present') are expressed by zero morphs. It seems more adequate to contrast *am-o* with all its neighbours simultaneously, just as we have done above. (As was pointed out above, it is not enough to say that a word-form has to be considered as part of its own paradigm; rather, it has to be considered as the intersection of all the paradigms in which it participates.) It will turn out that the meaning 'present' is expressed, not by a simple zero, but rather by a 'relational morph' which says 'no formatives between *am-* and the personal ending, as compared with other tenses' or, more precisely, 'the *least amount of formatives among the tenses*'. The same principle applies to the subjunctive present (*am*)-*e*-*m* ('I should/may love'), except that the form-meaning relations are a little more explicit insofar as -*e*- expresses the subjunctive while -*m* expresses the 1 person singular. – The WP model as applied to Latin inflectional (= conjugational) morphology is discussed by Matthews (1972). The analogical element implicit in the WP model is made explicit in Anttila's (1977b, 1991) 'field morphology'.

So far, the use of analogy in morphology seems fully justified and should, in my opinion, be regarded as *psychologically realistic*. But, as always, the role of analogy may also be exaggerated. In American structural linguistics it was assumed without question that linguistic levels should be represented as analogous to each other: "hence something analogous to the procedures that enable us to group allophones into phonemes ought to serve to group morpheme alternants into morphemes" (Hockett 1966:28). And Hockett adds that it was he himself who coined the term 'allomorph', on the analogy of 'allophone'. On reflection, however, it seems implausible that there could be a perfect analogy between phonology and morphology (apart from the obvious fact that, at both levels, the identity of a unit is determined by its relations to other units in the system). After all, morphemes are by definition form – meaning entities whereas phonemes are not, apart from the special case of sound symbolism (cf. the Hockett-quotation on p. 50).

A more revealing overall notion of morpheme might result from taking the situation of 'one meaning – one form', or 1M1F, as the default case (cf. Anttila 1989 [1972]:Ch. 7; Itkonen 1982a, 1983a:208–210), and from noting the violations of this norm. In the syntagmatic dimension, 2M1F is 'portmanteau morph' (and 1M0F is 'zero morph'), whereas 1M2F is 'discontinuous morph'. In the paradigmatic dimension, 2M1F is an instance of morphological ambiguity (or homonymy), whereas 1M2F is an instance of allomorphic variation. As noted above, the supposed analogy between phonology and morphology is based on the analogy 'phoneme : allophone = morpheme : allomorph'. But the temptation to view phonology and morphology as perfectly analogous to each other vanishes, once it is realized that 'allomorph' is just one of the four distinct types of violation of the 1M1F principle.

It is good to add that the 'analogical' relations that Paul investigates in synchronic morphology are identical with the relations which Saussure (1962 [1916]:173–175) calls 'associative' (*rapports associatifs*) and opposes to 'syntagmatic' relations. Later, of course, 'associative' was renamed 'paradigmatic'. Thus, denying the existence of analogy would amount to denying the existence of paradigmatic relations. Moreover, Paul (1975 [1880]: 109) extends the analogical relations also to phrases and (simple) sentences, as shown by the examples in (14) and (15):

(14)   pater : mortuus ('dead father', masc.) = filia : pulchra ('beautiful daughter', fem.) = caput : magnum ('big head', neuter)

(15)   spricht : Karl? ('does K. speak?') = schreibt : Fritz? ('does F. write?')

In just the same way, Saussure (1962 [1916]: 179–180) assumes that his associative/paradigmatic relations hold not only between word-forms but also between sentences. For instance, a sentence like *que vous dit-il?* ('what does he say to you-PL?') acquires its identity or 'value' (*valeur*) from the fact that it stands in systematic opposition to such sentences as *que te dit-il?* ('what does he say to you-SG?') and *que nous dit-il?* ('what does he say to us?').

2.5 Syntax

We have seen that in phonology and morphology units, i.e. *sounds* and (inflected) *words*, are defined by their (analogical) relations to other units. Such relational networks constitute corresponding systems. Phonological systems are relatively easy to visualize. This is no longer true of morphological systems because one unit typically participates in several paradigms simultaneously, which means that the corresponding systems must be multidimensional. (Notice, incidentally, that the notion of 'paradigm' is not restricted to inflecting languages, because e.g. adpositional constructions of isolating languages are clearly organized into paradigms of their own.) It would be logical to expect that the notion of (relational) system applies to syntax as well. The basic unit would be *sentence structure* (or 'construction' or 'pattern'), and – as always – the identity of a given unit would be defined by its place in the system, i.e. by the relations it entertains to other units. Indeed, it seems clear enough that this is precisely how sentence structures are defined, and exist, as a matter of fact (as suggested by Paul's and Saussure's simple syntactic analogies). However, there are problems of delimitation insofar as not only simple sentence structures but also 'basic' types of complex sentence structures should be included; but the latter notion is far from unambiguous. Thus, due to the complexity of syntactic relations, syntactic systems are seldom spelled out explicitly, in the form of (sets of) syntactic 'paradigms'. Instead, they have to be inferred from the overall syntactic descriptions.

A.   The Arabic tradition

The central methodological notion employed by Arab grammarians was *qiyās* (literally 'measuring'), which was used also outside linguistics, especially in jurisprudence. It is clear from the following passage that the meaning of this term is something like 'reasoning by analogy': "Building a *qiyās* consists in exploring an unknown configuration of data and trying to recognize in it a patterning already met and which, in other situations, lent itself to analysis" (Bohas et al. 1990:23). Thus, the aim was to "identify a new situation as basically similar to an older one" (p. 24).

The functioning of *qiyās* in grammatical analysis may be explained more concretely as follows (cf. op. cit.: Ch. 3). The basic descriptive device was the notion of *government*, as explained in detail by Owens (1988). The unit which governs must precede the one which is governed, and the two must belong to distinct word-classes. There are three word-classes, which are defined in terms of government. Verbs govern and are not governed. (For simplicity, I shall here ignore the fact that the mood of the verb was thought to be governed by either a visible or an invisible particle.) Nouns do not govern and are governed. Particles may or may not govern, but are not governed. The justification of these definitions may be illustrated with these two traditional examples (16 and 17):

(16)   daraba   zayd-un   rajul-an
       hit&3sg&m   Zayd-nom   man&sg-acc&Indef
       'Zayd hit a man'

(17)   marra   zayd-un   bi   rajul-in
       went&3sg&m   Zayd-nom   past   man&sg-gen&Indef
       'Zayd went past a man'

The verb *daraba* governs the two nouns *zaydun* and *rajulan* by 'causing' them to be in the nominative and in the accusative.[4] Similarly the particle (i.e. preposition) *bi* governs the noun *zaydin* by 'causing' it to be in the genitive. The prepositional phrase is understood as analogous to a noun in the accusative. Neither the verbs *daraba* and *marra* nor the particle *bi* are governed whereas the nouns *zaydun*, *rajulan*, and *rajulin* do not govern. Incidentally, defining the noun as non-governing makes it necessary to analyze possessive genitives (e.g. *gulāmu Zaydin* = 'Zayd's servant-boy') as underlying prepositional phrases (= *gulāmun li-Zaydin* = 'a servant-boy [belonging] to Zayd').[5] It may be added that, due to the *VSO* order, the subject was thought to be more closely connected to the verb than the object, which means that the notion of *VP* was inconceivable.

These examples represent the *clear cases* of word-classes which constitute the starting point of grammatical analysis. When the nature of less than clear cases has to be decided, *qiyās* is put to work. Here are some examples (cf. Itkonen 1991: 132–134). The active participle (of a transitive verb), although in some respects similar to a noun, may govern a noun in the accusative, and therefore it is decreed to be a (noun-like) verb. It is rather uncontroversial to regard indeclinable pronouns as analogous to nouns (as in *daraba-hu Zaydun* = 'Zayd hit him'). However, since verbs must govern their subjects, personal endings are regarded as analogous to pronouns, and thus ultimately to nouns (as in *darab-tu-hu* = 'I hit him'). The emphatic word *inna* (= 'indeed') governs the topic in the accusative and the comment in the nominative, but since it lacks both verbal inflection and verbal meaning, it is regarded as a (verb-like) particle. Inversely, the past tense of the copula (3SG&M = *kāna*) is regarded as a (particle-like) verb because, although without any definite semantic content, it inflects like a verb and governs the topic in the nominative and the comment in the accusative.

The force of *qiyās* is shown most dramatically in how the nominal sentence is analyzed. This is the traditional example (18):

(18)   *zaydun rajulun*
       TOPIC   COMMENT
       'Zayd is a man'

On the face of it, this sentence type is clearly different from the prototypical verbal sentence. However, since nouns are governed by definition, it follows that there must be some sort of *invisible* entity preceding these two nouns and governing their nominative endings. (The precise form, and content, of this entity remained a matter of dispute.) On the other hand, the nominal sentence also exerted an analogous influence on how the verbal sentence was interpreted. It was rather natural, especially in connection with intransitive verbs, to reinterpret the verb as the comment and the noun (= subject) as the topic. The two aspects may be depicted as in Figure 2.12, where N N and V N stand for nominal sentence and verbal sentence, respectively, and the arrows represent the relationship of government.

In sum, the 'government' model, exemplified by the verbal sentence, was first analogically extended to the nominal sentence. Then, the topic–comment

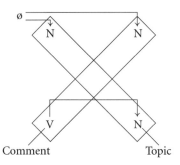

Ø

N   N

V   N

Comment   Topic

Figure 2.12 Simultaneous application of the 'government model' and of the 'topic – comment' model in the Arabic grammatical theory

model, exemplified by the nominal sentence, was analogically extended to the verbal sentence.[6]

It may be added that *qiyās* means not only theoretical analysis, but also the practical, routinized application of inflectional paradigms to produce new forms. As one Arab grammarian put it, "Don't you see that neither you nor anybody else has ever heard all the nouns of the paradigm *fa'il* or *maf'ul*? You have heard some forms and then you have proceeded by analogy to produce others" (Langhade 1985:111).

In conclusion, it is interesting to note, as a point of comparison, that analogy plays a less explicit role in Panini's tradition. This is due to the fact that Panini's system is 'vertical', in the sense of deriving forms from meanings in a step-by-step fashion (cf. Itkonen 1991:38–44). By contrast, as we have just seen, the Arabic tradition regards syntax as a 'horizontal' level of its own. And it is easiest to formulate analogies between units of one and the same level, for instance, between units belonging to a single paradigm.

B.   Generative linguistics

Over the years, several attempts have been made in the generativist circles to demonstrate that analogy is not needed in syntax. It can be – and has been – shown, however, that those very examples which are meant to prove the futility of analogy cannot be adequately analyzed except by resorting to the notion of analogy. And what is more, this notion can be *formalized* with full precision (cf. Itkonen & Haukioja 1997; and here, Appendix). Three representative types of examples will be dealt with in what follows.

Chomsky (1986) repeatedly discusses the following set of sentences (19)–(22):

(19)   John ate the apple

(20)   John ate

(21)   John is too stubborn to talk to Bill

(22)   John is too stubborn to talk to

As he sees it, the relation of (22) to (21) is analogous to the relation of (20) to (19). And yet, *John* is the subject of *ate* both in (19) and (20), while *John* is the subject of *talk* only in (21). Chomsky takes this to mean that analogy fails; and because analogy cannot explain why (22) is construed differently from (21), it follows (or seems to follow) that only some innate mechanism can do so.

Chomsky's argument here can be presented in the form of a binary proportional analogy, thus:

$$\frac{(19)}{(20)} = \frac{(21)}{X}$$

For Chomsky, the notion of analogy requires X to be replaced by (22). To see the error in this reasoning, consider the following analogy:

$$\frac{(19)\ \text{John ate the apple}}{(20)\qquad \text{John ate}} = \frac{(23)\ \text{John talked to Bill}}{X}$$

According to Chomsky's way of thinking, X stands for the following sentence:

(24)   *John talked to

This is wrong, however, because (24) is known to be an incorrect sentence whereas (25) is known to be correct:[7]

(25)   John talked

That is, the child learns by direct experience that sentences like (19), (20), (23), and (25) are sentences of his language, whereas a sentence like (24) is not (because it never occurs). Therefore the following equation represents (part of) his basic knowledge of sentences and their elliptical counterparts:

$$\frac{(19)}{(20)} = \frac{(23)}{(25)}$$

This equation functions as the basis for (analogical) inferences about sentence-types of which the child may have no direct experience. In the present context this means that when the child has to solve our first proportional analogy above, the solution cannot be (22). Rather, it has to be this:

(26)   John is too stubborn to talk

What about Chomsky's key sentence, i.e. (22)? What is the *right* analogy for it? It is to be found in equations like the following one:

$$\frac{\text{(27) The teacher discusses the question}}{\text{(28) The question is too difficult to discuss}} = \frac{\text{(23') Bill talks to John}}{\text{(22) John is too stubborn...X...}}$$

It is here – and only here – that the sentence (22) (= *John is too stubborn to talk to*) has its rightful place. Notice that there is not only a semantic, but also a formal analogy between (27):(28) and (23'):(22). This analogy *explains* Chomsky's original puzzle, i.e. why (22) is understood in the way it is: the role of *John* in (23') is the same as the role of *question* in (27); and since the latter remains the same in (28), so does the former in (22). John is not the agent, but the person who the action is directed to; he is not talking, he is being talked to. – The question still remains: Can this analysis be made more precise, i.e. can it be formalized? In the Appendix it will be shown that it can.

Let us proceed to discuss the next problem. Hoekstra and Kooij (1988:38) analyze the following two sentences:

(29)   Where did John say that we have to get off the bus?

(30)   Where did John ask whether we have to get off the bus?

(30) can be understood in one way only, whereas (29) has two interpretations, namely as a question either about the place where John said what he said (= 29a) or about the place where we had to get off the bus (= 29b). Thus we have here an instance of *syntactic ambiguity*.

How do we know the difference between (29a) and (29b)? – according to Hoekstra and Kooij, because we have "access to complex principles of UG". Why are they needed? – because "this piece of knowledge [, although] shared by all native speakers, ... can hardly have been established on the basis of induction". Why? – "simply [sic] because there are no data from which induction could conceivably proceed". But of course there are such data, and self-evidently so. Consider the following two analogies:

(31) John slept		(33) John said that we have to get off the bus
——————————	=	——————————
(32) Where did John sleep?		X

(34) John said that Bill was there		(36) John said that we have to get off the bus there
——————————	=	——————————
(35) Where did John say that Bill was?		X

It is obvious that (29) is the correct solution to both of these analogies. It is just as obvious that (29) has different meanings, i.e. (29a) and (29b), in the two cases. As for (30), only analogies of the first kind are available. Hence the impossibility of an ambiguity of the kind associated with (29).

Again, the facts are quite straightforward. The only interesting question is whether the above analogies can be formalized. In the Appendix it will be shown that they can.

Let us finally consider the third problem. Chomsky (1975b: 30–32) takes up the following sentences:

(37)   The man is tall

(38)   Is the man tall?

(39)   The man who is tall is in the room

(40)   Is the man who is tall in the room?

(41)   *Is the man who tall is in the room?

He then raises the following question: Why is it that questioning (39) happens by means of a structure-dependent rule, producing (40), and not by means of a structure-independent rule, producing (41)? Or, to put it more perspicuously, why do we have 'X = (40)', rather than 'X = (41)', in the following analogy?

$$\frac{(37)}{(38)} = \frac{(39)}{X}$$

According to Chomsky, "there seems to be no explanation [for structure-dependency] in terms of 'communicative efficiency' or similar considerations". It follows (or seems to follow) inexorably that "UG contains the principle that all such rules must be structure-dependent". This argument has often been repeated, e.g. in Lightfoot (1982: 67–68) and Crain and Nakayama (1987).

Now, this argument is vitiated by the fact that, contrary to what it claims, the explanation of structure-dependency is self-evident. Linguistic structure reflects perceptual structure. When you see a tall man eating a red apple, you see the tallness together with the man and the redness together with the apple (rather than vice versa). The (complex) NPs of your language reflect this fact: the words *tall* and *man* occur together, constituting a complex NP, and if this NP is moved, it is moved *as a whole*.[8] Similarly, when you see a boy eating an apple, a woman kissing a man, and a dog chasing a cat, you see the boy together with the apple, the woman together with the man, and the dog together with the cat. The sentence-structures of your language reflect this fact: this is the only reason why you put the words *boy* and *apple* in the same sentence, instead of separating them by two sentences speaking about the woman, the man, the dog, and the cat.[9] An NP may be moved out of an S or a complex NP only on condition that its connection with the 'extraction site' is still understood. Whether or not this is the case, depends on various semantic factors, with the consequence that a principle like subjacency has a huge number of syntactically unmotivated exceptions (cf. Deane 1991). Nevertheless, the contiguity of linguistic categories remains the null hypothesis, motivated by ontological-perceptual facts.

The preceding paragraph is plain common sense. Bolinger (1968:218) made the same point as follows:

> If two things react upon each other in our experience and we want to talk about them, whatever the device that is normally used for one (say, X) or for the other (say, Y), the result in what we say is going to be an XY or an YX. The words *cat, bite, dog* may be arbitrary, but if a dog bites a cat we can reasonably expect that these words will keep close company ... because the togetherness of words reflects the togetherness of things and events.

The explanation given e.g. by Givón (1990:970) or by Croft (1990:179) in terms of 'proximity principle' or 'iconic-distance hypothesis' is basically the same.

For the present purposes, the most important point to note is that there is a quite natural way to produce the right analogy, i.e. to view (40) as the result of an analogical generalization. That is, the analogical relation between (37):(38) and (39):(40) is mediated by sentences like (42) and (43) which contain NPs more complex than those in (37):(38) and less complex than those in (39):(40).

(42)   The man in the room is tall

(43)   Is the man in the room tall?

To sum up: The problem that has to be solved is defined by the three representative examples given above. Each of them illustrates the case where three sentences A, B, and C fit the pattern A:B = C:X, and where we intuitively feel that we can solve X, because its relation to C is the same as the relation that B bears to A. The problem is to find a systematic way to formalize this intuition. The solution will be given in the Appendix. It derives its interest from the claim, made by Chomsky and his followers, that the problem is unsolvable.

Up to now, I have been concerned to show that the data of generative analysis conforms to the concept of analogy. In the remainder of this subsection I shall consider the role of analogy in the generative theory-construction.

First, generativism has adopted a discrete or bivalent attitude towards the data, which is dictated by theoretical considerations, rather than by the nature of the data itself. More precisely, the discrete attitude is justified by the so-called clear case principle, which is in turn based on analogy: The nature of sentences with an equivocal grammaticality status has to be decided *in analogy with* the unequivocally (un)grammatical sentences:

> In many intermediate cases we shall be prepared to let the grammar itself decide, when the grammar is set up in the simplest way so that it includes the clear sentences and excludes the clear non-sentences. ... A certain number of clear cases, then, will provide us with a criterion of adequacy for any particular grammar.   (Chomsky 1957: 14)

It is obvious that the clear case principle is identical with the notion of *qiyās*, as it is applied to decide the class-membership of particular words. Remember that in the Arabic tradition it has been decided a priori that each and every word must belong to one of the three word-classes (cf. 2.3, A).

Secondly, there is an equally pervasive use of analogy also within generative theory-construction. This was well illustrated by the traditional 'depth vs. surface' distinction. Surface structures derived from one deep structure were (structurally) similar or analogous, precisely because they exemplified a common, more abstract structure. The 'performative hypothesis' serves as an example (cf. p. 5). Inversely, surface structures which looked similar were not really similar (or analogous) if they were derived from two distinct deep structures. The two sentences *John is easy to please* and *John is eager to please* serve as an example.

To choose a more recent example, let us consider some central aspects of X-bar syntax. It contains the lexical categories N, V, A, and P. These are certainly valid categories of the English grammar. Cross-linguistic evidence shows, however, that – as purportedly universal categories – they are not at all on an equal footing. N and V seem well-established.[10] By contrast, A is an 'intermediate' category in the sense that it is absent in many languages, and in many other languages it is a closed class. Moreover, P is 'transitory' (rather than intermediate) because it generally develops out of other categories; and it is just absent e.g. in most Australian and North-American Indian languages. In brief, the situation is as Bloomfied (1933: 198–199) describes it:

> It is a mistake to suppose that our [English] part-of-speech system represents universal features of human expression. If such classes as objects, actions, and qualities exist apart from our language, as realities either of physics or of human psychology, then, of course, they exist all over the world, but it would still be true that many languages lack corresponding parts of speech.

Thus, there is no empirical reason for treating N, V, A, and P alike. Why, then, are they treated alike in X-bar syntax (as part of Universal Grammar)? The reason appears to be the compulsion exerted by two distinct types of analogy. First, there is the *concrete* analogical model provided by the English part-of-speech system. Second, there is the influence of *theoretical* analogy: it is so 'neat' to think that all lexical categories are similar (in spite of the fact that in different languages they behave quite differently). Notice also that, as is usually the case, analogy is here a directional process. It is the 'strong' members N and V which constitute the basis for analogical reinterpretation of the 'weak' members A and P, rather than vice versa.

Because lexical categories are (postulated to be) similar, they share the same structure, namely specifier, adjunct, head, and complement. The head is obligatory, and whether or not it has a complement, is stipulated in the lexicon.

Next, the structure of the lexical categories is *analogically* generalized to the structure of the non-lexical category S. This generalization is made possible by taking S to have the tripartite structure NP-AUX-VP, where AUX functions as the head. AUX is reinterpreted as I (= 'Inflection'), which stands for Tense and Agreement. Thus, S(entence) turns out to be IP (= 'Inflection Phrase').

AUX is a lexical category. In English the postulation of AUX is supported by the temporal/modal verbs *will*, *can*, etc. and by the *do*-support, whereas the auxiliary verbs proper, i.e. *be* and *have*, are taken to originate within VP. As we just saw, AUX is reinterpreted as the functional category I, and S is reinterpreted as IP. This reinterpretation is far from natural because the specifier of IP, i.e. the subject NP, differs from the specifiers of other categories in being obligatory, and a separate rule is needed to stipulate this. Thus, the real reason for postulating IP turns out to be, once again, the compulsion exerted by theoretical analogy: it is just so neat to assume that all categories, both lexical and non-lexical, have the same structure. In fact, this justification has been given quite openly:

The principles of X-bar Theory arguably will gain more credibility if it turns out that the structural representation of the non-lexical categories is funda- mentally *similar* to that of lexical ones.   (Ouhalla 1994: 102; emphasis added)

It seems that the non-lexical category IP (alias S) can successfully be assigned a structure consistent with the principles of X-bar Theory. The *theoretical ad- vantage* of the revision introduced relates to the desirability of the [analogical] generalization that the structural representation of all categories (both lexical and non-lexical) is governed by the *same* principles.

(*ibidem*: 105; emphasis added)

In what precedes, the structure of S was modeled after that of NP. There is an interesting sequel to this maneuver. If the head of IP is a functional cate- gory like I, how can it be that the head of NP is a non-functional category like N? Here theoretical analogy sees a new opening: In reality, the head of NP is not N but the determiner (e.g. the definite article *the*), which means that NP must be reinterpreted as DP (= 'Determiner Phrase') (cf. Ouhalla 1994: 179– 182). Thus, the structure of IP (formerly S) is *analogically* generalized to that of NP (henceforth DP), after the structure of NP had first been *analogically* generalized to S.

The foregoing account was simplified insofar as theoretical analogy had already been at work in the definition of S: because the subordinate clauses are generally preceded by a complement (in English by *that*, for instance), and because it is neat to assume that the subordinate clauses and the main clauses share the same structure, it seems natural to make the *analogical* generalization that main clauses too are preceded by a complement (cf. Ouhalla 1994: 62–65).

Let us, in addition to this breath-taking sequence of analogies-after- analogies, consider one more example of how generative linguistics exploits the general notion of analogy. The existence of a VP constituent, i.e. verb and its complements (in particular, the object), is assumed in generative descrip- tions, with the understanding that V and Object-NP must be *contiguous*. This causes no problems for languages with either SVO or SOV, which are hierar- chically analyzed as S[VO] and S[OV]. Languages with VSO are, however, a problem. Accepting at the face value VSO, as it occurs in a sizable number of languages, would mean accepting a non-hierarchical or 'flat' structure V-NP- NP. This would entail that, if one NP is dropped, the remaining sequences VO and VS would be structurally indistinguishable. But there must be some way to distinguish them from each other. This problem is solved by postulating a deep structure with an underlying SVO order and then either raising V or lowering S to get VSO (cf. Carnie & Guilfoyle 2000: 4–5).

This chain of argumentation contains steps that are far from cogent. Why are V and O so often contiguous? Or, in Tomlin's (1986: Ch. 4) words, why is there such a thing as 'verb-object bonding'? The natural answer would be that their syntactic contiguity reflects, and is motivated by, their semantic closeness. Generativists must, however, leave this question unanswered since they deny any semantic motivation of autonomous syntax. But why must V and O be presented as contiguous even in those cases where they quite obviously are *not* contiguous? Two unspoken reasons conspire to bring this attitude about. The first is of purely aesthetic character: it would be just too messy (i.e. not at all 'neat') to let the branches of a tree-diagram cross. The second reason is, once again, the *analogy* exerted by the English sentence structure. For many years, English provided the sole data base for generative linguistics. Among the world's languages, English has a uniquely rigid word order – as shown by Bates and McWhinney (1989: 46–47) – and it is indeed SVO, i.e. the branches do not cross. This has raised SVO to a canonical status.

But is there any real danger that, in a language like Classical Arabic, the sequences VO and VS might get confused? And is there no other way to keep VO and VS separate than to postulate (at the 'deep' level) a nonexistent SVO structure? To these questions, the answers are 'no, there is no such danger' and 'yes, there are other ways'. In Classical Arabic, O and S are marked differently, i.e. by accusative and by nominative, respectively, so there is no way that they could get confused. Besides, it is also well known that O and S are semantically different insofar as the latter tends to be animate and definite while the former tends to be inanimate and indefinite, which means that they cannot be easily confused. (Interestingly, Carnie and Guilfoyle admit the existence of this difference on p. 5.) The reason why generativists cannot distinguish between VO and VS, except by postulating a 'deep' SVO structure, is the poverty of their descriptive apparatus, i.e. the over-reliance on (configurational) tree diagrams, combined with the analogical influence of the canonical, i.e. English-like, sentence structure. Sometimes this influence is openly admitted, as when Baker (1995: 13) recommends that noun incorporation in Mohawk should be described by "base generating *ordinary* (i.e., *English*-like) complementation structures" (emphasis added).

It is good to remember that the indigenous Arab grammarians took it for granted that the VSO sentences of their language have the internal structure [VS]O. In the preceding examples that were taken from generativist literature we have seen *qiyās* practiced with an intensity that might have startled Arab grammarians. Now, as argued in Section 1.7, there can be no objection against the use of *qiyās*, or theoretical analogy, as long as its role as a merely descriptive device is clearly understood. Objections arise, however, if the unlimited use of analogy is coupled with the claim to psychological reality, as is the case with generative descriptions. Objections acquire some additional urgency from the fact that, among the various schools of linguistics, it is only generativism which has explicitly denied the existence of analogy.

C.   Cognitive linguistics

It may seem a bit incongruous to deal with cognitive linguistics under the stark label of 'syntax', given that cognitive linguistics, adopting Saussure's notion of linguistic sign, considers form and meaning simultaneously. Nevertheless, my approach seems justifiable in the present context insofar as I shall concentrate on *construction grammar*; and constructions (in this technical sense) are claimed to represent the "syntactically relevant aspects of verb meaning" (Goldberg 1995:28).

Consider the following sentences:

(44)   John sneezed

(45)   John slept

(46)   John kicked the wall

(47)   John hit the ball

(48)   John pushed the napkin off the table

(49)   John gave Mary a letter

(50)   John sneezed the napkin off the table

(51)   John kicked Mary the football

Goldberg (1995:Ch. 1–2) makes inter alia the following claims on behalf of construction grammar. The sentences (50) and (51) exemplify 'non-basic' meanings of *sneeze* and *kick*. Postulating the existence of such meanings as independent units would be ungainly. It is more reasonable to assume that the non-basic meanings have been assigned by the *constructions* into which the two verbs have 'integrated' their basic meanings. For *sneeze* and *kick* the constructions are the caused-motion or *S-V-O-Obl* construction and the ditransitive or *S-V-O-O2* construction, respectively. In both cases, it is the construction itself which contributes additional participant roles to the verb meaning. Thus, constructions have meanings of their own, which are necessarily more abstract than verb meanings (apart from the meanings of such maximally abstract verbs as *go, put, make, do, give*).

Now, analogy plays the following role in this framework. The sentences (44) and (46) exemplify the basic meanings of *sneeze* and *kick*, which means that the two verbs in turn exemplify the intransitive *SV* construction and the transitive *SVO* construction, respectively (even though Goldberg has little to say about these maximally general constructions and their meanings). This means that (44) and (46) are *analogous* to (45) and (47), respectively. This is the self-evident or, if you wish, *trivial* sense of analogy, also exemplified by Sapir's and Jespersen's examples (cf. Figure 1.5). Sentences (48) and (49), in turn, exemplify in a straightforward fashion the two constructions which (50) and (51) exemplify in a less straightforward fashion. Thus the *S-V-O-Obl* and *S-V-O-O2* constructions, exemplified by (48) and (49), have been *analogically* extended to (50) and (51). This means that (50) and (51) are *non-trivially* analogous to (48) and (49), respectively. – Even if the role of analogy is overlooked by Goldberg, it is (eo ipso) not contested by her. This is a significant difference vis-à-vis generative linguistics.

There is one more aspect of analogy which has to be mentioned here. In discussing inheritance relations between different constructions, Goldberg (1995: Ch. 3) makes the following point. Not only verbs but also constructions have basic meanings. Non-basic meanings are *extensions* from the basic one. An extension is produced by a 'link'. For instance, there is a 'polysemy link' between the basic meaning of the ditransitive construction (= 'X causes Y to receive Z') and one of its non-basic meanings (= 'X enables Y to receive Z'). There is another such link between the basic meaning of the caused-motion construction (= 'X causes Y to move Z') and one of its non-basic meanings (= 'X enables Y to move Z'). Intriguingly, Goldberg notes explicitly (p. 76) that the two links are "quite analogous". She further assumes (p. 77) that frequently occurring links may "be applied to newly learned constructions". This is analogy at a relatively high level of abstraction. It is no longer just constructions being extended to new verbs, but links between constructions being extended to new (pairs of) constructions.

It is generally thought that the *Peri syntaxeōs* by Apollonius Dyscolus (c. 200 A.D.) is the oldest extant treatment of syntax in the Western tradition. This is not quite accurate, however, because Apollonius' actual object of study is the sentence, i.e. both its form and its meaning. On the first page of his book, Apollonius states the general principle of sentence-construction: "For the meaning which subsists in each word is, in a sense, the minimal unit of the sentence, and just as the minimal units of sound compose syllables when properly linked, so, in turn, the structural combining (*syntaxis*) of meanings will produce sentences by combining words." Later, this principle has come to be known as the principle of *compositionality*.

The pervasive *non*-compositionality of language has been one of the basic insights of cognitive linguistics. According to this view, there are no longer any general rules that would mechanically combine words (or word meanings) to produce sentences (or sentence meanings). For instance, Sinha and Kuteva (1995) show in great detail how the location of a thing, instead of being expressed by a single word, may – depending on the language – be expressed simultaneously by several words. Thus, meanings are expressed by entire syntactic 'chunks' or gestalts. The same is true of Goldberg-type constructions. In particular, this insight undermines the applicability of categorial grammar, as in Montague grammar or in Jackendoff-type syntax-cum-semantics. (This difficulty has been recognized in part by Jackendoff 1996:7.) But if the notion of general, mechanically applicable rules has to be rejected, what is the remaining alternative? As Zlatev (1997:7.4) has pointed out, referring to Itkonen and Haukioja (1997), it is *analogy*, i.e. either subsuming some cases under existing gestalts (or constructions) or extending these to other cases. How this happens, has been illustrated above by means of the Goldberg-type use of constructions.

The true extent of non-compositionality has been discovered so recently that the large majority of linguists, not to speak of philosophers, may not have fully digested it yet. The mainstream philosophy of language as well as the philosophy of cognitive science takes compositionality for granted. For instance, Fodor and Lepore (1992, esp. 175–176) vividly show that the entire edifice that philosophers and logicians have been constructing ever since Frege threatens to collapse if compositionality is abandoned. (To be sure, it shall remain an indispensable part of *formal* languages.) They admit that "idioms and other 'holophrastic' constructions are all exceptions"; but – they assume – these are "exceptions that prove the rule". However, this position, or a black-and-white distinction between 'holophrastic' and other constructions, can no longer be maintained. This becomes evident as soon as one considers examples more complicated than Fodor and Lepore's favorite example *brown cow*, whose meaning arguably results from the meanings of *brown* and *cow*.

To understand the true nature of non-compositionality, it needs to be related to more familiar notions. Most examples given by Sinha and Kuteva (1995), for instance, exemplify the notion of *redundancy*, which means – roughly – that 'one thing is said twice'. (Notice that all forms of agreement, for instance, illustrate the notion of redundancy.) The opposite of redundancy is *ellipsis*, which means – roughly – that 'two things are said only once' (or that one thing is not said at all, but only implied). It is obvious at once that compositionality is the syntactic equivalent or analogue of the morphological principle 'one meaning – one form' (discussed in 2.4), which means that non-compositionality is in turn the syntactic equivalent of any violation of this principle. Moreover, the fact that idioms are prime examples of non-compositionality shows the intimate connection between (non-)compositionality and (non-)*productivity*.

However, we should not exaggerate the scope and importance of non-compositionality. It still remains true that, in some sense, a 'whole is constituted by its parts'; but this sense remains to be specified more precisely. On the one hand, it is true that in the following two German sentences the notions of horizontality and verticality are expressed at least twice, which means that they are expressed redundantly or non-compositionally: *Das Buch* **liegt auf** *dem Tisch* ('The book is on the table') vs. *Das Bild* **hängt an** *der Wand* ('The picture is on the wall'). On the other hand, it would be nonsensical to claim that these sentences are *totally* unanalyzable wholes, or that there is *no* sense in which the former sentence (-meaning) is constituted – inter alia – by the word(-meaning)s *Buch*/'book' and *Tisch*/'table', whereas the latter sentence(-meaning) is constituted – inter alia – by the word(-meaning)s *Bild*/'picture' and *Wand*/'wall'.

2.6 Semantics

It is a very old idea that language is, or at least should be, a picture of the reality. The vicissitudes of this idea within the Western linguistic tradition, from antiquity via the Middles Ages to the end of the 20th century, have been described in Itkonen (1991: Ch. 5). The current concern with *iconicity* is just the latest stage in this development.

Because iconicity is defined as structural similarity between linguistic and non-linguistic entities, it is of course a straightforward exemplification of the general notion of analogy. Moreover, it is the non-linguistic term of the iconicity relation which is assumed to cause, and thus to *explain*, the constitution of the linguistic term, and not vice versa. There is reason to distinguish here between two basic types of non-linguistic entities, namely ontological-cum-conceptual and merely-conceptual. For brevity, the terms 'ontological' and 'conceptual' will be used in what follows (cf. Itkonen 1994).

'Ontology' means here the way that the language-external reality is conceptualized by ordinary human thinking. Alternative ontologies exist, but will be ignored here. At least the following ontological dimensions are relevant to the notion of iconicity: quality, quantity, order, and cohesion. Qualitative ontological distinctions include 'thing vs. action', 'agent vs. patient', 'human vs. non-human', 'animate vs. inanimate'. Quantitative ontological distinctions include 'one vs. many', 'less vs. more'. The basic ontological distinction of order is 'before vs. after'. The basic ontological distinction related to cohesion is 'perceptually (or causally) close vs. distant'. Research conducted by representatives of the typological-functionalist school has shown that all these distinctions tend to be reflected in cross-linguistic data (for an informative, and early, survey, see Haiman 1985).

Consider the ontological distinction of *order*. Let us assume within a single complex sentence the two simple sentences S1 and S2 that refer, respectively, to the consecutive observable events E1 and E2. In many languages both the order S1 & S2 and the order S2 & S1 are possible. (For instance, 'When John came home, he took a shower' vs. 'John took a shower, when he came home'). But there are also many languages where the order S1 & S2 is obligatory. And most importantly, there are no languages where the order S2 & S1 is obligatory. This is a genuine *linguistic universal*, and it is *explained* by the notion of ontology-based iconicity.

Notice, in particular, that the order of events and the order of (uttered) sentences can be compared in an objective and transparent way, without any danger of circularity. The same is true of the other ontological distinctions as well. To be sure, one and the same phenomenon may be construed as either 'one' or 'many', depending on the context, but it is again an objective fact whether, if compared in the same context with something else, it exemplifies 'one' or 'many' (or 'less' or 'more').

Next, let us consider the ontological vs. conceptual distinction. *Negation* is a prime example of a conceptual, non-ontological phenomenon. While an affirmative sentence like *A is hitting B* pictures an event in the world, its negation *A is not hitting B* does not. Rather than being something that ('objectively') exists in the world, negation is an operation performed by humans. The same is true of the operation of *identification*. There can be no picture, photographic or verbal, of the state of affairs truthfully referred to by a sentence like *John is my best friend* (let alone a sentence like *John is not my best friend*).

Does it follow, then, that there is no reason to speak of concept-based iconicity? Not necessarily. Insofar as conceptual or cognitive phenomena can be shown to be prior to, or independent of, language it is legitimate to consider language as 'caused by', and therefore as a 'picture of', the former. Indeed, recent research on preverbal cognition seems to indicate that the operations of negation and identification exist already before the emergence of language.

This issue is controversial, however, and therefore it seems wise to stick to the ontology-based iconicity as much as possible.

Iconicity is a point of convergence between typological-functional linguistics and cognitive linguistics. Its centrality to the former approach has already been indicated . As for the latter approach, it underlies Langacker's (1991b: 12–15) view of 'grammar-as-image' as well as Goldberg's (1995: 42–43) view of constructions as expressing 'basic scenarios of human experience'.

In the recent literature some doubts have been expressed concerning the viability of iconicity. As far as I can see, such doubts result from an inability to keep (uncontroversial) ontology-based iconicity apart from (controversial) concept-based iconicity (cf. Itkonen 2004).

Iconicity may be characterized as 'vertical' (directional) analogy, or analogy that goes from non-linguistic to linguistic. There is within semantics also 'horizontal' (directional) analogy. This distinction may be illustrated as follows. According to Givón (1995: Ch. 4), it is meaningful to distinguish between two 'super-modalities', viz. 'fact' and 'non-fact', expressed by affirmative-indicative and negative and/or subjunctive markings, respectively. Identifying sentences in subjunctive with 'non-fact' is unproblematic. By contrast, identifying negated sentences too with 'non-fact' might at first seem surprising. From the logical point of view, p and not-p are considered as symmetrical, and therefore if the former expresses 'fact', it may be difficult to accept that the latter expresses 'non-fact'. From the standpoint of the *psychology* of logic, however, p and not-p are *not* symmetrical. Rather than expressing a fact, a true negative sentence (in the indicative mood) is thought to express the "denial of a falsehood", which is something more complicated than, and hence different from, a simple fact (cf. Evans 1982: 28). At the same time, denial is necessarily less specicific than the (alleged) fact that is being denied. Thus, there is a twofold difference vis-à-vis affirmative-indicative. In consequence, we have reason to accept Givón's position.

In a given language the markings for the two 'super-modalities' are either asymmetric or symmetric. Both cases can be explained by analogy and, what is more, only by analogy.

In the *asymmetric* case, we have to do with vertical analogy or iconicity: from the ontological point of view, 'fact' is much more differentiated than 'non-fact', and linguistic structure reflects this difference between 'fact' and 'non-fact'. The asymmetric way to express the two 'super-modalities' is exemplified by Modern Tamil. The affirmative-indicative verb, which expresses 'fact', inflects in person/number/gender and in three (basic) tenses. By contrast, the negative-indicative verb has four distinct forms (= a, b, c, d), of which the first three are uninflected: (a) expresses any tense and any person/number/gender; (b), being based on nominalized present tense, expresses habituality and any person/number/gender; (c), being based on nominalized past tense, expresses the past and any person/number/gender; only (d), which expresses the future, inflects in person/number/gender (cf. Asher 1985:175). Apart from the negation, the super-modality of 'non-fact' is expressed either by the conditional mood or by one of several modal auxiliaries. The corresponding verb-forms, whether affirmative or negative, never inflect in person/number/gender, and only rarely in tense (*ibidem*: 165–166, 181–182).[11]

When the two super-modalities are expressed *symmetrically*, we have to do with horizontal (or language-internal) analogy: the structure of affirmative-indicative is extended to that of negative and/or subjunctive. This case is exemplified – approximatively – by Latin. Affirmative-indicative and negative-indicative are fully symmetric (the latter being expressed by negative particles, conjunctions, or pronouns). Both in the indicative and in the subjunctive, there is the same number of non-future tenses (= present, imperfect, perfect, pluperfect). However, in the subjunctive there are no counterparts to the two future tenses (which means that the symmetry between fact and non-fact is not complete). It is quite obvious that, semantically, the four tenses of the subjunctive have become more or less confused. The reason is, of course, that their ontological motivation is less than that of the indicative tenses. That they are maintained nevertheless, must be due to the analogical influence exerted by the latter.

Let us consider another example. All languages have a standard structure to express a genuine action, i.e. an action that exemplifies the agent – patient relation, but languages differ among themselves as to whether they generalize or extend this structure to express other relations (e.g. the experiencer – experienced relation) as well. This generalization, called 'coercion' by Croft (1991:5.2), is an obvious instance of horizontal analogy. At this point, it may seem that analogy 'explains too much'. But what would be the alternative explanation? There is none. To be sure, there is the additional question why one language chooses the vertical analogy (= ontological motivation) rather than the horizontal analogy (= morpho-syntactic motivation). It is unlikely that this question (which must remain unanswered in the present context) could also be answered by resorting to analogy.

Haiman (1998:158–162), for instance, uses the term 'analogy' so as to restrict it to the 'routinization' or 'ritualization' of the linguistic form, i.e. to the case where linguistic form ceases to be motivated by semantic (or ontological) facts. Accordingly, Haiman restricts 'analogy' to horizontal analogy. This position is comprehensible, and has its roots in traditional linguistic thinking. However, for reasons expounded in Chapter 1, it seems more illuminating to adopt a more comprehensive notion of analogy, i.e. a notion which, in addition to routinization, also allows vertical analogy (= iconicity), on the one hand, and creative analogy, on the other. Why is this more illuminating? Because it enables us to grasp the generalization or the superordinate analogy that subsumes different subtypes of analogy.

It may be added that Haiman de facto espouses this more comprehensive view of analogy, given the number of sweeping analogies in biological, cultural, and linguistic evolution that he is himself willing to envisage:

> Another word for this [gap between the signifier and the signified] in every human language is the design feature of displacement ... [W]e will recognize that [the fundamental process of the genesis of displacement] has *analogs* in many other fields. ... [W]e may hazard some respectable speculations about the origins of human language by investigating well-articulated theories of *similar* processes in the development of other human cultural institutions ... These, in turn, are cultural *analogs* of the biological process of emancipation,
> ....   (Haiman 1998: 128–129; emphasis added)

2.7 Diachronic linguistics

As was mentioned above, in antiquity 'analogy' was synonymous with 'regularity'. Therefore it is interesting to note that in the Neogrammarian theory of linguistic change 'analogy' came to mean the irregular force which counteracts the otherwise regular advance of sound change.

> Sturtevant phrased this as a paradox: sound change is regular and causes irregularity; analogy is irregular and causes regularity. That is, the mainly regular sound change can pull regular paradigms apart; analogy is in general irregular, in that it does not occur in every case where it could, but when it does, the result is greater regularity in morphology.   (Anttila 1989 [1972]: 94)

The Neogrammarian terminology was misleading insofar as it restricted the functioning of analogy to morphology (and, less systematically, to syntax), instead of viewing analogy as a general force which equally operates on all linguistic levels. As pointed out by Anttila (*ibidem*: 88), "the regularity of sound change is also analogical: when a sound x changes under conditions y in a word A, it also changes in word B under the same conditions". Moreover, in the synchronic dimension Hermann Paul, the leading theoretician of the

Neogrammarian school, continued to uphold the traditional view that analogy equals regularity and systematicity.

The closely related principles of 1M1F and analogy are at work in morphological change. Following Anttila (1989 [1972]:Ch. 7), I shall let the symbols '|', '∨', '||' and '∧' stand for, respectively, 1M1F, 2M1F, 2M2M, and 1M2F. Now, the prototypical interplay of sound change and morphological change can be pictured as the following two successions (cf. Itkonen 1982a:105–107):

(52) $| > \wedge > |$

(53) $|| > \vee > ||$

The symbols | and || represent the ideal or 'symmetric' state which is constantly disrupted by sound changes giving rise to less-than-ideal states represented by the symbols ∧ and ∨. According to Paul's (1975 [1880]:198) eloquent formulation, "Der Symmetrie des Formensystems ist also im Lautwandel ein unaufhaltsam arbeitender Feind und Zerstörer gegenüber gestellt" (= "The sound change is an enemy and destroyer that continuously works against the symmetry of the paradigm").

More precisely, succession (52) represents the ubiquitous fact that once sound changes have produced needless formal variation, it tends to be eliminated 'by analogy'. For instance, in Latin the first vowel of the verb 'to love' was uniformly a-, for instance *ámo* ('I love') and *amátis* ('you-PL love'), which exemplifies the situation |. In Old French the differential stress produced the variation *aime* ≠ *amez*, or the situation ∧. This 'harmful' situation was eliminated, and the situation | was re-established, by changing the vowel of the latter form on the analogy of the vowel of the former form from a- to ai- (which came later to be pronounced as [ɛ]): (*j*') *aime* = (*vous*) *aimez*, re-establishing the situation |.

Succession (53) represents the inverse fact, namely the ubiquitous tendency to avoid grammatical ambiguity. Either the situation ∨ (produced by some sound change) is *cancelled* by re-establishing, or 'producing' the situation ||, or the situation ∨ is *prevented* from coming about. Accordingly, these two phenomena may be called 'productive (morphological) change' and 'preventive (morphological) non-change'. Both are based on analogy, as will be shown now.

In pre-Classical Greek there was a sound change which deleted an -s- between two vowels. Thus, the singular of passive/medial indicative and subjunctive present of e.g. the verb *paideúein* ('to educate') underwent the changes and non-changes presented in Figure 2.13.

1SG	paideúomai	> paideúomai	paideúōmai	> paideúōmai
2SG	paideúesai	> *paideúē*	paideúēsai	> *paideúē*
3SG	paideúetai	> paideúetai	paideúētai	> paideúētai
	Indicative		Subjunctive	

Figure 2.13 A fragment of the medial/passive paradigm in Classical Greek

paideúō	paideúsō
paideúeis	paideúseis
paideúei	paideúsei
Present	Future

Figure 2.14 A fragment of the active paradigm in Classical Greek

While the 1SG and 3SG forms remain the same during the time interval under consideration, there is a change in the 2SG forms. The change from *paideúesai* (or *paideúēsai*) to *paideúē* must have been mediated by a form like *paideúeai* (or *paideúēai*). This sound change is harmful insofar as, first, it destroys the regular alternation of the endings -*mai*/-*sai*/-*tai* (which is retained in the perfect tense), and second, it eliminates the distinction between indicative and subjunctive in 2SG. Yet, the harmful effects of the sound change remain within 'reasonable limits' because in both paradigms the markings for 1SG, 2SG, and 3SG remain clearly distinct.

Now consider the paradigms of active indicative present and future singular of the same verb, given in Figure 2.14. If the intervocalic -*s*- were deleted here too, then the two tenses would merge, i.e. the future would lose its distinctive marking. Now, the future marking -*s*- is maintained elsewhere, e.g. after voiceless occlusives, as in the verb *trépō* ('I turn') vs. *trépsō* ('I will turn'). Therefore, -*s*- is maintained also in the intervocalic position, as in the form *paideúsō*, which means that the change is *prevented* from happening; or, alternatively, -*s*- was reinstated, if it had already been deleted, which means that the change is *cancelled*. In both cases, there is the following analogy at work:

$$(54) \quad \frac{\text{trépō}}{\text{trépsō}} = \frac{\text{paideúō}}{\text{X}} \quad \text{X} = \text{paideúsō}$$

This is a prototypical example of a 'functional' explanation in diachronic linguistics. (Notice that the forms of 1SG stand for all persons of the respective paradigms and, more generally, for all verbs either with occlusive + *s* or with *VsV*.) Many more examples are adduced in Anttila (1989 [1972]: Ch. 5 and 7).

It is interesting to note that, for whatever reason, Bybee (1985:78, n. 2) sees herself forced to replace the traditional term 'analogical change' by a more neutral term 'morphophonemic change'. However, the phenomena she deals with can *only* be understood as being subsumable under analogy: the relation *leap* : *leapt* was replaced by the relation *leap* : *leap-ed* on the analogy of (e.g.) the relation *walk* : *walk-ed* (p. 51); and the Old English relation *dō* : *dēst* : *dēth* was replaced by the Middle English relation *do* : *do-st* : *do-th* on the analogy of (e.g.) the relation *dyde* : *dyde-st* : *dyde-th* (p. 64). Under the label of 'morphophonemic change' Bybee gives the standard account of analogical changes, noting that "they tend to eliminate alternations between closely related forms". Thus, the underlying principle at work is our 1M1F, which means that the change of language is explained by the goal of "creating the same sound-expression for what is functionally the same" ("für das funktionell Gleiche auch den gleichen lautlichen Ausdruck zu schaffen"), as Paul (1975 [1880]:227) put it.

Some practitioners of diachronic linguistics find this type of explanation-by-analogy deeply unsatisfying. They want to know why the Greek -*s*- was lost in one case and retained in the other, or why the English verb system has not eliminated all irregularities. To put it more precisely, they want to have a metric of dysfunctionality which would *predict* when changes of this type do or do not occur. They can see no value in functional post hoc explanations (cf. Lass 1980, 1997).

This deep sense of dissatisfaction is motivated by an equally deep misunderstanding concerning the true nature of historiographical research. Some general tendencies for, or constraints on, linguistic change may of course be formulated. At bottom, however, all interesting and detailed historical explanations must be post hoc. This results from the fact that their explananda have been brought about by *rational agents*. As Whitney (1979 [1875]) put it, "the work is all done by human beings, adapting means to ends" (p. 73); "there is nothing in the whole complicated process [of linguistic change] which calls for the admission of any other efficient force than the reasonable action, the action for a definable purpose, of the speakers of language" (p. 144; similarly Itkonen 1981, 1982a, 1984; cf. here 1.8 and the end of 2.2).

The preceding examples may give the impression that analogy explains only more or less unsystematic or low-level changes. Therefore it is good to point out that also such large-scale changes as affect the entire structure of a given language have to be subsumed under analogy. For instance, it is often assumed that across the world's languages the 'head vs. modifier' (or 'head vs. dependent') order tends to be 'symmetric' in the principal constructions, i.e. either V+O, ADP+N, N+A, N+GEN or O+V, N+ADP, A+N, GEN+N (where

ADP = adposition, i.e. preposition or postposition). Notice, first of all, that here 'symmetric' is a misleading term which should be replaced by 'analogous'. Now, if for some reason (like language contact) the 'head vs. modifier' order changes in one case, it is generally assumed that there will be a chain reaction which re-establishes the earlier (analogical) uniformity. This was already suggested by Vennemann (1972), under the informative title 'Analogy in Generative Grammar'. To be sure, so many counter-examples to this putative regularity have been unearthed over the years that it can have statistical validity at most (cf. Croft 2003: 77).

In reality, students of diachronic linguistics have always practiced explanation-by-analogy, regardless of whether or not they have used this term. For instance, in the generative analysis of linguistic change in the early 70s, the term 'analogy' was replaced by a conglomeration of such neologisms as 'distinctness condition', 'leveling conditions', and 'paradigm coherence', which made it difficult to see that what was at issue was in fact a unitary phenomenon (cf. Anttila 1977a: 98–99). More recently, Kiparsky (1992) has attempted to replace analogy by 'optimization'. As he sees it, this term is preferable because it takes into account both linguistic structure and directionality of change. However, there is no reason to view analogy as non-structural and non-directional (cf. 1.1 and 1.4). When this misconception is corrected, there seems to be no principled difference between analogy and 'optimization'. To be sure, the 'optimization' account gratuitously makes language appear quite different from all other areas of the human life. Everywhere else analogy plays a central role (cf. Helman 1988; Vosniadou & Ortony 1989; Boden 1990; Holyoak & Thagard 1995; Hofstadter 1995; Gentner et al. 2001a), it is only in language that there is 'optimization' instead of analogy; it is only in language that "analogy is simply an inappropriate concept in the first place", as Chomsky (1986: 32) put it.

The remainder of this section will be devoted to discussing the role that analogy plays in *grammaticalization*. Contrary to the prevailing misconception (cf. Hopper 1998: 149; Haiman 1998: 147; Pintzuk et al. 2000: 4), the notion of grammaticalization was not invented by Meillet (1958 [1912]). Already the predecessors of the Neogrammarians, i.e. those working in Indo-European linguistics around 1850, took it for granted that "*die ersten Grundlagen der Wortbildung und Flexion durch das Zusammenwachsen ursprünglich selbständiger Elemente geshaffen sind*" ("the first foundations of derivation and inflection have been created by the coalescence of originally independent elements"), as Paul (1975 [1880]: 350) put it. Paul was the leading Neogrammarian, and therefore, having mentioned what became later Meillet's standard example, i.e. the change *amare habeo > j'aimerai*, he could afford to make the following comment (p. 349–350): "*Doch es scheint mir überflüssig aus der Masse des allge-mein bekannten und jedem zur Hand liegenden Materials noch weitere Beispiele zusammenzutragen*" ("But it seems to me unnecessary to give more examples to illustrate the huge amount of data which is generally known and accessible to anyone"). While today most students of grammaticalization concentrate on the development 'lexical > grammatical', Paul had the good sense to realize that this is just the conclusion of a larger development which he called *Komposition*: It starts with 'word group' (*Wortgruppe*), in which – in agreement with the principle of compositionality – each element still retains its autonomous form and meaning, and then the elements gradually coalesce and loose their auton-omy to an increasing extent. Thus, Paul established in Chapter 19 the following cline (55):

(55)   word group > compounding > derivation > inflection

It takes no great acumen to realize that Paul's *Komposition* is de facto synony-mous with Givón's (1979:Ch. 5) 'syntacticization'. Among his many examples of *Komposition* Paul mentions (p. 344) the German development *hiu tagu* ('on this day') > *heute* ('today'), an example that Hopper (1998:148) characteristi-cally attributes to Meillet, the putative inventor of grammaticalization.

In what follows, I shall accept the *opinio communis* according to which grammaticalization, and morphosyntactic change in general, is a two-stage process consisting of *reanalysis* and *extension* (cf. Hopper & Traugott 1993; Harris & Campbell 1995). The notion of grammaticalization will now be re-lated to the notion of hypothetico-deductive method, as explicated in Section 1.5; but it may be added that the analogy between linguistic change and scien-tific change was explored already in Itkonen (1982b).

First of all, reanalysis and extension correspond to the two stages of the hypothetico-deductive method (= abduction and prediction) which have been illustrated by means of the two inferences in Figures 1.19 and 1.20 There is, however, one important qualification to be made. The hypothetico-deductive method applies to events that occur in the outside world. Reanalysis-cum- ex-tension applies to language which is a *normative practice*; that is, extension as an analogue of deducing new predictions is not about new *events* to be observed, but about new *actions* to be performed by the speaker himself. Moreover, the analogue of deducing (new) true predictions consists in performing (new) ac-tions that will be accepted by the linguistic community. New predictions are *discovered* to be *true*, but new actions are *accepted* to be *correct*. Some amount of reflection is needed to grasp this distinction fully.

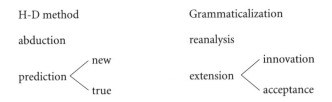

Figure 2.15 Analogy between hypothetico-deductive method and grammaticalization

$$\frac{[[\text{legit}]\ \text{librum}]}{[[\text{legit}]\ \text{libros}]} = \frac{[[\text{habet lectum}]\ \text{librum}]}{X} \qquad X = [[\text{habet lectum}]\ \text{libros}]$$

Figure 2.16 Analogical extension

Establishing linguistic analogues to deducing *new* and *true* predictions neatly captures the *psychological* and *social* aspects of linguistic change. At the same time it validates the customary distinction between innovation and acceptance (or acquisition and diffusion) in linguistic change: new predictions = (psychological) innovation; true predictions = (social) acceptance.

Rather than saying that grammaticalization (= reanalysis & extension) instantiates the hypothetico-deductive method, it should said that the two equally instantiate some superordinate concept (and thus are structurally similar or *analogous* to each other). This analogy is spelled out in Figure 2.15.

It is good to illustrate the claims made above. Consider the well-known case of the emergence of the active perfect tense in Romance languages. To begin with, a Latin sentence like *habet lectum librum* was analyzed as [*habet* [*lectum librum*]] (= 'he has a/the read book'), which means that it was taken to exemplify the structure [$V[A+N]$]. Then it was reanalyzed as [[*habet lectum*] *librum*] (= 'he has-read a/the book'), which means that it was taken to exemplify the structure [[$AUX + V$]N]. Thus, *habere* acquired the status of an auxiliary verb. The analogy to abduction as practiced in the natural sciences is evident at once. Next, a new form *habet lectum libros*, analyzed as [[*habet lectum*] *libros*] (= 'he has-read (the) books'), was produced by extension or, equivalently, the new action of uttering this new form was 'predicted'. This process is based on solving an *analogical* equation of the kind presented in Figure 2.16, where on the left-hand side we have two ordinary VP's, i.e. *legit librum* ('he is reading a/the book') and *legit libros* ('he is reading [the] books').

Finally, this new form was accepted by the linguistic community. It is the origin of the Italian, Spanish, and French constructions (with definite objects)

$$\frac{\text{liber est lectus}}{[\text{liber [est lectus]}]} = \frac{\text{habet lectum librum}}{X} \qquad X = [[\text{habet lectum] librum}]$$

Figure 2.17 Analogical model for reanalysis

ha letto i libri, ha leído los libros, and *il a lu les livres*. Again, the analogy to the natural-science prediction is fully transparent.

Notice, however, that up to now I have explained the emergence of the proto-Romance active perfect tense only in the sense of showing *how* it happened. I have not yet tried to answer the ulterior question as to *why* it happened; and some people doubt that this kind of question can ever be answered.

I submit that insofar as the WHY?-question can be answered at all in connection with renalysis, it can only happen by seeking a *model* for this process. For instance, what was the model for reanalyzing *habet lectum librum* as [[*habet lectum*] *librum*] ? As far as I can see, it was the construction with the auxiliary verb *esse* ('to be'), as in [*liber* [*est lectus*]] ('the book was read'). This process was based on solving an analogical equation of the kind presented in Figure 2.17.

Maybe this is the right answer, maybe not. The main thing is, however, that if no model can be found, then the WHY?-aspect of reanalysis remains unexplainable. This claim might be countered by referring to the (probable) existence of universal and therefore explanatory 'pathways' of reanalysis. This is no genuine counter-argument, however, because universal capacities tend to be exemplified in one way or another at any particular time; and 'exemplification of a universal capacity for reanalysis' equals '(analogical) model for a particular reanalysis'.

It is generally recognized that extension is an analogical process. In fact, Hopper and Traugott's (1993) term for extension is 'analogy'. It is less often recognized that, as shown above, analogy plays a role in reanalysis as well. A *significant generalization* is achieved by showing that both components of grammaticalization, i.e. reanalysis and extension, involve the superordinate notion of analogy.

Givón (1995:95) too subscribes to the view that grammaticalization is based on analogy. Logically enough, he uses the terminology that is current in the analysis of metaphor: "The grammaticalization of source domains into target domains is guided by *functional similarity* of potential sources and targets" (emphasis added). He illustrates this thesis by showing (p. 73–75) how, in different languages, structures recognizable as passives have emerged from such multifarious structures as adjectival-stative, nominalization, reflexive, L-dislocation, and inverse clause.

There is one more question to be asked and answered: *Why* are (analogical) models used in reanalysis? The answer has to do with the kind of uniformity that analogy imposes upon the data, and thus with *economy* (cf. below). But then there are more specific questions which are likely to remain unanswered: Why this model and not some other? Part of the answer is provided by the overall structure of the language in question. But ultimately, one simply has to accept the 'brute fact' of free will and/or chance.

In keeping with what has been said so far, it may look like new constructions only result from applying analogical extension to constructions that have been the object of reanalysis. It seems clear enough, however, that new constructions may emerge also in a more random fashion. They are referred to as 'exploratory expressions' by Harris and Campbell (1995: 72–75). Similarly, Lass (1997: 318–320) distinguishes what he calls 'exaptations' from 'analogical processes' and 'abductions', on the grounds that they are genuine innovations: "In exaptation the 'model' itself is what's new." His example is the emergence of the progressive *be* + *V-ing* construction in English. It is quite clear, however, that the model for this construction was provided by the copula sentences, i.e. the structure *be* + *X* was already there. Harris and Campbell (*ibidem*) are explicit on this point: 'exploratory expressions' are produced by the *existing* grammar (and if they catch on, they may become the basis for reanalysis). Lass's (1997) view of completely novel linguistic changes can be regarded as a diachronic analogue of Chomsky's view that, synchronically, speakers can produce and understand completely novel sentences (cf. 2.2). I submit that, on reflection, both views turn out to be without foundation.

According to Peirce, "the leading consideration in Abduction [is] the question of Economy – the Economy of money, time, thought, and energy" (Hookway 1985: 226). This reveals the incontrovertibly *rational* character of reanalysis. In making the data conform to the result of reanalysis, extension too is 'economical' and therefore rational. It follows that grammaticalization, and linguistic change more generally, is amenable to 'rational explanation' (cf. 1.8).

2.8 The analogy between oral languages and sign languages

A discussion of sign languages, i.e. manual-visual languages used by the deaf, shows in a striking fashion that analogy is not just a matter of idle speculation, but possesses a power that may change people's lives. It had always been evident that what the deaf did with their hands served the same purpose as acts of speaking, namely communication. But communication may be achieved by non-linguistic means too, e.g. by pantomime. In fact, this is, by and large, how the communicative system of the deaf was conceptualized, until Stokoe (1978 [1960]) showed, 'beyond reasonable doubt', that it is a genuine language. It is almost trivial, but still very significant, to state that what Stokoe did was to discover the analogy between oral languages and sign languages. From the moment this analogy was grasped and accepted, it has had deep and lasting effects for the deaf community (cf. Wilcox 2001).

It was noted in Section 1.1 that the analogies that underlie the typological research of oral languages are not overly difficult to grasp: in practice, the common functions (i.e. the common meanings to be expressed) have always been taken for granted, and the capacity to translate from one language into another already guarantees that any given sentence of one language can also be seen as structurally similar to some sentence of another language, in the sense that the two sentences turn out to have the same number of equifunctional 'parts' (cf. Figure 1.7). It is more difficult to show what, precisely, are the structural counterparts between a spoken sentence and a signed sentence. Therefore it seems advisable to explore the basis for this difficulty.

There are four basic *physical* dimensions, namely vertical, horizontal, diagonal, and temporal. Speaking takes place in one basic physical dimension only, namely *time*, with the qualification of course that time manifests itself here as a sequence of sounds. This statement may seem to entail that speech is 'one-dimensional' and lacks hierarchy, which is clearly wrong. Notice, however, that the view of hierarchy as something 'two-dimensional' (in the sense of horizontal-cum-vertical) is merely a result of the habit to represent hierarchies in the form of tree diagrams. If they are represented with the aid of brackets (as in formal logic), the illusion of two-dimensionality vanishes. In speech, brackets can be thought to correspond to *pauses*; and it is self-evident that an alternation of sound and silence takes place in one dimension only, namely time. (It is interesting to note that in constructing his 'cosmic language', Freudenthal (1960) exploits this idea insofar as e.g. in a formula like $[(p \ \& \ q) \lor r] \rightarrow s$ the round brackets ( ) are represented by shorter pauses than the square brackets [ ].) The physical dimension of time contains both the qualitative differences between successive (sequences of) sounds as well as such simultaneous intonational properties as loudness and/or pitch. What is most important, however, is to realize that – regardless of how many hierarchical levels we may distinguish (in addition to, say, 'phoneme < morpheme < word < clause') – it is impossible to determine this hierarchy in purely physical terms, or without resorting to *meaning*. But notice that, although sound and meaning exist side by side, as it were, it would be nonsense to say that meaning is an additional *physical* dimension. Therefore, to repeat, speech takes place in one physical dimension only (in addition to taking place in non-physical dimensions).

In this crucial respect, sign languages are quite different from spoken languages because they make use of *all* of the four physical dimensions. Signed expressions are perceived to be produced by several 'articulators', namely two hands, the eyes, the face, and the body. In speech, by contrast, the notion of 'articulator' has no clear analogue. Of course, spoken expressions are produced by the articulatory organs, but they are not perceived to be produced in this way. What is perceived are, rather, the speech sounds as such. Because of its multi-dimensionality, signing contains simultaneous elements to a much higher degree than could be possible in speaking. On the other hand, this type of simultaneity is required for signing to convey the same amount of information as speaking, because the former is inherently slower than the latter.

Up to now, we have seen to what extent spoken languages and sign languages are *dis*analogous. Therefore it may seem quite remarkable, and almost miraculous, that there are nevertheless quite close structural counterparts between the two types of language. This means that their similarity must reside at higher levels of abstraction and that their all-too-obvious differences can be demonstrated to be merely apparent. It is well to start this demonstration with the by now familiar notion of *iconicity*, because the traditional arguments against the genuinely linguistic character of signing refer to its iconic (or, in some cases, pantomime-like) character, which contrasts – or seems to contrast – with the non-iconic character of the spoken language.

The iconic nature of the sign language may be brought out as follows. When the signer is telling a story in which he himself is not a participant, he constructs in front of himself a miniature model of the world. In it, he places the participants of the story, and afterwards he refers to them by pointing (or merely gazing) at their respective places. The places will be changed in accordance with the requirements of the story, and the signer as well as his cosigners must continuously keep track of who is at which place.

When presented in this way, the sign language certainly looks rather different from the spoken language. This difference can, however, be made to disappear, in the following steps.

First, Wittgenstein (1969 [1921]) envisages the so-called picture theory (*Abbildtheorie*) according to which it is possible to construct an ideal (written) language whose sentences correspond in an iconic (or 'isomorphic') fashion to states of affairs in the extralinguistic reality. Now, Wittgenstein has reported that he got the inspiration for his picture theory when he once observed how a traffic accident was reconstructed by means of a miniature model. The analogy between a miniature model consisting of cars and houses and a miniature model consisting of signs is obvious at once. It can further be shown that Wittgenstein's notion of ideal language can be modified so as to apply to natural languages as well (cf. Itkonen 1970). Now we have the following series of analogical transitions: etralinguistic reality → (representation by) miniature things → (representation by) signs → ideal (written) language → natural (written or spoken) language. In the process, the iconic nature of representation by signs ceases to look anything unique.

Second, and perhaps more robustly, it is generally accepted today that spoken languages too are iconic in character (cf. 2.6). This insight eliminates the basic 'barrier' between signing and speech.[12] In constructing his 'miniature model', the signer has to name the participants of his story, and the names are analogues of the nouns of spoken language; the pointing or gazing signs are analogues of pronouns; and the signs that connect participants and change their places (in accordance with the events to be told) are analogues of verbs. It can be freely admitted that signing is more iconic than speaking, because this is a difference of degree, and not a difference of kind. For instance, iconicity of (temporal) order, quantity, and cohesion/proximity is basically the same in oral and sign languages. As far as the notion of quality is concerned, by contrast, signing is more iconic than speaking insofar as signs for things (= 'nominals') actually resemble things in being more restricted and static than signs for actions (= 'verbals') which in this respect resemble actions. By contrast, the difference between oral nouns and verbs is 'iconic' in the weaker sense that it merely corresponds to the difference between things and actions, but does not reflect it in any more substantial sense (cf. Engberg-Pedersen 1996). Moreover, it goes without saying that in any sign language some signs are inherently, and predictably, iconic (e.g. 'go up', 'go down').

Third, the fact that the sign languages are iconic, and – in particular – more iconic than the spoken languages, does not deny their *symbolic* character. For instance, based on the manuscript version of Schaller (1991), Sacks (1990:Ch. 2) has described in vivid detail the difficulties faced by deaf people who learn a sign language only in their adulthood. At first, they are unable to grasp the fact that an even prima facie iconic sign may in a permanent or conventional way stand for something else. But once they achieve this insight, a 'naming explosion' follows (assuming that there are no otherwise unfavorable circumstances).

Fourth, although most individual signs have either an iconic or a metonymic origin, this is in general something that only etymological research can reveal. From the synchronic point of view, these signs are opaque or genuinely symbolic. To think otherwise would amount to committing the familiar diachronistic fallacy (cf. 1.6).

Fifth, even those signs which remain recognizably iconic, are not iconic for someone who does not master the sign language in question, for the simple reason that they are signed so rapidly. For an outsider, they become comprehensible only if he is allowed to watch them in slow motion. For a Finnish-speaking person, for instance, Finnish Sign Language is a foreign language just like Spanish.

So far, I have showed, at least in outline, that there are no obstacles against accepting the analogy between sign languages and oral languages. Next, I have to show that such an analogy exists as a matter of fact. To do so, I shall choose one sentence meaning and then observe how it is expressed in one sign language and in a number of spoken languages. The sentence meaning is 'N1 gave/showed N2 to N3' (where the N's may vary) plus its pronominal version 'He gave/showed it to her' (or some variation thereof). The sign language is the Finnish Sign Language (= FSL), and the spoken languages are Japanese, English, Latin, Finnish, West Greenlandic, Wari', Swahili, Yagua, and Yimas.

Let us consider the sentence-meaning 'The man gave a book to the woman' (ignoring for the present purpose the role of the past tense). In FSL 'to give' is expressed iconically as a curved movement from the giver X to the recipient Y, symbolized as V (cf. Figure 2.21). The signs for 'man' (= N1), 'woman' (= N2), and 'book' (= N3) are given in Figures 2.20, 2.19, and 2.18. The first two signs are originally metonymic (= tipping one's hat or profiling the female breast), whereas the third iconically depicts the opening of a book (= first, pressing the palms of a hand together and then opening them).

The practice of giving context-independent example sentences is relatively unfamiliar in FSL, but the closest signed equivalent to the sentence 'The man gave a book to the woman' is uttered as follows. First, N1 is signed and then placed into (what will be) the X-position; second, N2 is signed and then placed into (what will be) the Y-position. Third, N3 (identifiable as the patient Z) is signed and then placed into the X-position, i.e. the position which reveals itself as the X-position at the next moment when the V-sign or the curved movement from X to Y is articulated. During this movement the handshape is either neutral or retains (some of) the characteristics of N3. These facts are summed up in Figure 2.22.

Figure 2.22 does not, and could not, represent the positions where N1, N2, and N3 are signed (because N1 and N2 are signed on the forehead and on the chest, respectively, whereas N3 is signed in the neutral space in front of the

Figure 2.18 'book' in FSL

Figure 2.19 'woman' in FSL

Figure 2.20 'man' in FSL

Figure 2.21 'give' in FSL

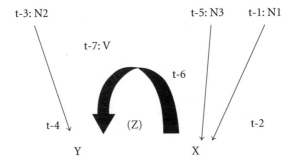

Figure 2.22 'The man gave a book to the woman' expressed in Finnish Sign Language

signer). The acts of placing (which are performed either by pointing or by gazing or by both) are represented by straight arrows. Thus, for instance, N1, having been signed at time t-1, is placed in X at time t-2; N2, having been signed at t-3, is placed in Y at t-4; and so on. Time t-7 represents the entire movement from X to Y. The round brackets around Z represent its optional status.

The role of the nouns N1, N2, and N3 in this sentence seems unproblematic. The structure of the verb V is more interesting. It might seem to be a conceptual truth that V must contain the 'marking' for X and Y, i.e. agent and recipient, because a movement must, by necessity, have a starting point and an end point. In careless signing, however, the exact place where the V-sign starts need not coincide with X. This is true of the sign for 'give' in American Sign Language as well (cf. Meier 1987).

As was mentioned above, it is generally assumed that pointing and/or gazing have a 'pronominal' function. In its barest form, the pronominal version of our example sentence would just consist of the movement from X to Y. The agent and the recipient (who would have been previously introduced) would be expressed implicitly, whereas the patient (having been previously introduced) would remain unexpressed.

Next, I shall examine a set of more or less synonymous sentences taken from a set of structurally more or less dissimilar spoken languages. The examples will be presented in the order from the least to the most analogous to the FSL example; but, as will be seen, there is some latitude for interpretation.

> (56)   Japanese (Nobufumi Inaba, personal communication):
>
> *otoko ga onna   ni   hon   o   age-ta*
> man   AG woman REC book PAT give-PRET
> 'The man gave a book to the woman'

(56) is a typical case of dependent-marking. The verb is uninflected (except for tense), and agent, recipient, and patient are expressed by *ga*, *ni*, and *o*, respectively. The full pronominal version would be *kare ga kanojo ni sore o ageta*. Depending on the context, any of the (pro)nominal arguments can be dropped. Most significantly, if some persons debate whether or not a friend of theirs will or will not buy a book to his girlfriend, and if afterwards one of them says '*ageta*' to the others, the utterance of this verb alone constitutes a perfectly grammatical sentence.

> (57)   English:
> The man gave a book to the woman

The verb is uninflected in (57) as in Japanese, but the semantic roles are less explicitly expressed. Unlike in Japanese, the pronominal version (= *He gave it to her*) cannot normally omit any of the pronouns.

> (58)   Latin:
> *Vir-ø*   *femin-ae*   *libr-um*
> man-NOM&SG woman-DAT&SG book-AKK&SG
> *dedit*
> give-ACT&IND&PERF&3SG
> 'The man gave a book to the woman'

This example differs from the previous ones insofar as the verb agrees with the subject/agent. In the pronominal version (= *eum ei dedit*) the subject is dropped, which means that the verb does not really agree with the agent-expression, but rather expresses the agent.

(59) Finnish:
    Mies-ø   *anto-i*   *nais-e-lle*
    man-NOM&SG give-ACT&IND&IMPERF&3SG woman-SG-ALL
    kirja-n
    book-AKK&SG
    'The man gave a book to the woman'

Sentence (59) is structurally identical with the Latin one; the 'allative' case performs the same function as the dative. The only difference vis-à-vis Latin is that
in the pronominal version (= *hän antoi sen hänelle*) the subject usually cannot
be dropped.

(60) West Greenlandic (Fortescue 1984: 89):
    angut-ip   *qimmi-ø*   *niqi-mik*   *tuni-vaa*
    man-ERG&SG dog-ABS&SG meat-INSTR&SG give-AG=3SG & REC=3SG
    'The man gave meat to the dog'

The inflectional morpheme -*vaa* is a portmanteau morpheme, which expresses
the person and number of two arguments in (60). In basic verb forms they normally are agent and patient, but in connection with *tuni-* ('give') the second
argument is recipient. The word *tunivaa* constitutes in itself a complete sentence (with an unexpressed object/patient). Therefore our example sentence,
with three overt nouns, is decidedly artificial (but not ungrammatical).

(61) Wari' (Everett & Kern 1997: 125, 131):
    mi' na-m   *kon*   *hwam narima' tarama'*
    give AG=3SG-REC=3SG&F PREP&3SG&M fish   woman man
    'The man gave a fish to the woman'

The form *na-m* exemplifies a clitic whose first part expresses the person and
number of the agent (plus tense/mood) and whose second part expresses the
person, number, and gender of some other semantic role (here: recipient). In
this example, *na* and -*m* agree with *tarama'* and *narima'*, respectively (exemplifying the VOS order of Wari'), and the patient *hwam* is expressed with the aid of
the only preposition of Wari' (which inflects in person, number, and gender).
The combination *mi' nam* is a complete sentence. Like in West Greenlandic,
the cooccurrence of three overt nouns in a single sentence is artificial, but not
strictly speaking ungrammatical.

(62)   Swahili (Perrot 1957: 54, 63):

m-tu   *a-li-m-pa*   *m-wanamke*   *ki-tabu*
CL&SG-man   AG=3SG-PRET-REC=3SG-give   CL&SG-woman   CL&SG-book
'The man gave a book to the woman'

Like in West Greenlandic, the verb (= *alimpa*) in (62) contains the markings
for (human) agent and (human) recipient, and therefore constitutes a sentence
of its own (with an unexpressed patient).

(63)   Yagua (Payne & Payne 1990: 256, 368):

sa-sāāy-siy   *Alchíco-níí*   *sa-deetu-rà*   *pāā*
AG=3SG-give-PAST3   Alchíco-REC=3SG   3SG-girl-PAT=INANIMATE   bread
'Alchico gave the bread to his (= somebody else's) daughter'

In (63), the agent is expressed by the verbal prefix whereas the recipient and the
patient are expressed by clitics attached to the end of the preceding word. Thus,
Alchico, *sadeetu* ('his daughter') and *pāā* ('bread') agree with *sa-*, *-níí*, and *-rà*,
respectively. Under certain conditions clitics may be dropped. The corresponding pronominal version is *sa-sāāy-siy-níí-rà*. (If the patient were animate, e.g.
a fish, the corresponding sentence would be *sa-sāāy-siy-níí-níí*.) Thus, all the
three arguments are coded on the verb only when there are no overt nouns.

(64)   Yimas (Foley 1997: 358):

uraN   *k-mpu-tkam-r-mpun*
coconut&CL6&SG   PAT=CL6&SG-AG=3PL-show-PERF-REC=3PL
'They showed them the coconut'

Thus, the classifier *k-* agrees with *uraN*, and *-mpu-* = 'they', *-tkam-* = 'show',
-r- = PERF, and *-mpun* = 'to them' in (64). This example differs from all the
others insofar as it contains only one overt noun. Because of the polysynthetic
structure, "the great majority of Yimas clauses in ongoing text consist of just the
verb" (Foley 1997: 360). As noted above, the same disinclination against using
more than one noun in one clause is evident in West Greenlandic, Wari', and
Yagua. Of these three, West Greenlandic is strongly and Yagua mildly polysynthetic whereas Wari' is analytic (with a lot of clitics and particles). The Yimas
example is important because it is the only one where ditransitive verbs like
'give' or 'show' contain obligatory and explicit markings for all three arguments
in all situations. (Remember that if a Yagua sentence contains an overt (postver-
bal) noun for agent, neither recipient nor patient can be marked on the verb.)
If overt nouns do occur in Yimas sentences, they are uninflected and stand in
an appositional relation to the verbal markings.

Basically, the sign-language sentence of Figure 2.22 consists of three nouns and one verb. It is obvious at once that all our oral-language examples (apart from the last one) have the same meaning ('X gave Z to Y') and the same four-part structure, which means that they are analogous to it in the general sense defined in connection with Figure 1.7. In addition, however, the verb of the sign-language example is such as to contain the markings for agent and recipient obligatorily and for recipient optionally. In this respect, it is possible to set up a continuum where the number of the arguments coded on the verb are zero, one, two, and three, as shown in (65):

(65) $0 = ageta < 1 = dedit < 2 = alimpa < 3 = kmputkamrmpun$

The example of Figure 2.22 would be situated between 2 and 3, because the marking for the third argument or patient is optional. Thus, in this respect, Finnish Sign Language is most analogous to Swahili, on the one hand, and to Yimas, on the other.

One important qualification remains to be made. In the sign-language example, the markings for agent and recipient are not just obligatory but also conceptually necessary in the sense that they cannot be separated from the verb. (The movement that expresses 'give' starts with agent and ends with recipient.) Both in *alimpa* and *kmputkamrmpun* it is possible to single out the verb proper: it is *-pa* or *-tkam-*. In the curved movement that expresses 'give', by contrast, it is not possible to separate the starting point and the end point from the 'movement itself'. Therefore, if we wish to find a *perfect analogy* for this particular sign-language verb among oral languages, it should be a type of verb in which the markings for arguments are totally *fused* with the verb, prosodically or otherwise.

It is well known that the marking for subject/agent tends to get fused with the marking for tense/mood. This happens in Indo-European languages (like Latin), Amazonian languages (like Wari'), Chadic languages (like Hausa), and Papuan languages (like Hua). (Interestingly, the corresponding fusion between the markings for patient and tense/mood never occurs in the Papuan languages, for instance; cf. Foley 1986:136.) It is much less common that argument-marking would get fused with the verb root, because this presupposes that the number of verb roots is very restricted. A case in point is Vanimo, a Papuan language. The forms for 'I sit', 'you-SG sit', 'she sits', 'they sit' and 'I make', 'you-SG make', 'she makes', 'they make' are *ve, pe, se, hve* and *le, ble, pli, di*, respectively (cf. Foley 1986:134). From the synchronic point of view, it is impossible to distinguish here between the verb root and the subject/agent marking. Of course, this is still not a perfect analogy to the sign for 'give' because there is no fusion between the verb root and the object or recipient marking.

So far, I have been concerned to show that, in spite of huge differences as to their respective physical bases, there is a fundamental analogy between oral languages and sign languages. It should be kept in mind that this analogy is something that should not be taken for granted, but should rather be demonstrated (as I have tried to do above). It would be very odd if the physical differences between spoken and signed languages had *no* consequences as to their architecture. It is generally assumed that a typical sign is constituted at least by three components, namely the shape, the position, and the movement of the hand. If the sign itself is considered as an equivalent of the word (or morpheme), then the components might be considered as equivalents of phonemes. In fact, this analogy has been widely accepted. There is this *dis*analogy, however, that while phonemes are inherently meaningless, units exemplifying each of the above-mentioned components may have an inherent meaning; for instance, handshapes as classifiers, proximity (to the heart) indicating sympathy, self-explanatory movements upwards or downwards. Therefore, the analogy between the two types of languages should not be pressed too far. Rather it should be admitted that a dichotomy like 'phonology vs. morphology' does not apply to sign languages. Or, if one cannot bring oneself to give up these familiar terms, it should at least be admitted that they have different meanings in these two contexts.[13]

2.9 Conclusion

In what precedes, I have exemplified the functioning of analogy at such traditional linguistic 'levels' as phonology, morphology, syntax, and semantics, as well as in diachronic linguistics and linguistic typology (in relation to sign languages). My approach has been a 'moderate' one in the sense that, contrary to both stratificational linguistics (cf. 1.7) and generative linguistics (cf. 2.5, B), I have refrained from demanding that the descriptions carried out at different levels should also be analogous to each other. I have not dealt with such linguistic subdisciplines as pragmatics, psycholinguistics, and sociolinguistics, although I do think that, together with diachronic linguistics, they share the common feature of having to espouse one or another form of so-called rational explanation (cf. Itkonen 1983a). In this general sense, then, they should be considered as methodologically analogous to one another.

I have not dealt with language acquisition (except in passing, in Sections 2.2 and 2.5). According to the traditional view, language acquisition contains two successive and distinct stages of analogical thinking, i.e. stages which in terms of our taxonomy (cf. Figure 1.10) can be identified as discovery and application (cf. Figures 1.21 and 1.22): First, the child discovers a structure common to several utterances that he has heard; second, he applies this structure to produce new utterances.

Paul (1975 [1880]: 111) gives a classical formulation to the traditional view:

> Bei dem natürlichen Erlernen der Muttersprache ... hören [wir] nach und nach eine Anzahl von Sätzen, die auf dieselbe Art zusammengesetzt sind und sich deshalb zu einer Gruppe zusammenschliessen ... und so wird die Regel unbewusst aus den Mustern abstrahiert.
> (In the natural acquisition of our native language we hear little by little a number of sentences which are constructed in the same way and therefore constitute a group, and so it comes about that the rule is unconsciously abstracted from these models.)

Von der Gabelentz (1891: 63–66) echoes Paul's words, in claiming that the linguistic system is learned by the child on the basis of 'unconscious abstraction out of multiple experience'; and he adds: "*Die Wirkung dieser unbewussten Abstraction nennen wir Analogie*" ("The functioning of this unconscious abstraction is called Analogy").

Jespersen (1965 [1924]: 19), having noted that sentences made after the same 'pattern' or 'type' are called 'analogous', formulates the distinction between discovery and application as follows:

> Now, how do such types come into existence in the mind of a speaker? An infant is not taught the grammatical rule that the subject is to be placed first, or that the indirect object regularly precedes the direct object; and yet, without any grammatical instruction, from innumerable sentences heard and understood he will abstract some notion of their structure which is definite enough to guide him in framing sentences of his own.

As we have already seen in Section 2.2, in his 1955 dissertation Chomsky took this traditional view to be the very rationale of his generative undertaking. Here it is enough to repeat the words which are identical with those of Paul, von der Gabelentz, and Jespersen:

> [Language acquisition is based on the ability] to *abstract from* a corpus of sentences a certain structural *pattern*, and to construct, from the old materials, new sentences conforming to this *pattern*.   (p. 131; emphasis added)

As has been noted above, Jackendoff (1994), for instance, has returned to the traditional view:

> [The brain does not store] whole sentences, but rather words and their meanings, plus *patterns* into which words can be placed ... That is, 'making sense' involves, among other things, conformity to known patterns. (p. 12, 15; emphasis in the original)

Finally, Pinker (1994) too has returned to the traditional, analogy-based view. So much is evident from his claim that language-acquisition is based on detecting 'similarities': because these are not material similarities, they must be structural similarities; and if they are structural similarities, they must be analogies. Pinker wishes to emphasize that the analogies in question are of linguistic character, or operate within the innate linguistic module. This may or may not be the case. (In Chapter 3 I will argue that it is not the case.) When such representatives of the traditional view as Paul and Jespersen argued for the analogy-based mechanism of language-acquisition, the issue of innateness was neither here nor there. All that matters is that their view of how language-acquisition takes place is the same as the one that Pinker now adopts:

> For language acquisition, what is the innate similarity space that allows the children to generalize from sentences in their parents' speech to the "similar" sentences that define the rest of English? Obviously, "Red is more similar to pink than to blue", or "Circle is more similar to ellipse than triangle", is of no help. It must be some kind of mental computation that makes *John likes fish* similar to *Mary eats apples*, but not similar to *John might fish*; otherwise the child would say *John might apples*. ... That is, the "similarity" guiding the child's generalization has to be an analysis into nouns and verbs and phrases,
> ....   (p. 417)

It goes without saying that Paul and Jespersen formulate their 'similarities' in the way suggested by Pinker, namely in terms of "nouns and verbs and phrases". What we have here is one and the same position and, what is more, a position which received its definitive formulation already in the 19th century.

But whatever happened between 1955 and 1994? (Remember that during that time similarities of even the most innate kind were banned from generativist theorizing.) A satisfactory answer to this question would require a rational reconstruction of arguments that cannot, in my opinion, be rationally reconstructed. (An interpretative effort in this direction was made, nevertheless, in Section 2.2.) The empirical problem of language acquisition, with which Paul and his successors were concerned, was replaced by the 'logical problem of language acquisition'. For reasons of mathematical elegance, this logical problem was conceptualized as the problem of how forms without meanings are learned by the child. In solving this problem, analogy turned out to be dispensable. But this was just as well. It is to the credit of analogy that it is not needed in solving a nonexistent problem (nonexistent, because forms without meanings are not – and cannot be – learned by the child) (cf. Nuyts 1992: 158–159; Itkonen 1996: 483–486).

CHAPTER 3

Analogy and/or overlap between language and other cognitive domains

3.1 General remarks

In this chapter I shall investigate what linguistic analysis (as distinguished from psycholinguistic or neurolinguistic analysis) can reveal about the nature of the (human) mind. In so doing, I have to define my position vis-à-vis the question about the 'modularity of mind'.

In conformity with his wish to emphasize the *innateness* and the uniqueness of language, Chomsky (1972:90) explicitly denied any analogy between language and other cognitive systems:

> There seems to be little useful analogy between the theory of grammar ... and any other cognitive system that has so far been isolated and described; similarly, there is little useful analogy between the schema of universal grammar ... and any other known system of mental organization.

This position was given a sharper formulation when Chomsky (1975b) launched the idea that language might be a mental module, or 'mental organ', on the analogy (sic) of physiological organs like heart, lungs, or wings. Originally, he delineated language against what he called "(conceptual system of) common-sense understanding".

Fodor (1983) elaborated on this idea. He defined modules as input systems which function rapidly and are "informationally encapsulated" vis-à-vis one another. All sensory modalities plus language constitute modules of their own. On more careful analysis, e.g. vision alone turns out to contain several modules. Modules are contrasted with a 'mysterious' central system which functions according to different principles, i.e. it is non-automatic and integrates the information coming from different (input) modules. The processes characteristic of the central system have a 'global' character. "The more global a cognitive process is, the less anybody understands it. *Very* global processes, like analogical reasoning, aren't understood at all" (p. 107).

Jackendoff (1987, 1992, 1994) points out the obvious fact that modules (assuming that they exist) must have an output function too and, as examples of modules, he mentions language, vision, music, and 'social cognition'. The taxonomy of modules is further developed in Jackendoff (1996), where a distinction is made between 'representation modules' (represented by boxes) and 'interface modules' (represented by arrows between boxes). Language turns out to be a composite module, consisting of two representation modules (= phonology and syntax) plus the interface. One single central system à la Fodor is replaced by at least two 'central' or 'slow' (representation) modules, namely conceptual system and spatial representation. ('Body representation' is mentioned as a third candidate in Jackendoff 1994.) Logic is located in the conceptual system, which qualifies as non-linguistic (or 'supra-linguistic') insofar as it interfaces with several modules (including language).

Pinker (1994) raises the number of modules to as high as 19, including 'intuitive biology', 'number', and '(fear of) contamination'. He further assumes that each module has its own 'similarity space' within which (analogical) generalizations are made. As pointed out in Section 2.9, this entails that analogy *within* language (or the 'linguistic module') is no longer ostracized in generative thinking.

In Fodor's conception, modules were originally defined as 'encapsulated' and 'fast', and they were contrasted with the (non-modular) central system which is both non-encapsulated and slow. The modularity thesis has been considerably watered down by Jackendoff who, as we just saw, calls the central systems too 'modules', while admitting that they are quite different from the original, Fodor-type modules. However, referring to Jackendoff's work, van der Zee and Nikanne (2000: 4) still characterize as "domain specific and informationally encapsulated" those three interface modules that link Conceptual Structure with Spatial Structure, Language (= Syntactic Structure & Phonological Structure), and Motor Structure.

There are three basic arguments against the view that language is a mental module (assuming that this term still has a coherent sense). First, language is not encapsulated vis-à-vis the extralinguistic reality, as shown by *iconicity*, or the structural similarity between the two realms. Second, language is not encapsulated vis-à-vis other cognitive domains, as shown by the fact that (contrary to what Chomsky claims) there are obvious analogies between all these domains, which suggests their ultimate unity. Third, language is not encapsulated vis-à-vis such cognitive domains as vision, logic, and social cognition, because it is not just analogous to, but (partly) *identical*, or overlaps, with the latter. – These three points will be argued in what follows.

3.2 Iconicity revisited

While discussing modularity, we have to return to the notion of iconicity, which has already been touched upon in Sections 1.1, 2.4, and 2.8. The arguments for the innateness of language include the following. Linguistic operations (like making questions) are defined in terms of *categories*. There is, however, "no a priori justification" for this fact. Other, simpler ways to define linguistic operations are logically possible. For instance, it is logically possible "to formulate as a transformation such a simple operation as reflection of an arbitrary string (that is, replacement of any string $a^1 \ldots a^n$, where each a^i is a single symbol, by $a^n \ldots a^1$), or ... insertion of a symbol in the middle of a string of even length" (Chomsky 1965:56). As a matter of fact, however, such mathematically simple operations are excluded as candidates for transformations. Because, to repeat, there is no a priori justification for this aspect of language (namely, that operations are defined in terms of categories, and not of single symbols), it must be innate. – This is the argument from "structure-dependence" (cf. 2.3, B).

There is a gap in this argument. Why should the justification for structure-dependence be a priori, when it can be, and is, a posteriori or matter-of-fact? Linguistic operations are defined in terms of categories, because these are motivated by, or reproduce, their extralinguistic counterparts, as implied by the notion of *iconicity*.

There is an additional weakness in the above argument, as pointed out by Householder (1977). Some of the 'logically possible' operations mentioned by Chomsky (1965) presuppose that one always knows the exact length of a sentence (as measured in words) before one utters it. However, this is a factual impossibility. When one begins a sentence one never knows how, exactly, it will end. (One-word utterances may be the exception, but they play no role at all in the generative theory-construction.) Here, as in so many other places, Chomsky's argument is vitiated by his inclination to regard linguistic data as nothing but (ready-made) strings of meaningless symbols. Contrary to this position, however, forms without meanings could not be learned, which entails, inter alia, that the branch of formal linguistics known as 'learnability theory' is based on nothing at all (cf. the end of 2.9). Of course, it could be replied that even if it is never the case that one knows the exact length of the sentence to be uttered, this has nothing to do with language as such, or with 'competence', but is rather a matter of 'performance' only. But this ploy just accentuates the fact that 'competence' so defined is devoid of content. In its ordinary sense, competence is what one *can* do. But the generativist notion of competence seems to concentrate on what one can*not* do.

Apart from what precedes, it is the principal contention of this section that the notion of iconicity is apt to shed additional light on the current 'imagery debate'. One side, represented by Pylyshyn (1984), argues that thought is exclusively digital/propositional or language-like, whereas the other side, represented by Kosslyn (1980), argues that thought is partly digital and partly analog or picture-like; an alternative terminological distinction is 'algebraic vs. geometric' (for an overview, cf. Tye 1993). Thus, the former position endorses the existence of a *single code* whereas the latter position endorses the existence of *dual coding*. The distinction 'digital/propositional/algebraic vs. analog/pictorial/geometric' corresponds to the distinction between *arbitrary* and *motivated*.

It may be added that the advocates of digitalism do not deny the introspective or phenomenal existence of mental images. However, they separate the question of the introspective existence of X from the question as to how X is *represented* in the (unconscious) mind; and in the name of overall simplicity they decide that mental images are represented in the digital form.

First of all, it needs to be noted that the single-code position is opposed to the modularity hypothesis. Because knowledge of any kind is assumed to be represented in an abstract digital code, it retains no trace of its original source modality. Also the dual-coding position contests the modularity hypothesis because 'images' are of course not restricted to the visual modality.

Secondly, in order to do full justice to the analog/pictorial/geometric position, some background assumptions of cognitive science have to be stated explicitly. The entire edifice of cognitive science is based on two broad analogies. First, the unconscious mind is assumed to be analogous to the conscious mind, in particular in having beliefs and goals:

> Indeed the assumptions that underlie most contemporary work on information processing are surprisingly like those of the nineteenth century introspective psychology, though without introspection itself.   (Neisser 1976:7)

That is, what cannot be introspected is nevertheless assumed to be analogous to what can. If we eliminate the notions of unconscious belief and goal, then – as was already pointed out in Section 1.8 – we eliminate the notion of unconscious mind as such, and there will be nothing left for cognitive science to describe.[1] This is a general statement about the *structure* and *function*, not about the *contents*, of the unconscious mind. (In other words, it is irrelevant in the present context that a person's unconscious beliefs/goals may not be the *same* as his conscious beliefs/goals.) Second, mental operations are assumed to be analogous to behavioral operations. For instance, adding two numbers on a paper with the aid of a hand-held pen is at least a *starting point* for conceptualizing the corresponding mental operation. The computer analogy of the mind is just a refinement of this crude idea. The idea that mental operations are *sequential* (and not parallel) is clearly based on the fact that our conscious and public behavior of calculating or inferring is sequential. This analogy was the basis for the Turing machine (cf. 4.3); but it may well be misleading.

There is a large amount of experimental evidence, reviewed in Tye (1993), that supports the postulation of mental imagery (= mental rotation, scanning, zooming, and overflow, as well as the early demonstration that people can be led to confuse a perceived image with a mental image). There is no need to rehearse the relevant literature here. One point may be mentioned, however. When Pylyshyn and the others dismiss the introspective evidence for mental images, they also dismiss the first analogy mentioned above, without any genuine justification. That is, if having conscious beliefs counts as a reason for assuming that one may have unconscious beliefs, then having conscious mental images should count as a reason for assuming that one may have unconscious mental images. Moreover, the discussion has been one-sided in emphasizing that the idea of mental *images* is implausible. By the parity of reasoning, it should be realized that the idea of mental *sentences* is just as implausible. To be sure, introspective evidence may support this idea, but advocates of the digital position cannot appeal to this fact because – as we have just seen – they claim that introspections about X tell, in principle, nothing about how X is *represented*. The remaining alternative is the thesis, supported by connectionism, that thinking is really subsymbolic, and hence neither language-like nor picture-like, in character.

Next, we shall see that the notion of iconicity can, at least to some extent, resolve the digital vs. analog controversy. Let L, T, and R stand for 'language', 'thought', and 'reality' (i.e. 'reality-as-conceptualized'); let $A \rightarrow B$ mean 'A represents B', and let $A \Rightarrow B$ mean 'A produces the structure of B' (or 'B reproduces the structure of A'). Then the two sides of the debate may be presented as in Figure 3.1.

In brief, according to the first position, the structure of thought is produced by, and reproduces, the structure of language, whereas according to the second position it is produced by, and reproduces, the structure of reality(-as-conceptualized).

A few comments are now in order. First, the tripartite relation $L \rightarrow T \rightarrow R$, on which both sides agree, follows exactly the Aristotelian line of thinking,

The digital/propositional position:	L	→	T	→	R
		⇒			
The analog/pictorial position:	L	→	T	→	R
				⇐	

Figure 3.1 Elucidation of the digital and analog positions

according to which thoughts are signs of things just like words (or 'sounds') are signs of thoughts. As such, this position is open to the following traditional criticism, formulated already by Abaelard and William Ockham: words and sentences are, typically, *not* signs of thoughts, but of the *same* things and states of affairs which thoughts are signs of. If I say *Dogs bark*, I do not mean that (my) ideas of dogs emit (my) ideas of sounds; nor does the sentence-form, taken in itself, admit of such an interpretation (cf. Itkonen 1991: 175–176, 223–224, 245).[2]

Second, the digital position is more ambiguous than it seems at first, because it is committed to the view that thought is a *digital picture* of language. This is unwittingly admitted by those representatives of the digital position who claim that the relation between language and thought is *isomorphic* (cf. Fodor & Lepore 1992: 176). Briefly, digitalism entails its own version of iconicity.

Third, the possibility of $L \Leftarrow R$ has been overlooked in this debate. Iconicity shows, however, that language (= syntax) is a picture of reality. Therefore the whole opposition 'language-like vs. picture-like' vanishes, at least to some extent. (That is, language/syntax is an abstract or structural picture, not a concrete picture on a par with ordinary mental images.) The foregoing presupposes that if there is a non-digital relation between reality-as-conceptualized and language, then the 'intervening' level of thought cannot possibly be digital.

A few caveats still have to be added. As Wittgenstein has pointed out, a picture, whether on paper or in the mind, is never enough, because it may be interpreted in an indefinite number of ways. Therefore any picture must be complemented with its rules of interpretation. In the present context this general injunction could be understood as reasserting the inseparability of mental representation from mental process (cf. Anderson 1978).

To repeat a metaphor from Section 2.6, iconicity may be called 'vertical' analogy whereas the analogies between cognitive domains, to be discussed in the following sections, qualify as 'horizontal'. A significant generalization is achieved once it is realized that both cases exemplify one and the same concept. Moreover, the structural similarity between language and reality is not symmetrical. Rather, as pointed out above, there is a cause – effect relation between the two, such that the direction of causation goes from reality to language (cf. also the discussion in Section 2.6). And even if we restrict our attention to the relation between language and thought, the direction of causation is opposite to that assumed by digitalism:

> syntax presumably evolved as a means to express conceptual structure, so it is natural to expect that some of the structural properties of concepts would be *mirrored* in the organization of syntax. (Jackendoff 1992:39; emphasis added)

But concepts are not just inertly 'there'; rather, they are employed to interpret the extralinguistic reality. Thus, the Jackendoff-quotation really amounts to saying that the structure of syntax mirrors or reproduces the structure of the reality-as-conceptualized.

If there is an iconic relation between A and B, it does not make sense to claim that A and B are 'informationally encapsulated' from each other. To reformulate the issue in current modular terms, we have conceptual structure and syntactic structure (as part of the language module) and the "conceptual-to-syntactic-structure interface" linking the two. Van der Zee and Nikanne (2000) assume a pervasive analogy between conceptual structure and syntactic structure. For instance, a verb like *send* selects its "syntactic arguments" just like its conceptual counterpart selects its "conceptual arguments"; and van der Zee and Nikanne insist (p. 10) that "the linking between these linguistic representations and conceptual structures must be somehow *transparent*" (emphasis added). But if it is transparent (i.e. iconicity-based), it cannot 'informationally encapsulated', which means that it cannot be modular. The notion of module is just mistaken.

In the imagery debate the digital position has been made to appear more plausible than it really is, because the existence of *sign languages* has largely been ignored. In the syntax of sign language, space is used (e.g. by pointing) to directly represent either real or imaginary spatial relations; the language – world relation cannot get more iconic than that. It is impossible to assume that between the syntax and the referent (which stand in an iconic or non-digital relationship to each other) there is somehow an intervening conceptual level of digital nature. And this result can be generalized to the iconicity of spoken language too.

It is interesting to note that the syntax of sign language has in many respects the same structure as Johnson-Laird's (1983, 1996) *mental models*. To see this, one only needs to compare how such meanings as 'A is on the right of B' and 'B is in front of C' are represented in mental models (cf. 1996:446–448), and how the same spatial relations are expressed in American Sign Language (cf. Emmorey 1996:175–178). Needless to say, Johnson-Laird squarely bases his concept of 'mental model' on the concept of iconicity:

> The parts of the [mental] model correspond to the relevant parts of the situation, and the structural relations between the parts of the model are *analogous* to the structural relations between in the world. (1996:438; emphasis added)

Mental images are in turn defined as 'perceptual correlates' of mental models.

In addition to mental models, Johnson-Laird also accepts the existence of (arbitrary) propositional representations, thus subscribing to the dual-coding hypothesis. In the comprehension and the recollection of sentences and texts he assumes a very fine-grained division of labor, such that "subjects construct a mental model of *determinate* descriptions, but abandon such a representation in favor of a superficial propositional one as soon as they encounter an *indeterminacy* in a description" (1983:162; emphasis added).

McGinn (1989) represents a more straightforward attitude. The contents of thought are assumed to be constituted by mental models, and the process of thinking consists in manipulating them. Sentences, being of digital nature, differ 'toto caelo' from models, although the *meaning* of sentences may be explained in terms of associated models (p. 181, esp. Note 16). At most, the following concession is made to the propositional standpoint: "When a creature has a public language this may indeed seep back into its system of mental representation, but no such seepage is necessary in order that mental representation is possible" (p. 184). One of the principal merits of this 'modelling theory' is seen in the fact that the isomorphism between mental models and pertinent states of affairs explains why the former have the structure they have. To put it somewhat figuratively, this isomorphism solves the problem of *intentionality*, by making it possible to see which (type of) state of affairs a given (type of) mental model is directed to (p. 196–198). To be sure, it is added immediately that mental models should not be considered in abstracto, but as embedded in their actual use.

To sum up: First, iconicity refutes modularity. Second, the assumption of dual coding ('propositional vs. pictorial'), adhered to by Johnson-Laird, McGinn and others, is misconceived, because propositional *is* pictorial: language imitates, and is a picture of, reality and assuming that the structure of thought imitates the structure of language, the former is a 'picture' of the latter.

3.3 Language and vision

On the face of it, a juxtaposition like 'language *and* vision' is somewhat odd. Just like spoken language consists of sounds, or something to be heard, sign language consists of gestures and written language consists of figures, or something to be seen. In consequence, sign language and written language could be defined as 'language-*as*-vision'. Therefore, in order to be meaningful, the word 'vision' as used in the present context must mean 'vision applied to objects other than language'.

It is rather obvious that the understanding of sentences and the visual perception of figures are similar enough to illuminate each other. Thus, e.g. Hockett (1966 [1954]: 391) and Itkonen (1983a: 1–4) draw an analogy between a Necker cube and a syntactically ambiguous sentence: as a 'surface' phenomenon, the Necker cube is disambiguated by 'deriving' it from two distinct and unambiguous cubes situated at the level of 'depth'.

Taking Gestalt psychology as his basis, and arguing against Chomsky's 'Cartesian' tradition, Slagle (1975) pursues the analogy between language and vision, and wishes to *explain* it by postulating a common structure for perceptual experience in general:

> The real ... breakthrough [of Gestalt psychologists] came in discovering that similarity and contiguity are factors underlying *spontaneous* unification in perceptual fields (p. 330). ... This functioning [of similarity and contiguity] is, as Wertheimer (1923) and Köhler (1947) repeatedly emphasized, not limited to any given sense modality (p. 332). Similarity ... underlies the process of recognition and consequently the ability to categorize, categorization being of course the process through which we relate present experience to similar past experience (p. 333). Figure – ground differentiation [or 'perceptual focus'] is perhaps the most ubiquitous mode of perceptual organization. Indeed, there is some form of figure – ground differentiation in all domains of sensory experience (p. 336; see also Anttila 1977b).

The 'figure vs. ground' distinction has become central to today's cognitive linguistics. (Sometimes the terms 'trajectory' and 'landmark' are preferred.) Unless it is meant to be merely metaphorical (which does not seem to be the case), this terminology carries with it a strong methodological commitment to the ultimate unity of all types of perceptual experience, as suggested by Slagle above. Such a unity argues against any form of modularity. Similar remarks hold true of the notion of 'perspective', as utilized in cognitive linguistics.

When applied to language, the 'figure vs. ground' distinction holds, primarily, within the confines of a *sentence*. In no language is the sentence-structure entirely 'flat', or string-like. Rather, it exemplifies, to varying degrees, the concept of *hierarchy*. Insofar as 'independent' units can be considered as *heads* of those constructions in which they occur together with 'dependent' units, the syntactic structure may be qualified, more narrowly, as a 'headed hierarchy'. Interestingly, Jackendoff (1987:249–251) observes the occurrence of headed hierarchies not only in language, but also in vision and music. It may be added that, as van der Zee and Nikanne (2000:5–7) point out, headed hierarchies occur not just in linguistic, conceptual, and spatial representations, but also in motoric representations.

Surprisingly, the ubiquity of headed hierarchies does not shake Jackendoff's conviction that the domains where they occur (e.g. language, vision, and music) are separate modules. This is hard to understand. It is a very wasteful strategy to invoke innateness three times (or more), in order to 'explain' the fact that one and the same phenomenon X obtains in three (or more) distinct domains. It is both more economical and more plausible to postulate X only once and to assume that insofar as there are differences between the ways that X is manifested, this is due to differences of context. The latter option, which argues for the basic unity of the mind, also shows that what prima facie looks like 'different' domains, are on closer inspection not so different after all. Science has to reveal the deeper similarities (or analogies) which are often obscured by superficial dissimilarities. This was the lesson of Chapter 1.

Prior to Gestalt psychology, it had generally been thought that perception is a synthesis out of more elementary sensations. However, the phenomenon of 'apparent motion', for instance, shows that the perceptual structure may be something that the mind imposes upon sensory data. Why? – because in this case some of the sensations out of which the perception is assumed to be constructed just are not there (cf. Goldstein 1989:22–23). The analogous phenomenon (called 'phonemic restoration effect') is well known in the study of speech perception: people 'hear' sounds which are not there, but which they strongly expect to hear. In this sense, then, Gestalt psychology represents the 'top-down' approach. More recently, the influence of a wider (cultural) context on visual perception has also been demonstrated. Here the analogy to the process of understanding speech is overwhelming because, in conformity with the so-called 'reality principle', people hear (or think they hear) what *makes sense*.

On the other hand, it is obvious that in some sense visual perceptions must be constructed or computed out of smaller building blocks. Thus, there have to be both bottom-up and top-down processes going on simultaneously (*op. cit.*:Ch. 6). The same is of course true of speech processing. Again, it would be very surprising if this near-identity were a mere coincidence. And if it is not a coincidence, then it suggests the basic unity of the mind.

It is interesting to note that Jackendoff seems anxious to establish exactly the same point that I have been making here. For instance, he claims that "producing visual images is more or less *analogous* to speech production", and "linguistic imagery [i.e. 'hearing sentences in our heads'] is a precise *parallel* to visual imagery" (1992: 11; emphasis added). "The relation of images to image schemas (SRs) [= 'geometric' spatial representations] in the present theory is much like the relation of sentences to thoughts [= 'algebraic' conceptual structures]" (1996: 10). In other words, we have the analogy (1):

$$(1) \quad \frac{\text{sentences}}{\text{thoughts}} = \frac{\text{images}}{\text{image schemas}}$$

Interestingly, Jackendoff is unaware of the fact that by postulating in this way an analogy between language and vision, he flatly contradicts Chomsky, who, it will be remembered, denies the existence of any such analogy: "There seems to be no useful analogy between the theory of grammar ... and any other cognitive system that has so far been isolated and described" (cf. p. 129). Moreover, analogy is the governing principle not only between, but also inside Jackendoff-type modules: "The upshot is that the correspondence between syntax and CS [= conceptual structure] is much like the correspondence between syntax and phonology" (1996: 7). This (conjoined) analogy may in turn be represented as in (2):

$$(2) \quad \frac{\text{phonology}}{\text{syntax}} = \frac{\text{syntax}}{\text{conceptual structure (= 'thought')}}$$

Jackendoff (1996) accepts the hypothesis of dual coding in the sense that conceptual structure is 'algebraic' whereas spatial representation is 'geometric'. We have already seen that this type of dichotomy is misleading, at least to some extent. Conceptual structure cannot be (entirely) algebraic, because it mediates between morpho-syntax and (the conceptualization of) extralinguistic reality which stand in an *iconic* (= 'geometric') relation to each other (cf. 3.1).

The work of David Marr has been influential in the study of vision. His theory, as outlined by Gardner (1985: 298–308) contains three levels, namely 'computational theory', 'algorithm', and 'implementation'. The first of these defines the task, or *what* has to be done. The second shows *how* it is done, at the level of *abstract* instructions. The third shows *how* the instructions are carried out by some *concrete* mechanism. The first two levels correspond, respectively, to the set-theoretic and algorithmic definitions of a *function* (cf. Itkonen

1983a: 149–150). There is a close analogy between linguistics and the Marr-type theory of vision insofar as the three levels mentioned above correspond quite exactly to three distinct types of linguistic subdiscipline, namely autonomous linguistics, psycholinguistics, and neurolinguistics. Each of these three has its own ontology, on the continuum 'conceptual > psychological > neurological' (where the term 'conceptual' is used as in the expression 'conceptual analysis').

It is important to realize that the designations of Marr's three levels are likely to create misunderstandings. The term 'computation', as used e.g. by Minsky (1967) in the title of his foundational book, is identical with *algorithm*. As noted above, the *task* to be performed can be defined e.g. in set-theoretic terms, which do *not* entail computations (i.e. 'acts') of any kind. Therefore it is unfortunate that Marr applies the term 'computation' to this (de facto *non-computational*) level. This curious choice of terminology may have up to now obscured the basic analogy between language and vision.

Because vision provides the principal access to spatial cognition, it may be difficult to keep the two apart. Nevertheless, they have to be kept apart:

> Objects are perceived under the same conditions whether they are seen or felt. Objects do not appear to be apprehended by separate visual and haptic mechanisms but by a single mechanism that operates on representations arising either through vision or through touch.   (Spelke 1988:175)

This view has been dramatically confirmed by Kennedy (1993), who uses evidence from blind children's drawings to show that the same spatial cognition is achieved either by vision or by touch (plus language). Therefore it is misleading to treat Marr's (1982) *visual* 3-D model as a theory of *spatial* representation, as is often done.

In the beginning of this section I made the stipulation that the concept of vision should be restricted so as to exclude visual *languages*. This is an unnatural restriction, and now I have to give it up. Because sign language is a subtype of language, and because it is based on vision, not audition, there has to be a *direct* link between language and vision. This fact has not been appreciated by Jackendoff (1996:3), who represents the relation between language and vision as necessarily *indirect*, as in Figure 3.2.

Thus, one arrives from visual input to syntax only via (algebraic or digital) conceptual structure. Or, inversely, one arrives from syntax to spatial representation only via conceptual structure. As an account of meaning in sign language, this is certainly wrong. It would be odd to claim that representing space by space is *not* a matter of spatial representation, without any intervening algebraic or digital level. Of course, these defects can be *easily* amended, by

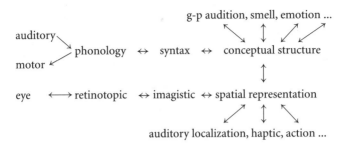

Figure 3.2 The relation between language and vision according to Jackendoff (1996)

adding a few arrows and/or boxes. But this points to a more fundamental flaw, namely how *easy* – quite literally – it is to practice 'modular psychology'.

In what precedes I have pinpointed some general similarities between language and vision (and some other domains as well). Of course, this does not imply that there are no differences between language and vision. There are both similarities and differences, which means that the situation is neither black nor white. But this is precisely my point. The 'modular' terminology is conducive to a black-and-white interpretation.

3.4 Language and music

According to Jackendoff (1992:71), music is a mental module or "a set of modules". The fact that the number of musical modules, insofar as they exist, is quite open indicates, once again, that the notion of 'module' is not as constrained as one might wish it to be. Let us now consider the relation between music and language more closely.

Jackendoff (1987:Ch. 11) offers a convenient starting point. He distinguishes between four distinct levels of musical structure. For instance, the opening line of Mozart, K. 550 has 20 notes, which constitute a 'grouping structure' in the following way: notes 1–3 (= A), 4–6 (= B), 7–10 (= C), 11–13 (= D), 14–16 (= E), and 17–20 (= F) are constituents of the lowest level; constituents of the next level are formed by A and B (= G) as well as by D and E (= H); constituents of the next level are formed by G and C (= I) as well as by H and F (= J); the one-line-length unit itself is constituted by I and J and will in turn be a constituent in higher-level units (cf. Figure 3.3). The constituents are held together by the standard gestalt criteria, i.e. similarity and/or proximity between

Figure 3.3 Grouping structure in the opening of Mozart's G minor symphony, K. 550 (from Jackendoff 1987:219)

units, and are – inversely – separated by the opposite criteria, i.e. dissimilarity and/or distance.

Next, there is a 'metrical structure' consisting of strong and weak beats. The 20-note line mentioned above contains 32 beats, as follows:

214121315121312141213121512131

The 'strength' of a beat is constituted by a heavy stress and/or by a relatively long duration. There is a tendency to put the strong beat at the beginning of the units of the grouping structure. Just like the grouping structure, the metrical structure too may be represented with the aid of a tree diagram.

The level of 'time-span reduction' introduces the distinction between a theme and its variation (or elaboration). The former represents what is important; it is the 'skeleton' enriched by the latter. The enrichment may be either sequential (= melody) or simultaneous (= harmony). At this level too, structures may be depicted with the aid of tree diagrams, with the qualification that the 'theme vs. variation' distinction becomes visible only by comparing *several* trees simultaneously.

Finally, the level of 'prolongational reduction' introduces the distinction between the building-up of tension and its relaxation. It represents the 'movement' within a piece of music. Correspondingly, while the elaboration of units at the previous level is symmetrical, it is asymmetrical at this level: "long periods of increasing tension [are] followed by relatively rapid relaxation".

It is quite easy to see the analogy (sic) between the musical structures and the linguistic structures. The grouping structure strongly resembles the constituent structure of a sentence. The fact that the same type of structure seems to be "involved in any sort of temporal pattern perception [and production!]" (Jackendoff 1987:221), does nothing to diminish the importance of this overall similarity. Rather, it constitutes a general argument for anti-modularity.

The metrical structure is practically the same in language and in music; for instance, Jackendoff (1987: 79) analyzes the metrical structure of the expression *American history teacher* as 121141131, in much the same way he analyzes the opening line of Mozart, K. 550 (cf. above).

At the level of time-span reduction, the distinction between theme and variation closely parallels that between obligatory and obligatory-cum-optional constituents (cf. *The boy ate an apple* vs. *The little boy hastily ate a red apple*); and both in language and in music, the obligatory constituents are the 'heads' of their respective domains. It is curious that Jackendoff does not point this out explicitly, especially since Sapir (1921: 36), for instance, applied the same term, i.e. 'reduction analysis', to the method of finding out the obligatory constituents of a sentence. (It may be added that this method was already practiced by Apollonius Dyscolus; cf. Itkonen 1991: 202–203.) The 'theme vs. variation' distinction is also paralleled, in the linguistic domain, by the distinction between a sentence in its basic form and any of its stylistic variants (*The boy ate an apple* vs. *An apple was eaten by the boy*, *It was an apple that the boy ate*, etc.).

Finally, the distinction between the levels of time-span reduction and prolongation reduction parallels that between the levels of sentence and text (or discourse). Again, Jackendoff fails to mention this obvious fact.

While Jackendoff is content to analyze the structural aspect of music in Chapter 11 of his 1987 book, he turns to the question of how music is processed (i.e. heard and understood) in Chapter 7 (= 'Musical parsing and musical affect') of his 1992 book. He notes explicitly (p. 125) that he will proceed "by analogy with evidence from the processing of language", a problem that he had addressed in Chapter 6 of his 1987 book. His solution is, briefly, that both language and music are understood by constructing parallel interpretations, from among which one will ultimately prevail. This is certainly plausible.

Jackendoff's overall argument contains the following oddity. On the one hand, he uses continuously such words as 'analogy', 'similarity', and 'parallelism'; and he clearly assumes that the plausibility of the hypothesis that language is processed in a parallel fashion *supports* the hypothesis that music is processed in the same way. On the other hand, as a "deeply committed Chomskian" (1992: 53), he accepts Chomsky's view that language and (e.g.) music are separate mental modules. But this is inconsistent: if language and music are independent of each other, then any similarity between the two is due to *chance*; and results achieved in one domain cannot possibly support hypotheses about the other domain.

In other words, Jackendoff takes the both structural and processual analogy between language and music in a purely *heuristic* sense: language just happens to illuminate music, and vice versa. It must be asked, however, what is the basis of this pervasive analogy. To me at least, it seems too implausible to think that it is a result of pure chance, or that it rests on some sort of 'pre-established harmony'. The only reasonable answer is that language and music emanate from a common source, or instantiate a more general capacity; that is, the analogy must be taken in a *realistic* sense. Because of his a priori commitment to the Chomskian modularity, Jackendoff is prevented from drawing this obvious conclusion. (To be sure, he assumes the existence of 'general properties of the computational mind', but the implications that this assumption has for the modularity thesis are never spelled out.)

All in all, the evidence presented by Jackendoff speaks strongly *for* the similarity of language and music (and thus against any modular interpretation of the relation between the two). Therefore, if we wish to find some evidence *against* the similarity of language and music, we must look elsewhere.

According to Thomas (1995: 12–13), the 20th-century musical theory has in general disregarded the possibility that music might have any referential or expressive functions, and has instead posited the existence of 'pure' or 'absolute' music. If we are interested in elucidating the relationship between music and language, it is not very meaningful to consider a position which simply ignores the possibility of any such relationship.

A more fruitful position in this respect is represented e.g. by Davies (1994). On the one hand, he rejects the notion of 'absolute music', because he assumes that music has at least some sort of relation to such a 'substantive' notion as *feeling*. On the other hand, however, he argues at great length against the view that music could be interpreted as (analogous to) a *symbol* of any kind, be it linguistic, pictorial, metaphoric, or 'representational'. According to him, there are first of all several reasons why music cannot be language-like: it lacks the distinction between illocutionary force and propositional content, i.e. it neither asserts (truly or falsely) nor asks nor commands; it lacks (counterparts to) logical connectives; it has no (counterpart to) metalanguage; etc. Second, music is not picture-like, because – quite obviously – no concrete things or events can be 'recovered' from a musical performance with anything approaching intersubjective agreement. Third, music is not metaphoric, because while metaphors can in general be paraphrased in non-metaphorical terms, this cannot be done to a statement like 'This piece of music is sad'.

Up to this point, it is easy to agree with Davies. However, this has hardly any bearing on the modularity issue. It would be quite unrealistic to demand a low-level point-by-point similarity between language and music. And Davies's general approach is so 'philosophical' that he never comes to grips with the systematic structural-cum-processual similarities between language and music that have been pointed out above. Thus, the argument for anti-modularity, or the 'common source' of language and music, remains intact.

Nevertheless, it is meaningful to ask whether Davies (1994) is capable of throwing any additional light on the issue. The opportunity to do so arises when he comes (pp. 123–134) to examine Langer's (1942) philosophy of music. According to Langer, language and music are similar in being symbolizations, but they are different insofar as language is a 'discursive' symbol while music is a 'representational' symbol. A representational symbol is supposed to symbolize the form common to all feelings (or, alternatively, the form common to the various instances of a particular feeling). It is based on the *iconicity* of music/art and feeling insofar as a sameness is experienced between the forms of works of art and the forms of feelings.

Davies rejects Langer's theory, on two accounts. First, the concept of representational symbol presupposes the view of the iconicity of language (as represented e.g. by the 'picture theory' of the early Wittgenstein); but – according to Davies – this view has subsequently been abandoned by everybody (including Wittgenstein himself). Second, because the nature of the representational symbol cannot be discursively discussed, it is simply obscure (or incoherent).

Davies's own view is as follows. Music neither symbolizes nor expresses feelings. Rather, in musical contexts we act just like we do in those "nonmusical contexts in which we attribute emotion characteristics to the appearances of people, or nonhuman animals [cf. the 'sad look' of Basset hounds], or inanimate objects [cf. the shape of the weeping willows which resembles the shape of people who are downcast and burdened with sadness]" (p. 228). This view is indebted to Wittgenstein's later philosophy which denies any strict separation between 'inner' feelings and 'outer' behavior.

Davies's view calls for some comments. First of all, it is of course wrong to claim that iconicity of language is an outdated doctrine (cf. 2.6). More specifically, it is wrong to claim that the 'use theory of language' of the later Wittgenstein contradicts his earlier 'picture theory'. Rather, the former simply contains the latter (see e.g. Kenny 1973: Ch. 12).

Secondly, Davies is quite right to point out the simple-mindedness of the notion that, on one side, there are the feelings and, on the other, there is that by which they are expressed (be it language, music, or ordinary behavior). Wittgenstein's private-language argument has demonstrated the impossibility of inner mental states that have no systematic public criteria (cf. Itkonen

1978: 4.2). In the current metatheory of psychology, including psycholinguistics, this simple-minded separation of mind and behavior is advocated by the 'Neo-Cartesian' school (cf. Itkonen 1983a: 5.1). It is not without interest to note that Jackendoff, a "deeply committed Chomskian" (cf. above), must be counted among the Neo-Cartesians.

From the fact that the levels of ('inner') feeling/thought and ('outer') behavior are conceptually interdependent, it does not follow, however, that they are identical. It is a matter of conceptual necessity that, in order to exist, a feeling or thought requires *some* public criterion *most* of the time; but the precise nature of this criterion is unpredictable, and sometimes it may be lacking. Therefore it is still admissible, *grosso modo*, to speak of feelings/thoughts and their expressions as if they were two distinct levels. In this way it seems possible to retain Langer's (1942) analysis, while doing justice to Davies's (1994) misgivings: sadness is attributed to certain characteristics of music just like it is attributed to certain characteristics of the human face; but in both cases, these characteristics do express the corresponding feeling, even if in a 'conceptually dependent' way. (By contrast, the 'sadness' of dogs and willows is metaphorical.)

Thus, the analogy between language and music seems to hold up rather well. But now an important qualification has to be made. When the term 'language' is used in this context, it is always *oral* language which is meant. This seems natural enough because music too is concerned with *sound*. However, sign languages are on a par with oral languages, and they must be viewed as exemplifications of a more abstract, i.e. non-auditory and non-visual, concept of 'language' (cf. 2.8). This means that the traditional notion of language has to be revised accordingly also in the present context where language is being compared to music.

This revision has the interesting consequence that from now on, while discussing music, we have to regard its auditory aspect as merely incidental. (To be sure, it could be argued that this change of perspective is not all that dramatic because both speech and music can be written and thus already exist in the visual mode.) The following structural levels remain intact: (a) grouping structure as the general hierarchical patterning of (symbolic) actions; (b) the distinction between a 'core structure' consisting of obligatory elements and its elaborations that add optional elements; (c) the distinction between 'sentence' and 'text' (or 'event' and 'story'). By contrast, the 'metrical structure' has to be reinterpreted so as to eliminate any reference to sound. What remains, is the distinction between emphatic and less emphatic; and it may be conveyed by a corresponding auditory distinction (cf. above) or visual distinction (= large and/or quick motion vs. its opposite) or tactile distinction (= more vs. less pressure).

Thus, just as there is an analogy between music and spoken language, there is also an analogy between music and sign language. It may be claimed, in addition, that sign language is not just analogous to music, but also has a 'music' of its own. (Hence there are in fact two analogies instead of just one.) Of course, the notion of 'music without sound' may seem preposterous at first. However, it can be made more comprehensible by pointing out that an expression like 'song in a language without sound' actually occurs in the title of a 1976 paper by Klima and Bellugi. They analyze the changes that are involved in the *artistic* use of American Sign Language, as compared with its everyday use.

More specifically, they observe three types of change that might be characterized as 'poetic': choice of vocabulary; increased tendency to use both hands; tendency to build uninterrupted transitions between particular signs, thus creating an impression of a 'flow of movement'. Even more interestingly, however, they also observe a change that they characterize as 'musical': the movements of the two hands are much enlarged, and they are placed in such a way as not to intersect. According to Klima and Bellugi (1976), this last-mentioned pattern is imposed upon signing just like, in a song, the melody (= one type of sound structure) is imposed upon the words (= another type of sound structure). (To be sure, it could be argued that there is something musical already in the attempt to emphasize the 'flow of movement' aspect of signing.) It may also be added that there is a striking similarity between the activities of conducting a symphony orchestra and conducting a chorus of signers.

One complication still has to be mentioned. In singing, it is always possible to eliminate the words and leave the music, which – presumably – exhibits the four types of structure mentioned above. At first, one might think that this phenomenon can have no analogue in sign languages. However, Terhi Rissanen (p.c.) has confirmed to me that there actually exists a comparable practice of 'pure' or 'merely-musical' signing, analogous to humming, among the users of sign language.

Up to now, I have been trying to show that there are plausible similarities between music and spoken language, on the one hand, and between music and signed language, on the other; and such similarities can be interpreted as pointing to a common source. Language has referential meaning whereas music lacks it. My argument would be strengthened if it could be shown that between music and (typical) language there is such a missing link as 'language without referential meaning'. Now, it is the central claim of Staal (1989) to have discovered precisely this type of phenomenon in the mantras of the Vedic age. They were uttered or performed according to strictly defined rules, but they just had no meaning, at least not in the referential sense. More obviously, the same phenomenon occurs in singing, because it is self-evident that singing often involves words (or 'words') with no or very little meaning.

Comparing language with music is apt to de-emphasize its referential aspect and to emphasize its *rhythmic* aspect. Moreover, the combination of rhythm and *iconicity*, as it occurs in Langer's (1942) theory of music, provides a new perspective on the iconicity of language. In rhythm, there is an inseparable connection between doing and understanding (or responding); one cannot be without the other. A notion like 'rhythmic iconicity' presupposes that there is rhythm not only in the symbol but also in that which is symbolized. Now, this is *not* how iconicity is generally understood in linguistic theory. In it, a sentence is taken to be a (structural) picture of a state of affairs; but the picturing (which inevitably has its own rhythm) is thought to be performed always alike, independently of whether that which is pictured is a man hitting a dog or the sun setting behind a mountain. But now the notion of rhythmic iconicity suggests that the primary case might be the one where there is doing (and understanding) both on the 'picturing side' and on the 'pictured side': one can picture only what one has done or can do oneself.

The foregoing could be taken to stress the metaphorical aspect of language (and thought): human action is primary, and everything else is understood on the model provided by it. However, this interpretation might be a little hasty. (Remember that the cave men also painted animals in at least apparent isolation either from men as such or from men hunting animals.) What this interpretation really points to, is something more subtle: the reality as a whole, i.e. both its human and its non-human aspect, has been equally conceptualized by man. Therefore we possess an intimate knowledge of this conceptualization. It is this truth that the doctrine of 'response-dependence' or 'response-authorization has recently rediscovered (cf. Pettit 1996: 195–203; Itkonen 1997, 2003b: 126–130 and Appendix 3; Haukioja 2000). The rhythm that language pictures is not that of actions (like a man hitting a dog), understood as antithecal to physical events, but that of conceptualizations in general, be it conceptualizations of actions (like a man hitting a dog) or of physical events (like the sun setting behind a mountain). – It is vital to understand the following distinction: the sun has not been made by man, but the concept 'sun' has.

In what precedes, I have argued for the view that language and music derive from a common source. This statement is meant to be taken in the *synchronic* sense, i.e. as being about the human mind as it exists now. It is tempting, although in no way mandatory, to take the statement also in the *diachronic* sense, i.e. as being about the (evolutionary) origin of language and music. In the present context I shall resist this temptation only in part and thus add a few words on the latter topic as well.

Staal (1989) was mentioned above as providing evidence for the synchronic commonality of language and music. However, he personally regards his analysis of the 'language without meaning', exemplified by the Vedic mantras, as a contribution to clarifying the origin of language. As he sees it, this type of non-referential, and hence 'musical', use of structured sound was the precursor of referential language: meaning was secondarily imposed upon sound that was already there. Of course, this sound too had to have some sort of function, but this was to express or sustain hard-to-define communal feelings.

Wallin (1991) reaches a similar conclusion from a rather different, i.e. biological and cross-species, point of view. According to him, language was, and still is, prefigured by the calls emitted by non-human vertebrates. He assumes a slow evolutionary process during which sound patterns acquire more and more differentiated meanings. This view is becoming more and more widely accepted. Dunbar (1998) sees the origin of language in 'grooming-by-sound', which on the one hand was an extension of the earlier 'social grooming' (i.e. grooming-by-hand) and, on the other, was later harnessed to convey information. Locke (1998) postulates both phylogenetically and ontogenetically a level of 'talking' which is intermediate between mere vocalization and (symbolic) speaking:

> In talking, the individual engages in sound-making in order to achieve and maintain cohesion with others. Cohesion is achieved through a range of social behaviors that promote meshing and synchronization, and are manifested in co-ordinated vocal turns, gaze patterns and bodily movements. (pp. 191–192)

The collective nature of this type of pre-language explains quite naturally how meanings, once they emerged, could be learned by all members of the community simultaneously. In this type of group performance, exemplified equally by song and dance, every participant has to *synchronize* his actions with those of every other participant. Consequently, behavior of this type literally *embodies* the notion of common knowledge (= 'everybody knows-1 X and knows-2 that everybody knows-1 X'). The theoretical importance of song and dance becomes evident when we recall that *language* exists only as an object of common knowledge (cf. the end of 3.5). Keeping in mind the analogy with song and dance, we are able to grasp better than before the sense in which, in a typical verbal exchange, the speaker and the hearer have to synchronize their respective actions in relation to what has been and is being said. (The term 'synchronize' is clearly more adequate than the fashionable term 'negotiate'.) – The analogy between language and dance qua cooperative undertakings is also employed by Clark (1996:3).

It is quite interesting to note that these modern views were anticipated in great detail by Jespersen (1922:392–442). In his speculations about the origin of language, he arrived at the view that referential language must have been preceded by singing, which in its turn was functional in fulfilling the need for sex (or love), on the one hand, and the need for coordinating collective work, on the other. These speculations have, in turn, their origin in Darwin's 1871 book *The Descent of Man*:

> we may conclude from a widely-spread analogy that this power [of sound] would have been especially exerted during the courtship of the sexes, serving to express various emotions. ... The imitation by articulate sounds of musical cries might have given rise to words expressive of various complex emotions.
>
> (quoted from Howard 1982:70)

The modern scholars mentioned above agree in rejecting the well-known scenario according to which language originated as a system of monosyllabic grunt-like sounds that had the (referential) function of pointing at things. Instead, they propose a scenario according to which referential meaning was slowly grafted upon nearly autonomous melodious sound. This is an ironic vindication of Chomsky's overall position. All along, he has been arguing for 'autonomous syntax', or the view that in human language, *as it exists today*, form is primary with respect to meaning. This view is patently false. The most obvious arguments against it are brought together in Itkonen (1996:483–486). But now, as a result of the foregoing excursus into theories about the evolution of language, we see that (relative) autonomy of syntax may well have been true of that type of vocalization which *preceded* language proper.

3.5 Language and logic

In this section I will examine the relation between language and logic. A more thorough discussion is given in Itkonen (2003a).

Jackendoff (1992:32, 54–55) locates 'logical inference rules' in a module called 'conceptual system', which, although separate from the language module, is assumed to constitute both the semantics and the pragmatics common to all languages. To substantiate this thesis, he refers to Jackendoff (1983:Ch. 5, 6, and 8). The following are examples of rules of inference à la Jackendoff: 'if x is a dog, then x is an animal'; 'if x is red, then x is coloured'; 'if x causes y to do z, then y does z'; 'if x is a red hat, then x is red and x is a hat'.

It is immediately obvious that Jackendoff uses the term 'rule of inference' in an idiosyncratic way. What he is dealing with are entailment relations between word meanings (or meanings of phrases, as in the case of 'red hat'). In Jackendoff (1983: 99–100), moreover, he erroneously assumes that an implication that occurs as a premise in a (deductive) inference must be an entailment, i.e. necessarily true. In the typical case, however, it is only the relation between the premises and the conclusion which is necessary; that is, what is necessarily true is the inference once it has been reformulated as an implication such that the premises constitute its antecedent and the conclusion constitutes its consequent. Jackendoff's (1992: 18) claim that he is dealing with 'logic' must be taken with a grain of salt.

Both propositional logic and predicate logic are truth-functional, and truth is indeed the basic semantic notion. In his approach to logic, Jackendoff may have been hampered by his wish to abandon the notion of truth altogether. According to Jackendoff (1992: 172), for instance, 'belief' and 'truth' are not part of scientific vocabulary, but merely belong to folk psychology, which "is full of all kinds of crazy things". In sum, when Jackendoff claims that logic and language are separate modules, the meaning of this claim is not clear. In the sequel, in any case, I will try to find out whether this claim is true or false, assuming that the words 'language' and 'logic' have their usual meanings.

To start with, it seems natural to think that logic is what formal logic is a formalization of. Formal logic is primarily concerned with connectives such as *not, and, or, if – then*, and *if and only if – then* as well as with quantifiers such as *all* and *some*. More precisely, it is concerned with the *meanings* of the connectives and the quantifiers. Husserl, for instance, understood clearly that, in reality, there is no purely formal or syntactic logic because all logical terms express, and are determined by meanings (which he took to be universal) (cf. Itkonen 1991: 285–286). Furthermore, it is natural to think that the meanings of the connectives and the quantifiers is more or less the same as the corresponding *grammatical meanings* (i.e. the meanings of *not, and*, etc.), as they occur in natural languages. What is at issue here is the exact significance of this 'more or less'. Therefore, in what follows, I shall compare several formal-logical notions to their natural-language equivalents and point out both similarities and dissimilarities between the two domains.

In two-valued propositional logic the relation of a sentence p to its negation $\sim p$ is symmetrical: if (and only if) p is true, then $\sim p$ is false, and vice versa. In natural language, by contrast, the relation between p and *not-p* is asymmetrical: the affirmation p is the primary case, and the negation *not-p* is the secondary case which denies a false affirmation (cf. Evans 1982: 196). It is one of the most consistent findings produced by experimental research on the psychology of logic that negation makes comprehension more difficult. Moreover, because p is primary, it is difficult to understand its secondary use in denying a false *not-p*.

Both natural language and propositional logic agree that a conjunction p & q is true if, and only if, both conjuncts are true, and it is false otherwise. Beyond this, natural language adds e.g. temporal and/or causal meanings to the word *and*, depending on the context.

In propositional logic the disjunction $p \vee q$ is normally taken in the inclusive sense, i.e. it is true if, and only if, at least one of the disjuncts is true, and it is false otherwise. It is also possible to define an exclusive disjunction, which is true if, and only if, exactly one of the disjuncts is true. The natural language connective *or* fails to consistently distinguish between the inclusive use and the exclusive one. The content of the disjuncts decides whether one or the other interpretation is adopted (cf. Evans 1982: 118). E.g. 'He managed to do it or he was killed trying to do it' permits only an exclusive reading.

Propositional logic and natural language agree that an implication $p \rightarrow q$ is true if both the antecedent and the consequent are true, and it is false if, and only if, the antecedent is true and the consequent is false. Beyond this point, propositional logic sharply diverges from natural language, namely in stipulating that $p \rightarrow q$ is true also when p is false, whether or not q is true, which gives rise to the 'paradoxes of (material) implication'. Logically untrained persons, i.e. ordinary natural-language speakers, find it difficult to accept the corresponding interpretations of *if – then* sentences. Their experimental behavior is far from uniform, but it seems to support the postulation of a 'defective' truth-table for the implication: *if p, then q* is true or false with the constellations 'True & True' or 'True & False', respectively, and neither true nor false otherwise (cf. Evans 1982: 120).

Nevertheless, it is possible to contrive examples that make the truth-functional interpretation of the implication comprehensible at least to some extent. That $p \rightarrow q$ is true when both p and q are false, can be understood on the basis of the intuitive principle that (it is true that) 'falsity follows from falsity'; just consider an example like 'If Hitler was a good man, then I am Mickey Mouse'. It is more difficult to understand that $p \rightarrow q$ is true also when p is false and q is true. But consider an example like 'If you ask me, Hitler was a bad man'. It seems natural to say that the sentence is true even if you do not ask me, i.e. when the antecedent is false; it is enough that the consequent is true. However, it is exactly the contrived and non-representative nature of such examples which shows that Johnson-Laird (1983:54–62) is probably right in claiming that, instead of being a unitary phenomenon, the natural-language implication is context-dependent or "creates its own context".

In propositional logic, $p \rightarrow q$ is equivalent to the following sentences (or, rather, sentence-schemas): $\sim q \rightarrow \sim p$, $\sim (p \,\&\, \sim q)$, $\sim p \lor q$. Of these three, the last one in particular is important because it transforms an asymmetric relation into a symmetric one. (That is, $p \rightarrow q$ is not the same as $q \rightarrow p$, but $\sim p \lor q$ is the same as $q \lor \sim p$.) It is interesting to note that only the second equivalence of these three seems to be psychologically real (cf. Evans 1982:137–138). The reason must be that, as we have seen, the falsity of the implication is more clear-cut than its truth; and $\sim (p \,\&\, \sim q)$ denies the only, and psychologically real, constellation, i.e. 'True & False', which makes $p \rightarrow q$ false. Yet, as before, it is possible to contrive examples which give at least a glimpse of the justification for the equivalence $(p \rightarrow q) \equiv (\sim p \lor q)$. For instance, 'If you still disturb me, you must leave' means much the same as 'You don't disturb me any longer or you must leave'. Notice, incidentally, that the corresponding equivalence $(p \lor q) \equiv (\sim p \rightarrow q)$, which transforms a (symmetrical) disjunction into an (asymmetrical) implication, is immediately comprehensible, without any contrived examples (cf. Evans 1982:190). For instance, 'John buys books or Mary sells newspapers' means obviously the same as 'If John doesn't buy books, then Mary sells newspapers'.

In addition to the (material) implication, propositional logic also postulates the existence of the (material) equivalence $p \equiv q$, which is true either when p and q are true or when p and q are false. The equivalence is translated as 'if, and only if, p, then q', which, when spelled out, amounts to 'if p, then q; and only if p, then q'. The equivalence is also called 'bidirectional implication', which means that it may be translated as 'if p, then q; and if q, then p'. This reveals the intuitively surprising fact that 'if q, then p' means the same as 'only if p, then q'.

Just as in connection with the inclusive vs. exclusive disjunction, natural-language speakers have difficulties in distinguishing between implication and equivalence. First, natural-language counterparts of the equivalence connective are unwieldy and infrequent, which means that their function is pre-empted by a simple *if – then*, even when this goes against the meaning to be expressed. Second, often the meaning allows only an equivalence reading, which makes a simple *if – then* sufficient (cf. 'If you mow the lawn, I'll give you five dollars'; Evans 1982: 151–152). Third, and as expected, people mostly fail to grasp the equivalence between 'if p, then q' and 'p, only if q', which means that they fail to grasp the (truth-functional) content of *only if* (cf. Evans 1982: 145–151). All these complications hamper an adequate understanding of the cognitive processes involved, without, however, making it impossible.

The use of natural-language connectives presupposes that the two sentences to be combined are somehow *relevant* to each other. No similar presupposition attaches to the use of the logical connectives, as is evident from the fact that, instead of genuine sentences, propositional logic can afford to make use of sentence-schemas or formulae. Most of the time, psychology of logic has been experimentally investigated in the same spirit, namely by using such 'abstract material' as in themselves meaningless letters or numbers. On the one hand, it could be maintained that this is the right way (and the only way) to disentangle the genuinely logical component of thinking from the 'merely' linguistic and/or common-sense components. On the other hand, it could also be maintained that this research paradigm is too artificial to produce meaningful results. Personally, I think that truth lies somewhere between these two extremes (cf. below).

Up to now, the existence of natural-language connectives *and*, *or*, and *if – then* has been taken for granted. Therefore it is important to add that there are many languages in which clear-cut counterparts to these (English-language) connectives are lacking. For instance, Mithun (1988) notes on three separate occasions that she has been surprised to find how wide-spread the lack of a coordinating conjunction (= *and*) is in the world's languages. This seems to be characteristic of most languages in Africa, Central America, and Australia.

Let us single out here the situation in two genetically unrelated Amazonian languages, namely Yagua and Wari'. In Yagua, "the primary means of indicating all types of clausal coordination [= *p and q*] is by simple juxtaposition" (Payne & Payne 1990: 294), that is, without any overt means of expression. This leaves open the question whether, or to what extent, the speakers of Yagua possess the concept of logical conjunction. Intriguingly, there seems to be some evidence that they actually lack the concept of logical disjunction: "In elicitation via Spanish, speaker after speaker simply responds *sí* 'yes' to an 'or'-type question, or else fails to answer it, treating it as unintelligible" (p. 297). By contrast, there seems to exist a reasonably unequivalent way to express conditionality, namely the clitic *-tiy* which is suffixed to the first word of the (complex) sentence (pp. 340–341).

The situation is rather similar in Wari', where "there are no simple equivalents of 'and'-, 'but'- and 'or'-coordination" (Everett & Kern 1997: 159). Rather, 'and' is expressed either by simple juxtaposition or by appending a comment equivalent to 'so it is' to a string of juxtaposed clauses (pp. 159–160), whereas there are three separate constructions that can be interpreted as conveying the meaning of 'or' (p. 162). By contrast, just as in Yagua, there is one standard way to express conditionality, namely the construction (equivalent to the antecedent clause *if p*) that contains the operator word *mo*, a tense/mood clitic, the finite verb, and a person/number/gender clitic; this construction is followed by the consequent or main clause (pp. 103–106). (There is a separate way to express contrafactual conditionality.) Thus, in Yagua and Wari' there is at least a systematic way to express conditionality. Therefore it is good to add that there are also (polysynthetic) languages like Cayuga (a member of the Iroquoian family) and Yimas (a Papuan language of New Guinea) whose syntax is so paratactic or 'flat' as to make explicit expression of subordination (including conditionality) practically impossible (cf. Mithun 1991; Foley 1997).

These findings seem to indicate that in some languages there may be no need to explicitly make conceptual distinctions that are made elsewhere as a matter of course. On the other hand, the fact that in these and similar languages the words for 'and' and 'or' have been or are being borrowed either from Spanish or from English shows that we are not dealing with any kind of 'alien logic'. The following interpretation offered by Boas (1964 [1911]: 18) still remains valid:

> It seems very questionable in how far the restriction of the use of certain grammatical forms can really be conceived as a hindrance in the formulation of generalized ideas. It seems much more likely that the lack of these forms is due to the lack of their need.

The same view has been reiterated more recently e.g. by Levinson (2003: 292–293).

While propositional logic is content to describe intersentential relations, predicate logic takes also the intrasentential structure into consideration. A sentence consists of one predicate like F, G, etc. and one or more arguments. These are either constants (= 'individual-names') like a, b, etc. or variables like x, y, etc. quantified either by $\forall$(= 'all') or by $\exists$(= 'at least one'). Here it is sufficient to note that there is a rough-and-ready correspondence between natural language and simple applications of predicate logic. That is, predicate logic fails to make a huge number of distinctions which are relevant to natural language, but the few distinctions which it does make (= predicate vs. argument and 'all' vs. 'some') can be understood without much difficulty. To be sure, interpreting 'all'-statements as universally quantified implications gives the paradoxical result that any such statement made about nonexistent entities

Modus Ponens (MP)	Denying the Antecedent (DA)
$p \rightarrow q$ p	$p \rightarrow q$ $\sim p$
q	$\sim q$
Affirming the Consequent (AC)	Modus Tollens (MT)
$p \rightarrow q$ q	$p \rightarrow q$ $\sim q$
p	$\sim p$

Figure 3.4 The four conditional inferences

(like unicorns) is true. More importantly, increasing the number of quantified argument-variables leads very quickly to total non-comprehension on the part of logically untrained persons.

Consider the sentence $\forall x \forall y Lxy$, meaning 'Everybody loves everybody'. Because the order of quantifiers of the same type is free, this sentence is equivalent to $\forall y \forall x Lxy$. Let us negate the two sentences, and let us move the negation-sign to the right, which necessitates reversing the type of the quantifier. At this point we have two equivalent sentences $\exists x \sim \forall y Lxy$ and $\exists y \sim \forall x Lxy$, meaning 'There is somebody who does not love everybody' and 'There is somebody who is not loved by everybody', respectively. They have the same truth-condition, i.e. there is no situation which would make one sentence true and the other false. It seems safe to assume, however, that this fact is not, and probably cannot be, understood by everybody. It is just as difficult to understand the equivalence between e.g. $\sim \exists y \forall x Lxy$ and $\forall y \exists x \sim Lxy$, or 'It is not the case that there is somebody who is loved by everybody' and 'Everybody has somebody who does not love him'. Thus, Johnson-Laird (1983:76) is certainly right to claim that "the quantificational calculus ... seems too powerful for a psychological model".

So far, we have reviewed the basic *structure* of expressions of propositional and predicate logic in relation to natural language. Next, let us consider a few *inferences*. The principal types of conditional inference are those shown in Figure 3.4.

MP and MT are *valid*, i.e. it is necessarily the case that if the premises are true, the conclusion is true. While both DA and AC are invalid, there is this difference between the two that, in a suitable context, AC confirms *p*, or offers a reason for accepting *p* as true, whereas DA has no meaningful use at all. If, however, the implication is misinterpreted as an equivalence, then DA and AC

$$\frac{\begin{array}{l} p \vee q \\ \sim p \end{array}}{q} \qquad \frac{\begin{array}{l} \sim p \vee q \\ p \end{array}}{q}$$

Figure 3.5 The differential role of negation in inferences

too are valid. Yet it is possible to ward off this kind of misinterpretation, at least in principle, by giving additional instructions to test subjects.

Experimental research shows that, as one might expect, MP is universally understood. By contrast, it is quite surprising that in separate experiments the same number of subjects (which varies between 50% and 80%) considers DA, AC, and MT as equally valid (cf. Evans 1982: 128–135). This finding is rather uncomfortable for those who insist on the rationality of human thinking, considering in particular the central importance that MT has in the philosophy of science. To be sure, the differential comprehension of MP and MT may be explained. First, reasoning involves a directionality such that it is easier to reason from the antecedent to the consequent (as in MP), rather than vice versa (as in MT). Second, the use of negation (as in MT) generally inhibits comprehension. Moreover, these results have been achieved with abstract material (like letters and numbers), and it is safe to assume that MT is grasped when it is applied to realistic material (cf. 'If John has come home, the lights are on; but the lights are not on; therefore John has not come home').

The situation becomes more complicated, when – in the implication $p \rightarrow q$ – either p or q or both are negated. MP still remains universally understood (which is at least some consolation for those who advocate the rationality of human thinking). However, when p is negated, the comprehension of the validity of MT falls to 40% or less, and in one experiment as low as 12%. Once again, this is quite remarkable. It is no less remarkable that, under the same condition, the tendency to mistakenly view AC as valid actually increases. There is no simple explanation for these facts (cf. Evans 1982: *ibidem*).

The asymmetrical nature of negation becomes obvious in disjunctive reasoning. Consider the two inferences given in Figure 3.5.

It is natural that not-p denies a previously given p, and therefore the first inference is easy to understand. By contrast, a negated disjunct $\sim p$, denied by an affirmative p, is unnatural, and therefore – quite predictably – the second inference creates considerable difficulties of understanding (cf. Evans 1982: 193–197). Because $\sim p \vee q$ is equivalent to $p \rightarrow q$, the second inference is, from the logical point of view, identical with MP. This identity is not, however, psychologically real.

Experimental work on deductive reasoning seems to have created the following dilemma. Most people make logical mistakes most of the time; but this means that they are illogical or irrational; but this is impossible (for ideological reasons); therefore people must be assumed to possess a *logical competence*, and their seemingly illogical behavior must be attributed to 'performance factors'; but such an assumption is infalsifiable and therefore indefensible. – Is there a way out of this dilemma?

Piaget assumed that adults have developed a self-contained system a 'formal operations', comparable to formal logic (cf. Inhelder & Piaget 1958). More realistically, Henle (1962) attributed errors in deductive reasoning to the fact that test subjects reinterpret the premises, i.e. they either add or delete premises or transform implications into equivalences and inclusive disjunctions into exclusive ones or perform illicit 'conversions' (like 'All A are B' = 'All B are A'); but from their *own* point of view they reason in an impeccable way. The accumulating experimental evidence, reported in Wason & Johnson-Laird (1972), Evans (1982), Johnson-Laird (1983), Manktelow & Over (1990), and Johnson-Laird & Byrne (1991) has made this view increasingly implausible. But the strong version of the rationality hypothesis still has its advocates, with the qualification that the idea of possessing formal logic *tout court* has been replaced by the idea of possessing a 'logical competence', modeled on the Chomsky-type grammatical competence (cf. Cohen 1981, 1986:Ch. 3).

It seems rather obvious that the alternatives 'completely logical' and 'completely illogical' cannot be exhaustive. Between these two extremes there must be something like 'logical in a restricted or elementary sense'. (This also seems to be the position of both Evans and Johnson-Laird, although they might phrase it differently.) There are a few inference types which are mastered by all normal adults: Modus Ponens, Modus Tollens in a moderately realistic context, disjunctive inference with the premises $p \vee q$ and $\sim p$, and Aristotle's favorite syllogism 'All A are B' & 'All B are C'; 'therefore: All A are C'. This is the bridgehead on which formal logic has been and is being built. That there would be *no* point of contact with formal logic and the way that people make inferences as a matter of fact is just as unimaginable as the idea that arithmetic has nothing at all to do with the additions and subtractions that people perform in their daily life. Notice, for instance, that practically every action we perform is based on the following type of Modus Ponens: 'If I want to have X, I must do Y; but I want to have X; therefore I must to do Y'. It would be simply too implausible to assume that although MP is central both in everyday language (or thinking) and in formal logic, these two have nothing whatever to do with each other.

Thus, I locate the origin of formal logic in everyday language (or thinking). Therefore I find it hard to accept Johnson-Laird's (1983:51) claim that, since his mental models for syllogisms contain no formal rules of inference, "logic is banished from the mind".

On the other hand, it is easier to accept the view that the construction of mental models (i.e. what I would call 'mental logic') "is nothing more than the proper comprehension of discourse" (Johnson-Laird 1983:131). This follows from the fact, already mentioned above, that logic is based on the comprehension of (grammatical) meanings expressed by such grammatical morphemes as *not, and, or, if – then, all, some,* etc. To put it more explicitly, ('logical') intuitions about validity are embedded in ('linguistic') intuitions about certain *grammatical meanings.* Thus, logic is a matter of understanding and producing certain form – meaning pairs as they occur in sentences and discourses. Therefore logic is part of language. And because it is part of language, it cannot be a module separate from language.

It is a historical fact that formal logic had its origin in natural language, as confirmed by Kneale and Kneale (1962:59):

> For many centuries all the [syllogistic] relations asserted by Aristotle were accepted without much questioning by the thousands who studied his work. It is therefore very likely that his work is a faithful reflection of the normal usage for sentences constructed with words like 'every' and 'some'.

Today's formal logic gives to universal sentences an interpretation which is different from Aristotle's. But it would be nonsense to claim that Aristotle, just because he followed "the normal usage", did not practice logic. Similarly, measured by today's standards, Aristotle's logic was only half-formalized. But, again, it would be nonsensical to claim that, just for this reason, what he investigated was not logic. Formal logic has gradually emerged from (certain aspects of) natural language.

Up to now, I have been concerned with similarities between linguistics and formal logic. But there is also a crucial difference between the two. Linguistics is governed by a *descriptive* research interest. Formal logic, by contrast, is governed by a *prescriptive* research interest insofar as, starting from a few intuitively obvious principles, it develops new and *better* means of making inferences, i.e. means that rapidly transcend the limits of untutored logical intuition. The analogy to mathematics is self-evident.

According to the view that we have reached up to now, language and logic share a common origin insofar as they are both concerned with socially binding rules (or norms) of linguistic behavior, namely rules for speaking correctly and/or inferring validly. This 'common origin', which consists in the inherent *normativity* of the data, explains the methodological similarity between formalized grammars and axiomatizations of e.g. deontic logic, on the one hand, and the methodological dissimilarity between formalized grammars and axiomatized theories of natural science, on the other (cf. Itkonen 1978: Ch. 10, 2003b: Ch. 11). Ringen (1975) and Katz (1981) have also argued for the basic similarity between grammatical and formal-logical descriptions.

It is true that the social-normative dimension is totally absent e.g. from the tree diagrams of generative linguistics and from the pictorial diagrams of cognitive linguistics; but, when looking at linguistic descriptions of this type, it is not too difficult to *imagine* this (invisible) dimension in addition to what is explicitly visible. In case of logic, however, the situation is more complicated. The standard formalizations of logic (represented e.g. by the inferences given above) are just as unable to capture the social-normative dimension as the standard formalizations of language are. But while the latter are not, in general, sufficient to hide the social-normative nature of language, the former have – at least up to now – been quite sufficient to hide the social-normative nature of logic. Fortunately, there is one exception, which I shall now proceed to discuss.

An adequate formalization of logic should be a *logic in use*; and in order to be social, in the sense of 'intersubjective', it should be (at least) *dialogical*, rather than monological. (Notice that an adequate formalization of language – whatever it will turn out to be – must satisfy exactly the same criteria.) Precisely such a type of logic has been developed by Paul Lorenzen and Kuno Lorenz from the late fifties onwards (cf. Kamlah & Lorenzen 1967; Lorenzen & Lorenz 1978; for an English-language presentation, cf. Lorenz 1989). In addition to its social or 'actionist' nature, the dialogical (or 'game-theoretic') logic has still other advantages over more traditional conceptions. First, both the connectives and the quantifiers are introduced in the same way (cf. below). Second, whereas in truth-functional logic the truth-value of a complex formula can be determined only if the truth-values of the atomary formulae are known in advance, i.e. if these formulas are 'value-definite', the dialogical logic need not accept this clearly unrealistic restriction. Rather, the truth or the falsity of atomary sentences may be established only in the course of the dialogue-game.

The game is a succession of attacks and defenses between two disputants, namely the 'proponent' and the 'opponent'. The connectives *and, or, if – then,* and *not* are introduced as follows. If the proponent asserts the sentence p & q, the opponent attacks it by questioning p and q in turn; if the proponent can defend both p and q, he has won; otherwise he has lost. If the proponent asserts $p \vee q$, the opponent attacks it by questioning it as a whole, and the proponent wins if he is able to defend either p or q; otherwise he has lost. If $p \rightarrow q$ is asserted by the proponent, the opponent attacks it by asserting p, and then the proponent attacks by questioning p; but if the opponent is able to defend p, then the proponent wins only if he is able to defend q. If $\sim p$ is asserted by the proponent, the opponent attacks by asserting p, and the proponent attacks in his turn by questioning p. The opponent wins or loses depending on whether he can or cannot defend p. ('Defending' p amounts to showing, by whatever means, that p is true.)

The rules for the use of the quantifiers, which are superimposed upon the above-mentioned rules, are introduced as follows. If the proponent asserts a universally quantified sentence $\forall x Fx$, the opponent attacks by picking out an object a which he thinks is a counter-example. If the proponent is able to defend Fa, he has won (which does not mean that he has proved the truth of $\forall x Fx$). If the proponent asserts an existentially quantified sentence $\exists x Fx$, the opponent attacks by simply questioning it, and then the proponent must pick out a suitable object b and defend Fb. If he is unable to do so, he has lost (which does not mean that the opponent has proved the falsity of $\exists x Fx$).

The game starts from the entire sentence and proceeds gradually to the atomary sentences of the type Fa. In order to win, the opponent *seeks* an object which could falsify a universally quantified sentence and the proponent *seeks* an object which would verify an existentially quantified sentence. Depending on whether objects of the required kind have been *found* or, perhaps, *produced*, the game has been either won or lost. If this aspect of the dialogue-games is emphasized, they could be called 'games of seeking and finding'.

A complex sentence is *empirically true*, if the proponent always wins, i.e. if he is able to defend it against any opponent, by defending those atomary sentences which he has asserted during the performance of any game connected with the complex sentence. If any opponent is able to win, the sentence is empirically false. A complex sentence is *logically true*, if the proponent has to defend an atomary sentence which has been previously defended by the opponent. In such a case, the opponent has been forced to defend and to attack one and the same (atomary) sentence, which means that denying the complex sentence has led to a contradiction. This notion of contradiction is independent of the meaning of the particular sentence which the opponent has both defended and attacked, which means that it is permissible to consider (abstract) sentence-formulae instead of (concrete) sentences. Logical implication is defined in such a way that p is said to be entailed by q, r, etc., if q, r, etc. are asserted by the opponent, and the proponent is able to defend p in such a way that the opponent is forced into a contradiction. – In sum, the truth, whether empirical or logical, is defined as the defensibility of a sentence or of a formula against any opposition, which is equivalent to the existence of a winning strategy connected with the sentence or the formula.[3]

From the philosophical point of view, it is the basic weakness of mainstream formal logic that it is monological or *non-social* (in addition to the fact, mentioned above, that the connectives and the quantifiers are defined in a non-uniform way). It is the soliloquy of some Cartesian ego who is omniscient to the point of knowing in advance the truth-values of all atomary sentences contained in any complex sentences that he is going to assert. It is the great virtue of dialogical logic that it explicitly captures the *social* nature of logic (and language), by representing the dialogue games as two vertical columns of moves, namely those of the proponent and those of the opponent. It seems natural to regard Lorenzen-type dialogue games as one possible explication of Wittgenstein's rather diffuse notion of *language-game*.

The thesis of this section, namely the common origin of language and logic, is summarized in the claim that "dialogue rules *reconstruct* part of the use of natural language" ("*die angegebenen Dialogregeln rekonstruieren umgangsprachliches Verhalten*") (Kamlah & Lorenzen 1967:161; emphasis added). It needs to be added that this common origin is in turn based on *behavior in general*. People can reason impeccably in spite of the fact that their native languages may happen to lack any explicit *words* (or affixes) for the logical connectives (cf. above). In such cases, people's reasoning capacities are both supported and evidenced not by their speech, but just their behavior.

It was noted in Section 3.1 that 'social cognition' has also been considered as a separate module, i.e. a module separate from language. It does not take much to refute this view. Wittgenstein's so-called private-language argument cogently demonstrates why it is not just a contingent, but a *necessary* fact that rules (or norms) of language are intersubjective or social in character; and this fact may in turn be explicated by claiming that language exists as an object of *common knowledge* (cf. Itkonen 1978:109–113; for a summary, cf. Itkonen 1996:475–476). But no such elaborate machinery is really needed. The existence of other people (in addition to the speaker) is encoded into sentence-forms that express questions or requests, and such sentence-forms exist in all languages of the world. Therefore language is necessarily social in character. To Whitney (1979 [1875]), for instance, this was a self-evident truth: "The simple fact [is] that language is not an individual possession, but a social ... That would have no right to called a language which only one person understood and could use" (p. 149).

3.6 Conclusion

Rather than attempting to give an explicit overall theory of the human mind, I have done here something more modest. In what precedes, I have shown that there obtain some pervasive relations of analogy and/or overlap between prima facie separate domains of the human mind. When such relations obtain between X and Y, then it can be inferred that X and Y, instead of being two separate domains, constitute in reality a single domain. Thus, the upshot of this chapter could be formulated as follows: "Language shares the general character of other faculties of the mind." Curiously, this sentence comes from Jackendoff (1994: 60), who considers himself as an advocate of modularity.

Modularity continues to be a live issue in cognitive science. It is a moot question, however, whether, or to what extent, this state of affairs is justified, as shown by Hudson's (1999: 257) following remarks:

> [Jackendoff] claims that these modules are informationally encapsulated in the sense of Fodor (1983), but on the same page he admits that "different representations can influence each other as soon as requisite information for connecting them is available", which strikes me as a fundamental denial of Fodor's position. It is a matter of basic logic that information in one module can only influence mental activity in another module when it is available, so the crucial question is whether modularity prevents available (and relevant) information from being applied. If Jackendoff's answer is no, as it seems to be, his modules have no effect whatever on the flow of information in the mind.

The results achieved in this chapter should be considered in their own right, and not just as arguments against the modularity thesis.

CHAPTER 4

Analogy (mainly) outside linguistics

4.1 General remarks

Having examined the role of analogy both within linguistics and within the larger area constituted by linguistics and some of its neighboring disciplines, I wish to conclude this book by giving at least some indication of the importance of analogy in areas external to linguistics. Three principal types of such areas suggest themselves: mythological (and especially cosmological) thinking, everyday or common-sense thinking, and scientific discovery ('discovery' subsuming, for simplicity, also invention). Of course, the last area contains discovery in linguistics as well, so it is not possible to write this chapter entirely without regard to linguistics. Nevertheless, linguistics will play a subordinate role here.

Moreover, of the three areas mentioned above, I shall leave out the second one, i.e. analogy in everyday or common-sense thinking. To give an example, the influence of analogy is evident e.g. in how the impending Gulf war was viewed by the U.S. population in 1990, i.e whether on the analogy of the World War II (= 'victory') or of the Vietnam war (= 'defeat'). This case and many others have been discussed in detail by Holyoak and Thagard (1995), and I find it difficult to add anything new to what they have said already. Still, it might be useful to mention one example, because of its historical influence. Those who made the Russian revolution were acutely aware of the fact that when something similar had been attempted previously, namely in the context of the French revolution, the end result, i.e. the imperial rule by Napoléon, was the exact opposite of the intended one. Hence the constant fear of 'Bonapartism'. Because Trotsky was the leader of the Red Army, Stalin succeeded in implanting the following analogy in the minds of his fellow Bolsheviks: 'French revolution : Napoléon = Russian revolution : Trotsky'; and the rest is history.

Thus, this chapter will be devoted to analogy in mythology and in science. It will be seen that the line of demarcation between these two types of thinking is much less clear-cut than one might perhaps expect; and this is true not only of the early stages of science. At the same time, good examples of *bad* analogies will be supplied.

4.2 Analogy in mythology/cosmology

A binary *distinction* between two realms of phenomena is based on the fig-ure vs. ground distinction: 'A vs. not-A' (e.g. 'man vs. not-man'). The relation between A and not-A is that of *complementarity* (i.e. not-A is the complemen-tary class of A). In this type of relation there are only two terms. The first is a positive one, whereas the second is defined merely negatively: it comprehends everything that is *not* A. A binary *opposition* is a 'stronger' relation than mere complementarity because now both terms have a positive content; thus, an op-position could be designated as 'A vs. B' (e.g. 'man vs. woman'). By concealing the precise nature of the relation that obtains between the two terms, this no-tation makes it clear at once that, unlike in complementarity, in opposition (or 'polarity') there are in reality *three* terms, i.e. not just A and B, but also the 'dimension' which they share, i.e. *tertium comparationis* or what Trubetzkoy (1958 [1939]) called *Vergleichsgrundlage*. For instance, the opposition between the two positive terms 'man vs. woman' is based on the dimension of (human) *gender*.

Lévi-Strauss (1966) argues that the world-view characteristic of 'primitive' thought is based on *binary classification*, which consists of oppositions gov-erned by the 'principle of homology' (also called 'principle of analogy'). Thus, binary classification is based on *analogy*, exactly like phonological systems à la Trubetzkoy (cf. 2.3). Therefore it is only logical that Lévi-Strauss adduces structuralist phonology as the theoretical model of his anthropological theory. To be sure, he constantly confuses the two notions of (binary) opposition and (binary) distinction (cf. Seung 1982:11–14).

In any case, it seems clear enough that every culture, 'primitive' or not, makes at least some use of strings of oppositions to bring order into its world-view. Needham (1967:447) offers a long list of such oppositions that are char-acteristic of the Nyoro culture (in East Africa), part of which is reproduced in Figure 4.1 (following Hallpike 1979:231).

Lloyd (1966) has investigated the functioning of binary classification in the pre-Socratic thinking. In Seung's (1982:22) words, "he has shown that the two structural principles of polarity and analogy (homology) are the basic modes of thinking and feeling not only in primitive societies, as Lévi-Strauss and other ethnologists have claimed, but also in the early stages of such illustrious cul-

$$\frac{\text{right}}{\text{left}} = \frac{\text{normal}}{\text{hated}} = \frac{\text{social intercourse}}{\text{sexual intercourse}} = \frac{\text{king}}{\text{queen}} = \frac{\text{chief}}{\text{subject}} =$$

$$\frac{\text{man}}{\text{woman}} = \frac{\text{health}}{\text{sickness}} = \frac{\text{welth}}{\text{poverty}} = \frac{\text{heaven}}{\text{earth}} = \frac{\text{white}}{\text{black}} = \frac{\text{life}}{\text{death}} =$$

$$\frac{\text{good}}{\text{bad}} = \frac{\text{even}}{\text{odd}} = \frac{\text{hard}}{\text{soft}} = \frac{\text{princess}}{\text{diviner}} = \frac{\text{clothed}}{\text{naked}} = \frac{\text{moon}}{\text{sun}}$$

Figure 4.1 Binary analogy in Nyoro cosmology

$$\frac{\text{odd}}{\text{even}} = \frac{\text{limited}}{\text{unlimited}} = \frac{\text{one}}{\text{many}} = \frac{\text{right}}{\text{left}} = \frac{\text{man}}{\text{woman}} =$$

$$\frac{\text{resting}}{\text{moving}} = \frac{\text{straight}}{\text{crooked}} = \frac{\text{light}}{\text{dark}} = \frac{\text{good}}{\text{bad}} = \frac{\text{square}}{\text{oblong}}$$

Figure 4.2 Binary analogy in Pythagorean cosmology

$$\frac{\text{light}}{\text{dark}} = \frac{\text{warm}}{\text{cold}} = \frac{\text{sun}}{\text{moon}} = \frac{\text{south}}{\text{north}} = \frac{\text{front}}{\text{back}} = \frac{\text{heaven}}{\text{earth}} =$$

$$\frac{\text{right}}{\text{left}} = \frac{\text{man}}{\text{woman}} = \frac{\text{life}}{\text{death}} = \frac{\text{joy}}{\text{sorrow}} = \frac{\text{hard}}{\text{soft}} = \frac{\text{dry}}{\text{moist}}$$

Figure 4.3 Binary analogy (= yin vs. yang) in Chinese cosmology

tures as those of ancient Greece and China". For instance, the Pythagoreans postulated the analogies given in Figure 4.2.

For comparison, it is interesting to consider a few of the oppositions that were understood as exemplifications and/or extensions of the 'yin vs. yang' opposition in ancient China (see Figure 4.3).

While being arbitrary to some extent, such analogies clearly reveal some cultural universals (or at least near-universals). It is difficult to think of a binary classification which would not have 'man vs. woman' as one of its oppositions. It may be a matter of chance whether 'man' is correlated with 'even', as in East Africa, or 'odd', as in Pythagorean Greece. But it seems to be not just a coincidence that in these two cases 'man' and 'woman' are correlated with 'good' and 'bad', respectively. Similarly, it seems to be no accident that both in East Africa and in China 'man' and 'woman' are correlated with 'life' and 'death', respectively. In all three cultures 'man' and 'woman' go together with 'right' and 'left'; and in ancient Greece also the following analogy was well known: 'man : woman = heaven : earth'. The attitudes reflected in these analogies are of course based on the fact that men have been in a dominating position vis-à-vis women. Among Amazonian Indians this has been explicitly expressed by the following analogy: 'man : woman = sacred : profane = superior : inferior'. In addition to such '(near-)universals of evaluation', there are also biological universals, as in the correlation of 'man vs. woman' with 'hard vs. soft' (or 'square vs. oblong'). Similar analogies are implicit in the classificatory systems of different languages. For instance, in some Papuan languages men (like other 'elongate' objects) 'stand', whereas women (like other 'round' objects) 'sit' (cf. Foley 1986:88–91).

Where counter-examples to assumed universals seem to occur, they can – at least sometimes – be explained. The Chinese correlate 'man' and 'woman' with 'sun' and 'moon' whereas the Nyoro do the opposite. However, in the latter case it is explicitly specified that the sun is regarded as 'maleficient'. That the Nyoro correlate 'man vs. woman' with 'princess vs. diviner', seems inconsistent at first. The inconsistency disappears, however, when the opposition 'right vs. left' as well as the relevant social customs are taken into account. Although left-handed people are hated and nothing may be given with the left hand, divination is an exception because it is practiced with the left hand; and a would-be diviner must demonstrate his possession of spirits by becoming a woman, as it were. By contrast, a princess is treated like a boy, has her teeth extracted in the same way as a prince, and is buried on her right side, like a man (Hallpike 1979:229–230).

Cross-cultural parallels may be mentioned here. In the ancient Rome, the following analogy was accepted: 'right : left = good : bad'. This analogy was the basis of the corresponding polysemy (*dexter* = 'right' & 'good' vs. *sinister* = 'left' & 'bad'), which still has repercussions in Modern English. However, just as among the Nyoro, the group of diviners (= *augures*) was the exception. In their language *sinister* meant 'good'. The seeming inconsistency is actually produced by the inherent limitations of the binary classification: an exception to a rule can be expressed only by reversing the rule. One is reminded of how, in the Dyirbal classificatory system, fish and birds are correlated with men and women, respectively, but exceptional (i.e. maleficient) fish and birds are – inversely – correlated with women and men, respectively (cf. Lakoff 1987:92–104).

Drawing upon the history of Greek philosophy, from pre-Socratics to Aristotle, Seung (1982:Ch. 2) postulates a basic dichotomy between a concrete and non-hierarchical mode of thinking, based on analogies between binary oppositions, and an abstract and hierarchical mode of thinking, based on such distinct-level dichotomies as 'genus vs. species' and 'universal vs. particular'. He also notes that the practice of *definition*, perfected by Plato and Aristotle, is based on the progressive use of binary distinction (and not of binary opposition): e.g. 'virtue' turns out to be what is left when everything that is *not* virtue has gradually been eliminated.

Seung's (1982) 'concrete (= horizontal) vs. abstract (= vertical)' dichotomy may be accepted as representing the two extremes of a continuum, but it needs to be complemented in several ways. (a) It is just wrong to identify 'primitive' thought with binary classification. There exists another basic mode of primitive thought, which consists in projecting the *human body* into the larger environment. This too is an analogy, but not a binary analogy. (b) In addition to binary classifications, there are ternary, quaternary etc. classifications, which are based e.g. on the elements or the cardinal points. Once again, these are analogies which go beyond the number two. (c) There are less than successful attempts at hierarchic systematization which hover somewhere between binary classifications and Aristotelian taxonomies. (d) It is by no means the case that 'civilized' (as opposed to 'primitive') thought has entirely got rid of binary classification. There seems to be a tendency to falsely assume that all the members of 'civilized' societies have perfectly understood and internalized the hierarchical or scientific way of thinking which is thought to be the hallmark of 'non-primitive' thought. – In what follows, these four points will be illustrated.

Probably all cultures exhibit the tendency to interpret the non-human nature on the analogy of human body and/or human behavior. This is the source of animism; and some indications of this way of thinking are contained already in the binary classifications reviewed above. The ubiquity of this phenomenon is well known: "children (and adults) tend to rely on the source analog of a *person* when they do not already know the facts about the target analog" (Holyoak & Thagard 1995:91; emphasis added).

As an example, let us consider the role of the human body in Hindu cosmology. The oldest sacred texts of Hinduism, transmitted orally through centuries, are the four *Vedas* (c. 1300–800 B.C.), the most literary of which is the *Rig-Veda*. It includes several creation hymns, and one of these, called *Purusha-Sūkta* ('The Hymn of the Man', item 10.90) is especially relevant to our topic, because it contains two successive applications of the (directional) analogy 'man → universe'. First, the human body serves as a model for the 'elemental man' or 'primordial giant' (simply called *Purusha*, or 'Man'), on whom the gods perform a sacrifice by dismembering him, in order to create the universe. Second, the universe created corresponds to the different parts of *Purusha*, in the following bipartite way. There is a quaternary analogy between *Purusha* and the social world insofar as the mouth, the arms, the thighs, and the feet correspond to the four castes of the classical Indian society, namely priests, warriors, common people, and servants. There is a more complex, seven-point analogy between *Purusha* and the physical world, as follows: head – eye – mind – mouth – ear – navel – feet = sky – sun – moon – wind – cardinal points – air – earth.

Moreover, the analogy between microcosmos and macrocosmos is not just a static one, as described above. Rather, it was the duty of sacrificial priests to re-enact the cosmic sacrifice, i.e. the creation of the universe:

> Between man and the world there is an analogy of being, and since creation is a sacrifice on a macrocosmic scale, so is this sacrifice renewed on the microcosmic scale a creative act which ensures the continued orderly existence of the universe (Zaehner 1962:44). ... the cultic act creates a magical rapport with the entire cosmos... (p. 21). If sacrifice and the world process are in some sense identical, then it becomes important that these correspondences or identities should be correctly understood, and the compilers of the Brāhmanas [= sacrificial texts] spend much of their time in establishing identities between each and every sacrificial object and cosmic phenomenon (p. 45).

Similar analogies, more or less fully elaborated, could be reported from any culture. Therefore it is enough in the present context to add just one more example, namely Stoic philosophy:

> Other philosophers, such as Plato in *Timaeus* (30b), had described the universe as *zōon* ['living']; but none had applied the analogy as extensively as the Stoics. In their cosmology, the universe, like a living being, was born, lived an allotted span of time, and died; like a living being, it reproduced itself. The universe, like a living body, was animated by a vital heat or vital breath that passed through its entire extent; again, as with an animated body, all its parts were interconnected.
> (Lapidge 1978:163)

This example is only the more interesting because, while the analogy between man and the universe hardly qualifies as 'scientific', the Stoics in some other respects certainly represented the most advanced science of their own time (and culture) (cf. Itkonen 1991:183–189).

It may be added that the use of body parts as points of general orientation, so prevalent in the adpositional systems of African languages, exhibits the same type of anthropocentric thinking as has been at issue here. That e.g. the meaning 'above' may be expressed equally well by 'head' and by 'sky', confirms the analogy that we came across in connection with the *Purusha* myth (cf. Heine et al. 1991:Ch. 5).

Considering the complexity and the longevity of (Sanskrit-language) Hindu philosophy, it is only logical that dissimilar (but partly overlapping) cosmological classifications were entertained at different points in time and in

priests	wind	east	morning
warriors	fire	south	day
common people	water	west	evening
slaves	earth	north	night
spring	golden age	white	
summer	silvery age	red	
autumn	bronze age	yellow-green	
winter	iron age	black	

Figure 4.4 Four-level analogy in Hindu cosmology

different contexts. For instance, the quaternary classification presented in Figure 4.4 establishes correspondences between social classes, elements, cardinal points, colours, and periods of time on different scales (and even different ways of throwing dice, which will be left out here).

It is often unclear whether the overall classification is directional, i.e. based on some primary differentiation. In this particular case, it seems that the caste system constitutes the starting point because, given the values that it embodies, the items on the other dimensions may be predicted rather accurately. The caste system applies only to those who are considered as human beings: "Out of the same system grew the curse of untouchability which degraded a large section of the population to a state of permanent ritual impurity that put them on a par with dogs and other unclean animals" (Zaehner 1962:109). – More complex classifications were also in use (for instance, a seven-level system based on the number of the planets).

Elaborate classifications occurred also in the ancient Tamil culture of South India. One of the most interesting is contained in the grammar *Tolkaappiyam*, which is an analysis, and the oldest extant document, of the ancient Tamil language. As a grammar, however, *Tolkaappiyam* is rather exceptional. While its first two parts (composed around the year 0 A.D.) deal with phonology, morpho-syntax and semantics, its third and last part (completed around 500 A.D.) is a treatise of poetics. More precisely, it teaches in great detail both the subject matter of (love) poetry and the way to write about it. As a whole, *Tolkaappiyam* describes norms at three separate levels, namely language, poetry, and social behavior (i.e. how to manage one's love-life both before and after the marriage). It is no exaggeration to say, with Zvelebil (1973:Ch. 6), that in addition to being a linguistic grammar and a poetics, *Tolkaappiyam* is also a 'grammar of love'. This is the type of synthesis that the semioticians of the 20th century have been hankering after. What makes it especially worthwhile is the fact that it manages to embed both the poetry and its subject matter into the overall cosmology of the contemporary Tamil culture.

The poetry is divided into two clearly separate types, namely love poetry (*akam*, lit. 'inside') and heroic poetry (*puram*, lit. 'outside'). *Akam* is further divided into seven subtypes, five of which represent 'suitable love' fit for high-cultured couples, whereas the remaining two represent 'unsuitable love' (overly lustful or unrequited), fit for servants. The five subtypes of suitable love represent the different phases of a typical love-relationship: sexual union, separation, confident waiting, anxious waiting, quarrel (due to the man's infidelity). These five phases are recursive in the sense that they occur, with variations, both before and after the marriage, and their order need not be fixed.

The synthesis of love and cosmology is achieved in the following way. The entities of the universe are divided in three classes, namely space & time, feelings (plus the corresponding situations), and 'things'. *Space* is divided into *five* subtypes: mountains, wasteland, forest, seashore, fields. *Time* is divided into *five* corresponding subtypes on the scale both of a year and of a day: autumn & midnight; spring/summer & midday; winter & sunset; afternoon & the whole year; sunrise & the whole year. To each of the five resulting space-and-time units there corresponds one *feeling*, i.e. one of the *five* 'phases of love' mentioned above, and in the prescribed order. Finally, *things* are subdivided into (at least) eight subclasses: god, food, beast, tree, bird, drum, occupation of the local population, (sound of) lyre, and so on; and each subclass is in turn divided into *five* subtypes, corresponding to the five space-and-time-and-feeling units mentioned above.

In practice, the classification works as follows. The sexual union of the lovers takes place at midnight in the autumn, in the mountains. The god of this region is Murugan, the prototypically Tamil (= non-Aryan) god. The "food is the five varieties of paddy and millet, the beasts are the tiger, wild hog, and elephant; the trees: eagle-wood, ebony, …; typical birds are the parrot and the peacock; drums of three kinds: … Typical activity of inhabitants: gathering honey, digging up edible roots, dancing and/or wandering about the hills, … The particular lyre (or harp) is called 'mountain-lyre'" (Zvelebil 1973:97–98). As a contrast, it may be mentioned that wasteland, the scene of separation between the lovers, is characterized inter alia by emaciated elephants (= 'beast') and vultures (= 'bird'), while the occupations of the local population are highway robbery, stealing, and murder.

Thus, apart from telling how one should write about how civilized people should conduct their love-life, *Tolkaappiyam* qua poetics manages to give an account of the following topics: periodization of time, geography, religion, gastronomy, flora, fauna, sociology, music, and so on. This is no mean achievement, and it is based on a five-level *analogy*, or series of correspondences, between the various realms of phenomena. – Itkonen (2000) offers an overall assessment of *Tolkaappiyam*.

As the civilization advances, analogical classifications grow more and more complex. At the same time, unless they are checked by some sort of empirical thinking, they grow more and more fantastic. Thus, starting from binary oppositions of the yin vs. yang type, there gradually developed in China a doctrine in which the five elements (= wood, fire, earth, metal, water) were correlated with seasons, cardinal points, musical notes, colours, numbers, etc. The ultimate goal was to explain the history and the constitution of the entire universe by means of a huge set of analogies in which units function as signs of one another. In particular, detailed correspondences were postulated between microcosmos (i.e. man) and macrocosmos (i.e. the 'numerical categories of Heaven') (cf. Fung Yu-lan 1953: 11–16, 91–96, 455–464, 546–551).

So far, we have seen that a primitive classification is typically a binary one. The number of items that are put in correspondence with one another may increase to three or four etc., but the classification remains 'horizontal' in the sense that all elements are situated at the same level of abstraction. Once the vertical dimension, with more than one level of abstraction, has been brought in, we have the beginnings of a scientific way of thinking. This was evident in the Tamil world-view, where the elements of the five-way classification exemplify superordinate concepts at three distinct levels of abstraction. For instance, Murugan exemplifies, in the ascending order, the concepts of 'god', 'thing', and 'entity' (*porul*). Everything in the universe, whether space or time or feeling or thing, is one or another type of *porul*.

It will be remembered that, according to Seung (1982), a scientific classification is e.g. a taxonomy of animals or plants organized in accordance with the Aristotelian principles of genus and species. It is important to note that the so-called folk taxonomies do *not* satisfy the criteria of a hierarchical, Aristotelian classification. According to Hallpike (1979: 204), they follow a 'sphere of influence' model rather than a hierarchical model, i.e. the units of a given domain are organized more or less ad hoc, according to similarities of form and/or function. Palmer (1996: 88–91) confirms this result. Notice that the heterogeneity of the internal organizations of distinct domains *eo ipso* means lack of analogy between those domains. By contrast, Aristotelian taxonomies, in whatever domain they may hold, are structurally similar or analogous. Thus, analogy turns out to be the one concept that unifies primitive (= preponderantly binary) classification and scientific classification, as long as they are carried out *consistently*.

Even when the classification is hierarchical, analogies have up to now been assumed to hold between entities that are situated at the same levels of abstraction. Varro's notion of 'conjoined analogy' (cf. 2.4), when properly applied, shows, however, that analogies may also obtain between entities at different levels. Thus, *Genesis* 1, 26–27 teaches that the relation between God and man is the same as that between man and animal. One needs only to extend this analogy 'downwards', so as to cover plants and minerals too, in order to arrive at the 'great chain of being', which, illustrated in outline in (1), dominated the Western thought till the end of the 18th century, and beyond (cf. Lovejoy 1936):[1]

$$(1) \quad \frac{\text{God}}{\text{man}} = \frac{\text{man}}{\text{animal}} = \frac{\text{animal}}{\text{plant}} = \frac{\text{plant}}{\text{mineral}}$$

It is not without significance that the notion of analogy, as applied to the relation between God and man, has been officially sanctioned by the Catholic Church. So maybe one should think twice, before declaring analogy to be null and void:

> Con questo è però chiaro che l'intima forma *d'Imago Dei* [*eikòon theoû*] dell'uomo coincide con ciò che fin da Aristotele e dal Concilio Laterano IV è stata chiamata l' 'analogia'. La charatterazione dell'uomo come Imago Dei significa che egli è bensì affine a Dio (in una tanta similitudo), ma che essendo creatura nella creazione presenta nei confronti di Dio una 'dissomiglianza ogni volta più grande' (una maior dissimilitudo).
>
> (Thus it is clear that the essence of man's being *Imago Dei* [= 'God's image'] is identical with what has been called 'analogy' since Aristotle and the 4th Lateran Council. Characterizing man as *Imago Dei* means that he is similar to God, but – being a product of creation – displays in his encounters with God 'a bigger and bigger dissimilarity'.)   (Przywara 1995: 477–478)

Actually, the idea of the 'great chain of being' is a confluence of (at least) two traditions, namely the Judeo-Christian thought and Greek philosophy. In *Timaeus* 30, Plato assumes a basic similarity between God and the creation: "[the creator] desired that all things should be as like himself as they could be." And he establishes an ascending order also at the lower echelon of the creation, i.e. among the elements: "as fire is to air so is air to water, and as air is to water so is water to earth" (ibid.: 31). Or, more explicitly as shown in (2):

$$(2) \quad \frac{\text{fire}}{\text{air}} = \frac{\text{air}}{\text{water}} = \frac{\text{water}}{\text{earth}}$$

Renaissance thought, as represented by Paracelsus (1493–1541), is characterized both by many-level analogy (*convenientia*) and by one-level analogy (*aemulatio*):

> L'homme occupe donc réellement une position privilégiée: il est, dit l'Ecriture, créé 'à l'image et la ressemblance' de la divinité [= many-level]; il est aussi créé à l'image et à la ressemblance du monde [= one-level]. . . . On peut déterminer à quels organes correspondent les planètes . . .: comme les unes règlent et dirigent la marche de l'univers, les autres règlent et dirigent la vie . . . de l'individu.
> (Koyré 1971 [1933]:87)

Although mythical in origin, the idea of the 'great chain of being' made it easier to grasp and to accept the idea of Darwinian evolution, just like the story about the tower of Babel prepared the way for understanding the notion of languages descending from a common proto-language as well as the fact of linguistic diversity in general.

One perennial question in sociological theory has been the following: where do institutions get their legitimation from? how do they manage to command loyalty? Douglas (1986) offers an imaginative answer to this question, summarized in the title of Chapter 4 of her book: 'Institutions Are Founded on Analogy'. The type of analogy that she is referring to is the one that has been examined above, namely the analogy that is embedded in the *Weltanschauung* of a given community:

> There needs to be an analogy by which the formal structure of a crucial set of social relations is found in the physical world, or in the supernatural world, or in eternity, anywhere, so long as it is not seen as a socially contrived arrangement. When the analogy is applied back and forth from one set of social relations to another and from these back to nature, its recurring formal structure becomes easily recognized and endowed with *self-validating truth*.
> (p. 48; emphasis added)

Douglas illustrates her thesis by means of the binary three-part analogy "male is to female as right is to left and as king is to people" (p. 49), which is actually contained in our Figure 4.1. The quaternary analogy that implicitly legitimates the Hindu caste system might have been an even better illustration.

4.3 Analogy in scientific (including philosophical) discovery

A. A brief historical survey

It is seldom, and maybe never, the case that a scientific discipline develops in a fully autonomous manner. Rather, it is guided by analogies of all sorts: either by the analogy of a neighboring discipline which is (considered as) more developed and/or more prestigious, or by the analogy provided by some concrete artifact; and if these are lacking, one can always fall back on the primordial analogy of the human body. In these cases, the source of analogy is *external* to a given science. In the science-*internal* sense, research is guided ex definitione by analogy, because it aims at making generalizations, and because there are no (scientific) generalizations without analogy (cf. 1.3). In the present context, it is possible to enumerate and comment upon only a tiny number of (science-external) examples that pullulate in the annals of the various sciences. As will be seen, some analogies have been successful, and others less so. – Some of the same terrain is covered in Shelley (2003).

a. Analogies outside Linguistics
Pythagoras discovered that musical harmony is based on definite ratios between the lengths of two (similar) vibrating strings, for instance: the octave = 2:1; the fifth = 3:2; the fourth = 4:3; the major third = 5:4; the minor third = 6:5. It seemed natural to him and to his disciples to generalize these ratios to the entire universe, or rather to see musical harmony as just one emanation of these cosmic ratios. (Notice how these alternative thought patterns recur e.g. in today's cognitive metatheory: Is 'possession' a metaphorical extension out of spatial configurations? Or are both space and possession exemplifications of some more abstract, common schema?) Aristotle gives the following account in *Metaphysica* (Book I, Ch. 5):

> Since ... in numbers [the Pythagoreans] seemed to see many resemblances to the things that exist and come into being ...; since, again, they saw that the modifications and the ratios of the musical scales were expressible in numbers; since, then, all other things seemed in their whole nature to be modeled on numbers, and numbers seemed to be the first things in the whole of nature, they supposed the elements of numbers to be the elements of all things, and the whole heaven to be a musical scale and a number.

The Pythagorean thinking left echoes e.g. in Plato's *Timaeus*, and it was continued through the Middle Ages up to the 17th century. It needs to be emphasized, however, that this 'number mysticism' also had thoroughly practical applications, especially in architecture (cf. Moessel 1926; Münxelhaus 1976). The Pythagorean tradition culminates in Kepler's *Harmonice mundi* ('Harmony of the world', published in 1619), in which he "applies his harmonic ratios to every subject under the sun: metaphysics and epistemology, politics, psychology, and physiognomics; architecture and poetry, meteorology and astrology" (Koestler 1964 [1959]: 396).

Ever since antiquity, *mind* has been conceptualized on the analogy of *language*: either in the sense, expounded by Plato, that thinking is identified with (silent) speaking; or in the sense, expounded by Aristotle, that concepts qua mental signs refer to things just like words qua linguistic signs refer to concepts (cf. Itkonen 1991: 172–176). William Ockham developed the notion of *lingua mentalis* ('mental language'), which, unlike the observable language, is free from ambiguities and other logical defects (*ibidem*: 244–249).This conception has remained influential ever since, and is perpetuated in today's digitalism (*ibidem*: Section 5.4; and here 3.2).

The question about the nature of mind (= 'language-like or not?') is logically preceded by the question about the existence of mind (= 'does it exist or not?'). In practice, this question has been understood as concerning the existence of *other* minds (because the one who asks the question generally takes it for granted that he, at least, does have a mind). Within the Cartesian tradition, the positive answer given to this question is based on the 'argument from analogy': if there are creatures which resemble me externally, I am entitled to infer that they resemble me internally as well, i.e. have a mind just like I do (cf. Itkonen 1978: 94–96). There may be better reasons for answering the question affirmatively (*ibidem*).

Aristotle based his conception of natural science on the anthropomorphic model. This is evident from his doctrine of the 'four causes', which was based on the *artisan analogy*. For instance, when someone is building a house, the entire process may be analyzed into the following components: the material which the builder uses (= 'material cause'); the idea or plan which the builder eventually realizes (= 'formal cause'); the builder's actions which put the house together (= 'efficient cause'); the purpose which the house is meant to serve (= 'final cause'). The applicability of these notions to the subject matter of physics is justified rather perfunctorily: "Now surely as in intelligent action, so in nature" (*Physica* 199a, 10). Today few people are convinced by this justification.

It is quite normal that one may feel the pull of several, even conflicting analogies at the same time. We have seen that in his astronomy Kepler followed the Pythagorean analogy of musical harmonies. However, he also subscribed to the *clockwork analogy*, which was becoming fashionable at the end of the 16th century:

> My aim is to show that the heavenly machine is not a kind of divine, live being, but a kind of clockwork (and he who believes that a clock has a soul, attributes the maker's glory to the work), insofar as nearly all the manifold motions are caused by a most simple, magnetic, and material force, just like all motions of the clock are caused by a simple weight.
>
> (quoted from Koestler 1964 [1959]:345)

Moreover, as shown by Laudan (1981:Ch. 4), Descartes too based his 'corpuscular' conception of physics on the clockwork analogy. This analogy was effective in more than one way. First, if the entire physical universe is nothing but matter-in-motion based on contact influence (like the gears of a clock), then some alternative conceptions are *excluded*. For instance, there is no room for vacuum, action-at-a-distance, or teleology. Second, the ultimate structure of the universe, like the mechanism of a clock, remains hidden, which necessitates a *hypothetical* approach, as opposed to the Baconian approach based on straightforward induction. Third, the clockwork analogy, when applied universally, permits a further analogy, insofar as unobservable things may be assumed to behave just like observable things. For instance, atoms too are pieces of matter in motion, but they are just too small to be seen. – It may be added that this characterization goes counter to the general opinion according to which Descartes was just as aprioristic in his physics as in his philosophy. In reality, however, he was fully aware that, even if he would have preferred to infer the physical theory from his (aprioristic) 'first principles', he was in fact unable to do so, which made the 'method of hypothesis' inevitable.

Laudan (*ibidem*) goes on to show that Newton too accepted the clockwork analogy, although it openly conflicted with the concept of gravitation. He also toyed with the idea that the use of microscopes might one day enable scientists to actually see the clockwork-like mechanism which for the moment remained hidden. – Also, let us not forget the analogy between superlunary (= source) and sublunary (= target) which made it possible that the concept of inertia as unending rectilinear motion was generalized to the apparently quite different circumstances prevailing on the earth.

For a long time, Euclid's geometry served as a model of scientific thinking in the West. (Panini's grammar occupied the same position in India.) Therefore it was unavoidable that attempts were made to extend this *axiomatic* model to new domains. One such attempt was made by Spinoza in his *Ethics*, which, in spite of its name, is a synthesis of metaphysics, epistemology (assuming a dichotomy between spurious and genuine knowledge), and psychology (viewing ordinary thinking as based on association and composition, and explaining actions by pain, pleasure, and desire). The book starts with axioms and definitions, and then 'propositions' (i.e. theorems) are literally *proved*. The principal difference vis-à-vis today's notion of axiomatics consists in the fact that, as in Euclid's geometry, the rules of inference which effectuate the proofs remain implicit. Hampshire (1996:xv) notes that, given Spinoza's topic, the axiomatic manner of presentation is not the best choice: "Readers will easily see that the proofs are far from being rigorous and that the definitions and other premises within the argument often presuppose the propositions allegedly deduced from them."

In the 17th and 18th centuries (and even much later), the success of first Galilean and then Newtonian mechanics raised these disciplines to the status of a model to be imitated by the human and/or social sciences. Galileo explained the actual motion of a cannon-ball as resulting from two hypothetical elementary motions, i.e. the rectilinear motion due to the impetus, and the (uniformly accelerating) downward motion due to gravity.[2] Hobbes was impressed by this use of the 'resolutive-cum-compositive' method, and in his *Leviathan* (1968 [1651]) he intended to apply it to the explanation of the 'commonwealth', or of the social life in general. He asserted, first, that actions of individual persons are caused, and explained, by two conflicting intra-individual *motions*, or passions (themselves presumably caused by motions of external objects), namely the avoidance of death and the seeking of power; and second, that the actual state of the society is caused by inter-individual motions, i.e. people coming into contact with one another in their constant attempts to avoid death and to seek power. This second point is established in two steps. If there were no restrictions on people's power-seeking activities, this would result in a 'state of nature', or in everyone's war against everyone else. Because this would benefit no one, people voluntarily impose restrictions upon themselves by investing some person or some assembly of persons with a sovereign power.

It is interesting to note that, although Hobbes's approach seems in inspiration quite different from Spinoza's, there is in fact an intimate connection between the two. Spinoza, taking axiomatic geometry as his model, assumed that socio-psychological behavior is *necessarily* caused by such basic passions as pain, pleasure, and desire. In very much the same way, Hobbes equates his own type of study with geometry, and opposes it to the natural sciences:

> Geometry therefore is demonstrable, for the lines of figures from which we
> reason are drawn and described by ourselves; and civil philosophy is demon-

strable, because we make the commonwealth ourselves. But because of natural bodies we know not the construction, but seek it from the effects, there lies no demonstration of what the causes be we seek for, but only what they may be.

(quoted from Neuendorff 1973: 33)

Thus, somewhat like Kepler's astronomy, Hobbes's political science too turns out to be influenced by two rather dissimilar analogies simultaneously, namely Galilean mechanics, on the one hand, and (Euclidean) geometry, on the other (for discussion, cf. Itkonen 1978: 8.1, 1983a: 6.2.3). Just like Hobbes, Hume too took his inspiration from contemporary mechanics, with only the difference that Galileo was now replaced by Newton. The subtitle of his *Treatise of Human Nature* (1962 & 1972 [1739–1740]) makes his intentions clear: "Being an attempt to introduce the experimental method of reasoning into moral subjects". The analogy between physical objects and human beings was based on a (putatively) common concept of *motion*:

> Two objects are connected by the relation of cause and effect, [not only] when the one produces a motion or any action in the other, but also when it has the power of producing it. And this we may observe to be the source of all the relations of interest and duty, by which men influence each other in society, and are placed in ties of government and subordination. A master is such a one as by his situation, arising either from force or agreement, has a power of directing in certain particulars the actions of another, whom we call servant (1962: 56). In judging of the actions of men we must proceed upon the same maxims, as when we reason concerning external objects (1972: 146).

In accordance with his stated goal, Hume (1972 [1739–1740]: 86–98) devotes an entire section to analyzing the "experiments to confirm this system". It is obvious at once, however, that what he is talking about are not *genuine* experiments, but rather *thought* experiments, of the same type as philosophers have always – either implicitly or explicitly – made use of. It would be impossible to practice conceptual analysis (as opposed to empirical research) without constantly asking oneself the following question: "What would I say or do if X were the case?" (cf. Cohen 1986: 77–79). Now, as Wittgenstein (1958 [1953]: I, §265) has pointed out, a thought experiment is not an experiment. As a consequence, there is a pervasive de facto agreement between Spinoza, Hobbes, and Hume, in spite of prima facie disagreements concerning the appropriate analogy for the explanation of human behavior (= 'geometry or mechanics?'), or concerning the appropriate interpretation of the chosen analogy (= 'does socio-psychological research based on the analogy of mechanics produce demonstrable or experimental knowledge?').[3] – The analogy between New-

THING   PERSON

$$\frac{\text{inertia}}{\text{gravity}} = \frac{\text{motion-away (caused by fear)}}{\text{motion-towards (caused by desire)}}$$

Figure 4.5 Analogy between physical behavior and social behavior

tonian mechanics (= source) and Humean social science (= target) may be spelled out as in Figure 4.5.

Alternatively, the two physical motions analogous to the motions caused by fear and desire, respectively, could be electro-magnetic repulsion vs. attraction. If Aristotle committed the mistake of thinking that the inanimate nature is animate, and even intelligent (cf. above), Hume as well as his latter-day followers commit the opposite mistake of thinking that the human, intelligent nature is inanimate or physical (and therefore ultimately non-intelligent).

The model of the natural sciences exerted its influence also on metaphysics. In the preface to the second edition of his *Kritik der reinen Vernunft* (1787), Kant explicitly appeals to the analogy (*Analogie*) offered by astronomy and by experimental physics to justify his own approach. He wishes to revolutionize metaphysics with his insight that our intelligence does not adjust to things, but – on the contrary – things adjust to our intelligence (= *"die Gegenstände richten sich nach der Beschaffenheit unseres Anschauungsvermögens"*). As he sees it, Copernicus had an analogous insight when he realized that the 'army of stars' does not turn around the observer, but rather the observer is turning around while the stars are standing still (op. cit.: B XVI). This analogy is preceded by a rather dubious one: just like in geometry and metaphysics one knows a concept only to the extent that one has constructed it oneself (cf. the Hobbes-quotation above), so in physics one can understand only that which one has produced according to one's own plan (= *"die Vernunft sieht nur das ein, was sie selbst nach ihrem Entwurfe hervorbringt"*; op. cit.: B XIII). Two additional analogies follow: first, the metaphysician has to imitate the natural scientist in letting 'experiments' either confirm or falsify the claims that he puts forth (op. cit.: B XIX); second, the metaphysician uses a method which resembles the 'synthetic procedure' of chemists (op. cit.: B XXI).

Instead of accepting analogies imposed upon him from outside, Hegel created analogies of his own, especially in his *Phänomenologie des Geistes* (1807). This remarkable book is divided into three parts which can, in accordance with Lukács (1973 [1948]), be seen as dealing with the subjective spirit, the objective spirit, and the absolute spirit. In each part there is a gradual ascent from the least to the most perfect which remains structurally the same, or *analogous*, the only difference being that the entity which performs the ascent is conceived differently in each case: it is first the individual, then the society, and finally the conceptual system. In other words, three historical processes are set here in parallel, namely the life-history of an individual person, the world history qua history of societies, and the quasi-logical development from lower to higher systems of thought. In each case, the driving force behind the ascent is (the experience of) *contradiction*, more precisely a contradiction between what is the case and what ought to be the case. From this vantage point it is possible to grasp the basic similarity, or (meta-)analogy, between Hegel's *dialectical* philosophy and the 'explicative' method of *analytical* philosophy. In both cases, *progress* (whether extra- or intra-scientific) consists in the elimination of contradiction (cf. Itkonen 1988).[4]

The 'natural theology' of the early 19th century applied the 'argument from design' to explain the orderliness of the natural world: if you discover an intricate mechanism like a clockwork or an eagle's eye, you have to infer that someone has designed it. Thus, an analogy was assumed to exist between human design and divine design (epitomized in the notion of 'divine watchmaker'). Darwin reacted to and refuted this analogy with his theory of evolution, which was in turn based on a cluster of analogies of his own.

First, once Lyell's geology had shown that continuous long-term evolution existed in the physical world, it became possible to generalize the same notion to the biological world as well. Second, Malthus' view of the struggle for existence in the contemporary societies could be analogically projected to the biological history, to explain why some species disappeared and others did not. Third, there was an easily detectable analogy between domestication (or 'artificial selection') and natural selection: "I have invariably found that our knowledge, imperfect though it may be, of variation under domestication afforded the best and safest clue" (Darwin 1998 [1859]: 5). "There is no obvious reason why the principles which have acted so efficiently under domestication should not have acted under nature" (*ibidem*: 352).

The three above-mentioned analogies are external to Darwin's theory of evolution. Theory-internally, analogy (or 'homology') plays the most obvious role in morphology, the "most interesting department of natural history and ... its very soul" (p. 328). The notion of homology becomes evident in the fact that "in homological organs, the parts may change to almost any extent in form and size, and yet they always remain connected together in the same order" (*ibidem*). However much the bones of a limb, for instance, may be modified in the course of evolution, "in all this great amount of modification there will be no tendency to alter the framework of bones or the relative connexion of the several parts" (p. 329). – Recent applications of Darwinism to the explanation of intellectual history will be mentioned below.

It is at least arguable that the most important analogy in the history of science, considering its practical after-effects, has been the one invented (rather than discovered) by Turing (1965 [1936]). It was the analogy between the mind and the machine.[5] In Turing's original conception, the functioning of the machine which was to bear his name was analogous to the actions of a 'computer', who – *nota bene* – was meant to be a *human* being, not a machine. In fact, the source for the analogy was the human computing behavior (carried out on a typing machine), and the Turing machine was the target. Thus, Turing imagined "the operations performed by the [human] computer to be split up into 'simple operations' which are so elementary that it is not easy to imagine them further divided" (p. 136). Thus, having previously defined the notion of a 'tape' divided into 'squares', he defined the 'simple operations' as follows:

> The most general single operation must … be taken to be one of the following:
> (A) A possible change (a) of symbol together with a possible change of state of *mind*.
> (B) A possible change (b) of observed squares, together with a possible change of state of *mind*.
> The operation actually performed is determined … by the state of *mind* of the [human] computer and the observed symbols.
>
> (p. 137; emphasis added)

It is only after these definitions which, to repeat, are meant to capture the basic structure of how a *human* being computes, that he adds: "We may construct a machine to do the work of this computer." Thus, the analogy, as Turing originally conceived it, went in the direction 'humans → machines'.

Contemporaneously with Turing (1936), Shannon (1938) discovered the analogy between electricity and logic, in the following way. First, the two states in an electric circuit, i.e. 'on' vs. 'off', can be viewed as analogous to the truth-values of two-valued logic, i.e. 'true' vs. 'false'. Second, switches which modify the electric current can be viewed as analogous to truth-functional connectives in such a way that the incoming lines correspond to atomary propositions and the outgoing line corresponds to the complex proposition. The 'not'-switch, the 'and'-switch, and the 'or'-switch are primary, and the 'if – then'-switch may be constructed in accordance with (e.g.) the equivalence $(p \rightarrow q) \equiv (\sim p \vee q)$, as shown in Figure 4.6 (where '1' and '0' correspond to 'true/on' and 'false/off', respectively).

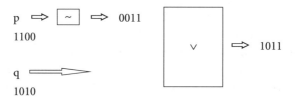

Figure 4.6 Analogy between logic and electricity

$$\left.\begin{array}{c}\dfrac{\text{input}}{\text{program}}\\\text{output}\end{array}\right\} = \left\{\begin{array}{c}\text{perception}\\\dfrac{\text{thinking}}{\text{action}}\end{array}\right. \qquad \dfrac{\text{software}}{\text{hardware}} = \dfrac{\text{mind}}{\text{brain}}$$

Figure 4.7 Analogies between machine and mind

In this way, Turing's fiction was transformed into fact, and actual comput-ers (in the sense of computing *machines*) were constructed, mainly under the influence of von Neumann.[6] But while for Turing the analogy had been 'hu-mans → machines', the analogy now went in the opposite direction, namely 'machines → humans'. That is, the computer became the dominating analogy for the human mind. There are well-known alternative ways to express this analogy, shown in Figure 4.7.

Today, there would be no cognitive science without the computer analogy of the mind. Yet, in my opinion at least, this analogy is inferior to Turing's and Shannon's analogies. Wittgenstein has conclusively shown that there are con-ceptual interdependencies between mind and behavior, on the one hand, and between behavior and context, on the other hand, which means – by transitiv-ity of implication – that there are also such interdependencies between mind and context. Yet, those who subscribe to the computer analogy of the mind have in general paid little attention to behavioral and/or contextual diversity. Still, this analogy can be *improved upon*, to the extent that it will be possible to take these aspects into account, e.g. by embedding the computer in a robot which interacts with its environment (for discussion, cf. Itkonen 1978:4.2.2–3, 1983a:5.1, 6.3).

It may be added that insofar as connectionism (also known as the theory of 'neural nets') is trying to shape its formalism on the model of the human brain, the direction of analogy in the unstable relationship between man and machine has changed once again. To sum up, the following shifts have occurred up to now: (humans → machines) > (machines → humans) > (humans → machines).

As a source of analogies or metaphors, Darwin's theory of evolution is comparable to Newtonian physics. From among recent examples, I choose only two. In tracing the history of astronomy from antiquity to Newton, Koestler (1964 [1959]) repeatedly emphasizes the non-rational element. Discoveries already made (like the idea of a heliocentric universe) were abandoned for no genuine reason, and articles of faith (like the circular motion of the planets) were upheld out of blind reverence for the tradition. As a result, the development of astronomy turns out not to satisfy the criteria of 'scientific progress', understood as a cumulative and rectilinear ascent towards Truth. It is obvious at once that Koestler (1964 [1959]) anticipated some of the central results of Kuhn (1970), and even did so in much greater detail than the latter.[7] Now, when he has to give a succinct explanation of the facts involved, Koestler falls back on the Darwinian analogy:

> All we know is that mental evolution cannot be understood either as a cumulative, linear process, or as a case of 'organic growth' comparable to the maturing of the individual; and that it would perhaps be better to consider it in the light of biological evolution, of which it is a continuation.
>
> It would indeed seem more expedient to treat the history of thought in terms borrowed from biology (even if they can yield no more than analogies) than in terms of an arithmetical progression. ... 'Progress' can by definition never go wrong; evolution constantly does; and so does the evolution of ideas, including those of 'exact science'....
>
> There occur in biological evolution periods of crisis and transition when there is a rapid, almost explosive branching out in all directions, often resulting in a radical change in the dominant trend of development. The same kind of thing seems to have happened in the evolution of thought at critical periods like the sixth century B.C. or the seventeenth A.D. After these stages of 'adaptative radiations', when the species is plastic and malleable, there usually follow periods of stabilization and specialization along the new lines.   (p. 524–526)

The analogy between scientific change and biological evolution was taken up e.g. by Popper (1972) and Toulmin (1974). Their argument remains, however, at a very general or 'philosophical' level. Lamb and Easton (1984) give some substance to this analogy, by showing that scientific discoveries can be viewed as exemplifying the notion of 'variation', insofar as (practically) no discovery is a unique phenomenon but is rather replicated, i.e. either anticipated or repeated, independently on a massive scale. As will be seen in the next subsection, a similar analogy between linguistic change and biological evolution has recently become fashionable.

The analogy between biological and intellectual evolution has been generalized by Dawkins (1976), who postulates the concept of (informational) 'meme', based on *imitation*, after the model of (biological) 'gene'. Whereas Koestler, Popper, and Toulmin are concerned with the survival and spread of (approximately) *true* beliefs, Dawkins – and, following him, Blackmore (1999) – are concerned with *any* beliefs (or 'representations'), whether true or false, as long as they will be accepted and transmitted by people. One should notice the differential status of analogy in the two cases. While Koestler's (or Kuhn's) view of scientific change stands on its own, or retains its interest also without the comparison with biological evolution, the concept of 'meme' would (pace Dennett 1991:202–210) lose whatever interest it may have if the analogy with genes were dropped. If one takes away the analogy with genes, the notion of 'meme' amounts to this: 'Some ideas spread, others don't; some are accepted, others are forgotten.'

As the final analogy, let us mention the structure of DNA and language. "Right from the beginning in 1953, the four nucleotide bases abbreviated by A, T, G, and C were called 'letters of the genetic alphabet'" (Raible 2001:105). Statistical analysis of literature on molecular biology reveals the frequent use of such terms as *reading, transcription, proof-reading, copy, editing, translation, coding,* and *(gene) expression (ibidem:* 105–106). Moreover, techniques developed in mathematical linguistics (like context-free rewriting rules) are employed to represent aspects of microbiological knowledge (*ibidem:* 115–116).

b. Analogies inside Linguistics

For consideration of the analogies that have been current during the history of linguistics, Winograd (1983:8–13) offers a useful starting point. He enumerates the following "metaphors for the study of language": prescriptive grammar – linguistics as law; comparative linguistics – linguistics as biology; structural linguistics – linguistics as chemistry; generative linguistics – linguistics as mathematics. This list calls for some comments.

The slogan 'linguistics as law' certainly has its use. It applies to the Arabic tradition (cf. 2.5, A), just like the study of ritual seems to have provided the original model for the Paninian tradition (cf. Itkonen 1991:78, 128). However, Winograd's conception of prescriptive grammar is erroneous. He assumes that linguistics (in the sense of *descriptive* grammar) investigates "what people actually say", which means that it can dispense with the concept of *correctness*. Things are much more complicated than that (as suggested in 3.5). The view of 'linguistics as biology' was indeed influential in the mid-19th century comparative linguistics (although Winograd's characterization of the latter as "tedious cataloging" is grossly misleading). 'Linguistics as chemistry' is a good analogy for structural linguistics (although I doubt that it is historically adequate). I agree with Winograd that 'linguistics as mathematics' is the analogy which best describes the essence of generative linguistics (although representatives of generative linguistics are sure to disagree). – What are the analogies needed to complement this list? At least the following come to mind.

Both Plato and Wittgenstein have regarded language (e.g. a word or a sentence) as comparable to an *instrument*. This analogy is apt to dispel the air of mystery that seems to surround the concept of *meaning*. Very few people seem to know what a meaning is, but everybody knows that an instrument has both a form and a function (= 'use'); everybody also knows how instruments are (meant to be) used (even if they may be misused now and then); and it would be odd for anybody to be puzzled about the 'ontological question' as to how the use of e.g. a hammer 'exists'. Seeing linguistic units as instrument-like entities consisting of form and function, and equating meaning with function, is likely to produce conceptual clarification. Notice, moreover, that in each particular case the one who is using an instrument must have some sort of 'mental representation' of what he is doing; but it would be a gross misunderstanding to confuse this individual-psychological entity with the (social, intersubjectively valid) function of the instrument.

The reference to Plato highlights the fact that, contrary to a generally accepted misconception, both for him and for Aristotle genuine knowledge was not, or not only, (theoretical or contemplative) "observer's knowledge", but (practical) "agent's knowledge", i.e. the knowledge possessed by the one who knows how to *do* something, especially how to use an instrument. The tradition of 'agent's knowledge' was continued e.g. by Hobbes and Vico. Today, it is easy to see that e.g. linguistic or logical intuition is an instance of 'agent's knowledge', or of how to speak correctly or infer validly. – These intertwined topics have been discussed in Itkonen (1978:8.1, 1983a:6.2, 1991:167–174, and – at length – 2003b).

Another influential analogy, employed e.g. by Saussure and Wittgenstein, is that between language and a *game*. This too is a good analogy, because it combines three essential aspects of language: it is normative; it is social (or intersubjective); and it is based on agent's (not observer's) knowledge. It has sometimes been objected that rules of language are not really analogous to rules of game because the latter must be *written* entities, whereas the former also exist in preliterate societies. This is far from convincing, however, because there are certainly games also in preliterate societies.

The concept of game manages to illuminate the social nature of language because it is obvious that those who play e.g. chess play one and the same game, i.e. a game whose rules are *common* to all of them. Each player must have internalized the rules of game, and these (individual-psychological, non-social) internalizations may well vary from one another; but this is irrelevant to the game of chess as such. Thus, two players share the rules of a game like they share a secret: there is only one secret which each of them has internalized in his own way. They do *not* share the rules of the game in the same way as two pieces of iron 'share' the same structure, because in the latter case 'sharing the same structure' means in fact that there are *two* similar structures. Finally, knowing a game means being able to *act* and to understand actions by others, just like knowing a language means being able to *speak* and to understand speech by others.

In the second half of the 19th century, August Schleicher accepted the analogy between evolutionary biology and diachronic linguistics whereas Hermann Paul and other Neogrammarians contested it. After more than one century of quiescence, this analogy has again become fashionable; cf. Haspelmath (1999), Kirby (1999), Croft (2000), Givón (2002). In this literature there are suggestions that we may not be dealing with an analogy, but rather with an identity: perhaps diachronic linguistics should be reinterpreted as a subtype of evolutionary biology. Thus Haspelmath (1999), for instance, assumes that such functionalist explanations as are used in typological-diachronic linguistics can, and should, be reinterpreted in biological terms. But he admits that innovation in linguistic change, unlike biological mutation, is prima facie a *goal*-directed activity. Therefore, for the analogy to obtain, e.g. the following goals (mentioned by Haspelmath) have to be explained away: "saving production energy", "avoiding articulatory difficulties", "eliminating threats to comprehensibility", "avoiding ambiguity". But it is far from clear how this explaining-away is to be carried out.

This is how Cohen (1986: 125) refutes Toulmin's (1974) Darwinist explanation of scientific change/progress:

> No evolutionary change of any kind came about through the application of intelligence and knowledge to the solution of a *problem*. That was at the heart of Darwin's idea. ... And that is why Darwinian evolution is so deeply inappropriate a model for understanding of scientific progress – as if scientific progress could occur without the application of intelligence and existing knowledge to the solution of new *problems*.   (emphasis added)

This criticism also applies to Lamb and Easton's (1984) improved version of Darwinist historiography of science.

As far as I can see, exactly the same criticism also applies to the Darwinist explanation of linguistic change. For instance, 'How to eliminate threats to comprehensibility?' is certainly a *problem*, i.e. a problem to be *solved* in one way or another. There is simply no possibility to conceptualize it in any other way. Remember also that grammaticalization, for instance, is generally conceptualized in terms of such cognitive processes as reanalysis (or abduction) and extension; and these are prime examples of the *application of intelligence*, which – as we just saw – must be absent from Darwinian evolution (for discussion, cf. Itkonen 2003b: Appendix 5).

In the 20th century, the principal influence on linguistics has been the 'methodological monism', or the view that all sciences (apart from logic and mathematics) are characterized by a common method, and more precisely a method that has been most fully developed in *physics*. But the 'linguistics-as-physics' analogy forces one to ignore important truths. For instance, coming to know a language means learning to *do the same* as one's research objects, whereas coming to know celestial mechanics or particle physics does not mean learning to 'behave' in the same way as planets or atoms (and this is not just a matter of difference in size). Thus, the analogy breaks down. Again, linguistics is practiced by its own research objects, i.e. speakers, whereas celestial mechanics is not practiced by planets, – another breakdown of the analogy. Then again, linguistic data must be inherently normative (because the research objects may both speak and understand either correctly or incorrectly), whereas physical data must not be; and so on. Thus, the 'linguistics-as-physics' analogy, if taken literally, is a prime example of a *bad* analogy.

In the general hierarchy of the sciences there is a pecking order such that the more prestigious sciences provide analogies for less prestigious ones. We have seen that many linguists have succumbed to the analogies provided e.g. by biology and physics. But there is also another side to the coin. Among the human sciences, linguistics is the prestigious one and provides an analogy for its less fortunate neighbors. The most obvious case is *semiotics*, or the 'general science of signs'.

Saussure (1962 [1916]) made a few remarks about the possibility of semiotics (*sémiologie*), which have been blown out of all proportion by some of his commentators. Hjelmslev (1963 [1943]), deliberately following Saussure's lead, was both more explicit and more consistent. He defined language (in the sense of 'system of signs') as follows. Language is a dualistic entity, consisting of 'expression' and 'content'. At both levels, units have both 'substance' and 'form', of which the latter may be defined as the 'value' of a unit in a larger structure. Language may be viewed from the viewpoint of either system (*langue*) or behavior (*parole*). Within the system, units stand to each other in paradigmatic relations based on alternativity ('either – or'), whereas within the behavior they stand to each other in syntagmatic relations based on succession ('both – and'). Both in the system and in the behavior, one of the following 'functions' obtains between units of 'form': 'interdependence' ('if A, then B, and if B, then A'); 'determination' ('if A, then B, and if B, then A or not-A'); 'constellation' ('if A, then B or not-B, and if B, then A or not-A'). – Hjelmslev's 'glossematics' is discussed at length in Itkonen (1968).

The high level of abstraction in Hjelmslev's edifice has been achieved at the cost of loss of information. The same can be said of Greimas's (1983: 82–90) attempt to reinterpret Aristotle's well-known 'square of opposition', without any kind of acknowledgment, as a 'semiotic square' (cf. Itkonen 1991: 180–181). In general, linguistics-based theorizing in semiotics suffers from the fact that the analogy is far from convincing. In linguistics, the data is unequivocal in the sense that, in the clear cases at least, the rules of language determine what is or is not correct. In other domains of 'meaningful behavior', by contrast, no equally determinate rules exist. And if they do not exist, they have to be imagined to exist, with the result that in one and the same domain (food, architecture, film, etc.) different semioticians will imagine different sets of rules.

B.   Objections against the importance of analogy

The results of the previous subsection could be summarized by the following quotations from James (1948 [1892]: 364–367):

> What does the scientific man do who searches for the reason or law embedded in a phenomenon? He deliberately accumulates all the instances he can find which have any analogy to that phenomenon; and, by simultaneously filling his mind with them all, he frequently succeeds in detaching from the collection the peculiarity which he was unable to formulate in one alone; ... Without [the association by similarity], indeed, the deliberate procedure of the scientific man would be impossible: he could never collect his analogous instances. ... Geniuses are, by common consent, considered to differ from ordinary minds by an unusual development of association by similarity.[8]

If analogy is as important as has been claimed here, then the following question arises. How is it possible that those who have represented the so-called received view of the philosophy of science, like Nagel (1961) and Hempel (1965), have in general adopted a rather indifferent attitude vis-à-vis the role of analogy in the natural sciences? The reason lies in the fact that it has been customary to make a distinction between the 'context of discovery' and the 'context of justification'; analogy has been regarded as part of the former; and because it is the latter which is thought to constitute the essence of science, it follows (or seems to follow) that analogy cannot be of decisive importance.

Examining the relation between a familiar (in particular, mechanical) model and some less familiar phenomenon, Hempel (1965: 436) defines 'analogy' as follows: "The relevant similarity or 'analogy' between a model of the kind here considered and the modeled type of a phenomenon consists in *a nomic isomorphism*, i.e. *a syntactic isomorphism between two corresponding sets of laws*." He then adds that the similarity between the two sets of laws may be only partial.

Nagel (1961: 110) in turn distinguishes between two basic types of analogy, viz. 'substantive' and 'formal':

> In analogies of the first kind, a system of elements possessing certain already familiar properties ... is taken as a model for the construction of a theory for some second system. ... In the second or formal type of analogy, the system that serves as the model for constructing a theory is some familiar structure of abstract relations, rather than, as in substantive analogies, a more or less visualizable set of elements which stand to each other in familiar relations.

As an instance of substantive analogy, Nagel mentions the prototypical example of our Type 2, i.e. the influence that the study of sound had on the wave theory of light (cf. 1.3). Formal analogy is in turn exemplified by "relativity theory and quantum mechanics, in both of which patterns of relations have been introduced in close analogy to important equations of classical mechanics" (p. 111). – It is clear that the notion of 'model' may be understood more or less strictly. Either it contains quite precise laws, or it merely suggests the existence of some laws. In the latter use, 'model' becomes nearly indistinguishable from 'metaphor'.

Nagel (1961: 114) has some sympathy for the view according to which "an analogy between an old and a new theory is not simply an aid in exploiting the latter but is a desideratum many scientists tacitly seek to achieve". However, he ends his treatment of analogy on a note of caution, pointing out that "a [familiar] model may be a potential intellectual trap". In just the same way, Hempel (1965: 434) views analogy as, essentially "reduction to familiar"; and he warns that this could be an obstacle to inventing new theories.

These views seem to entail a much too narrow notion of analogy. First, it is good to remember that Newtonian mechanics is based on taking the unfamiliar, i.e. the superlunary region, as the source analogue for explaining what is familiar, i.e. the sublunary region; thus, it is just wrong to simply identify analogy with "reduction to familiar". Second, in addition to being a scientific *model*, whether abstract or concrete, analogy may also be a *figure of thought* extended to new domains, in the following sense. Einstein had shown that what had been thought of as a wave was also a particle; therefore it was only 'logical' for de Broglie to draw the *analogous* inference that what was now thought of as a particle might also be a wave, which ultimately allowed him to establish the existence of 'matter-waves'. This type of (analogous) inference is available to anybody, whether or not he knows anything about physics.

Hempel tries (p. 439) to show the unimportance of analogy even more directly. Assume that there is a set of laws L1 pertaining to some familiar domain, and that a structurally isomorphic or analogous set of laws L2, pertaining to some new domain, is discovered. Now, L2 "*can* be used directly for the explanation of the new phenomena, without any reference to their structural isomorphism with the set L1. For the systematic purposes of scientific explanation, reliance on analogies is thus inessential and *can* always be dispensed with" (emphasis added). This is a surprising argument because its tautological character is barely hidden. Of course, once the set L2 has been discovered with the aid of L1, one *can* conceal this fact, i.e. one *can* act as if L2 had been discovered independently of L1, and one *can* proceed to "directly use" L2. One can do all this, but it would be *unreasonable* to do so (because one would deliberately be suppressing information). To put it differently, if one disregards the de facto relations between L1 and L2, one deliberately creates a non-analogical context and places L2 in it. But then it is surely vacuous to assert that in a non-analogical context, analogy "is inessential and can be dispensed with".[9]

Moreover, on pp. 441–445 Hempel does admit that analogy has a role to play in the context of discovery. As he sees it, however, this belongs to the 'pragmatic-psychological' area of science: "Surely, analogy thus *subjectively* conceived cannot be an indispensable part of *objective* scientific theories" (emphasis added). Again, it requires no great acumen to see the tautological nature of this claim: it goes without saying that what is defined as 'subjective' cannot – as a matter of conceptual necessity – be (defined as) 'objective'.

Accepting the view of analogy-as-familiarity, Pandit (1983:5.2) distinguishes between two senses of 'familiar' and, in so doing, further elaborates on Nagel's distinction between substantive and formal analogies. A theory may be 'familiar' in the ordinary sense, namely when it is based on a *picto-*

rial model; or it may be 'familiar' in the technical sense, namely when it is based on, or reducible to, the laws of the current scientific *paradigm*. In classical physics, it did not seem very important to distinguish between these two senses of 'familiar' because mechanical models were inherently pictorial in nature (perhaps apart from the weird notion of action-at-a-distance). Modern physics, with its non-Euclidean space and probability waves, shows, however, that a theory may be familiar in the technical sense and yet lack any pictorial model. In fact, the use of such models has been deemed downright outdated (cf. Hanson 1965:92). This creates an interesting tension (if not an outright contradiction). Popular books on modern physics, like Zukav (1979), repeat the thesis of non-pictoriality and yet make constant use of pictures to clarify the points they make.

Let us examine the following attempt to visualize the world such as it is hypothesized to be by modern physics:

> As early as the age of sixteen, [Einstein] had considered what he would see were he able to follow a beam of light at its own velocity through space. Here is a problem *picture* as graphic as any of the number with which he was to explain his ideas.　　　　　(Clark 1973:113–114; emphasis added)

There are two things to be noted here. First, such and similar musings eventually led to the Special Theory of Relativity. If Popper were right, i.e. if the context of discovery were totally irrelevant, they could have just as well led e.g. to the discovery of the phonemic principle; but they did not. Second, however, it turns out that, on reflection, the attempt at visualizing that we are speaking of here simply dissolves:

> [The fact] that light would thus travel with a constant velocity that was independent of the bodies emitting or receiving it ... would also answer Einstein's boyhood riddle of how a beam of light would look if you traveled at its own speed. The answer to the riddle was that this would be impossible since only light could reach the speed of light.　　　　　(Clark 1973:117)

We see that pictorial aids (if not literally 'models') are used anyway, and this fact certainly deserves to be acknowledged and accounted for. As Einstein's example shows, people have a tendency to use pictures which, if taken literally, are *contrafactual*. There are two options: either to abandon them or not to take them literally. I recommend the latter option. We make such contrafactual assumptions all the time. Consider a sentence like 'There is a skeleton in my closet always, and only, when no one looks in'. The meaningfulness of this sentence can be explained only by (implicitly) postulating the existence of a 'contrafactual observer' who sees what no one can see: "we use the omniscient, contrafactual observer to verify sentences we ourselves cannot verify" (Itkonen 1983a: 122). The (meta-)analogy to the use of pictures to depict something that cannot be depicted should be obvious. – In sum, substantive analogies retain their importance also in the era of modern science, and formal analogies are needed anyway.

C.   Implications for the philosophy of science

In the philosophy of science, analogy is important at least in the following three ways. First, even assuming that there is a distinction between 'discovery' and 'justification', analogy surely plays a role in discovery. Second, analogy must also play a role in justification, because there is, as a matter of fact, no (clear) distinction between discovery and justification; rather, only that is discovered which can be justified. Third, even after a theory has been discovered and justified, analogy continues to play a role: every theory achieves a *generalization*, either within one domain or across (what has previously been regarded as) several domains; and it is analogy which, being synonymous with generalization, keeps all this body of knowledge together. – It is good to comment on these three points in order.

If there exists some 'method of scientific discovery', then analogy is surely a prime candidate for exemplifying it. Now, as was preliminarily pointed out in the preceding subsection, there has been in some quarters a tendency to flatly deny that the context of discovery has any relevance for the philosophy of science. The classical argument for this view was given by Popper (1965 [1934]: 31–32):[10]

> The initial stage, the act of conceiving or inventing a theory, seems to me neither to call for logical analysis nor to be susceptible of it. The question how it happens that a new idea occurs to a man ... may be of great interest to empirical psychology; but it is irrelevant to the logical analysis of scientific knowledge. ... Accordingly I shall distinguish sharply between the process of conceiving a new idea, and the methods and results of examining it logically. ... My view may be expressed by saying that every discovery contains 'an irrational element', or 'a creative intuition', in Bergson's sense.

As influential as Popper's dichotomy has been, it is clearly fallacious. He conceptualizes scientific discovery as a choice between only two, diametrically opposite alternatives: either there is a strictly logical (or algorithmic) method for arriving at new theories; or new theories are arrived at on the basis of an irrational intuition about which nothing whatsoever (apart from the aspect of 'empirical psychology') can be said; and because the first alternative is false, then the second has to be true. Now, it is (nearly) self-evident that there is a third alternative between viewing discovery as either algorithmic or irrational, and what is more, it is precisely this alternative which is the true one. Of course, it is impossible to formalize creativity, either in science or anywhere else (cf. 1.8). However, in scientific discovery (and in discoveries of other types as well) there are thought patterns which are too general and too recurrent to be brushed aside as being merely subjective. Instead, they deserve to be studied; and, needless to say, analogy is the foremost among them. – Lamb and Easton (1984: 43) make the same point as follows:

> For Popper and Reichenbach the irrationality of discovery is derived from their conflation of 'rational' with 'logical'. ... Of the three modes of inference, [namely] induction, abduction, and deduction, only the latter has logical validity, which is not to say that the former two are irrational. ... Abductive inference moves from a universally recognized problem to a tentative, but nevertheless plausible solution. As such, discovery is ... not irrational and subjective as Popper and Reichenbach would have it.

Popper's stance may be made more comprehensible by noting that he was not fighting a straw-man. There seems to be something alluring in the idea that it could be possible, after all, to devise a method which would automatically guarantee that true theories will be achieved. Laudan (1981) extensively documents how, ever since antiquity, this fantastic idea has kept reappearing, in spite of repeated refutations.

Today the view that discovery cannot be rationally analyzed has lost much of its appeal, as shown by the proliferation of publications devoted to discovery in general and to analogy (or analogical reasoning) in particular; cf. Holland et. al (1986), Helman (1988), Vosniadou and Ortony (1989), Boden (1990), Holyoak and Thagard (1995), Hofstadter (1995), Gentner et al. (2001a). Still, it seems fair to say that the mainstream philosophy of science has maintained a slightly cautious attitude vis-à-vis discovery.

In the two preceding paragraphs, it was assumed, for the sake of argument, that a meaningful distinction can indeed be made between discovery and justification. Now it is time to take this assumption back. The reason for doing so has been given e.g. by Pera (1981: 158):

> There do not exist nor can there exist two distinct thought episodes – first blind invention and then the intervention of plausibility considerations; there is rather a single argumentative act: a hypothesis springs from the very same argument which provides the initial reasons of its plausibility.

In just the same way, it can be shown in linguistic metatheory that a strict distinction between 'discovery procedures' and 'evaluation (or justification) procedures' cannot be maintained:

> The grammar which [the grammarian] *discovers* is the one which he can best *justify* on the basis of considerations referring to the overall simplicity of the description. ... It may be true that it is impossible to devise exact and rigorous discovery procedures for grammars; but no exact and rigorous evaluation procedures for grammars have been devised either.   (Itkonen 1978:75)

The interdependence of discovery and justification can also be demonstrated by examining the concept of 'thought experiment'. In our discussion of Hume (cf. above), the emphasis was put on the first part of this compound: it was important to realize that *thought* experiments are not (genuine) experiments. But now there is reason to shift the emphasis on the second part of the compound: performing thought *experiments* entails that one does not just hit upon a new idea but also tries to figure out whether or to what extent it can be justified. In this sense thought experiments serve a useful function because they weed out new ideas which, on reflection, turn out to be unsound. Only such (plausible) ideas as *can be* justified are left; and then genuine experiments decide which one among them *is* justified.

Finally, it would be wrong to restrict the role of analogy to the stage of discovery (or, more precisely, discovery-cum-anticipated-justification). 'Analogy' equals 'generalization', and the latter is a typically ambiguous term: it may mean either the process or its result. (These two meanings correspond to 'dynamic' and 'static' analogy.) Once a generalization has been discovered *and justified*, it is there as a finished achievement. It would be odd to say that at this stage analogy has ceased to play any role, because what has been achieved is knowledge about structural similarity in the data, and this is analogical knowledge by definition. Now it is time to *consolidate* this knowledge, as Polya (1973 [1945]) would say (cf. 1.10). This aspect of analogy has been ignored in practically all discussions within the philosophy of science, where – to repeat – analogy has been identified as a thought pattern (= 'reduction to familiar') related to discovery only.

D.   Conclusion

Holyoak and Thagard (1995: 186–188) enumerate the following sixteen 'great scientific analogies': (1) Sound / water waves (Vitruvius, around 100 AD). (2) Earth / small magnet (Gilbert in 1600). (3) Earth / moon (Galileo in 1630). (4)

Earth / ship (Galileo in 1630). (5) Light / sound (Huyghens in 1678). (6) Planet / projectile (Newton in 1687). (7) Lightning / electricity (Franklin in 1749). (8) Respiration / combustion (Lavoisier around 1770). (9) Heat / water (Carnot in 1824). (10) Animal and plant competition / human population growth (Darwin in 1838). (11) Natural selection / artificial selection (Darwin in 1859). (12) Electromagnetic forces / continuum mechanics (Maxwell around 1860). (13) Benzene / snake (Kekulé in 1865). (14) Chromosome / beaded string (Morgan 1915). (15) Bacterial mutation / slot machine (Luria in 1943). (16) Mind / computer (Turing around 1950). Of these sixteen analogies we have had reason to mention eight in one connection or another. And we have adduced several other analogies as well, taking also the history of philosophy into account.

In spite of the examples enumerated above, Holyoak et al. (2001:6) claim that "the development of large-scale theories based on analogy is a relatively rare event in science". Personally, I find it difficult to accept this claim. The contents of Section 4.3, A constitute significant counter-evidence against it, and I could easily have mentioned more evidence of the same kind.

Finally, it needs to be explicitly repeated that in the context of scientific discovery analogy may play – and often does play – a twofold role. A generalization that unifies two apparently disparate realms of phenomena A and B is an instance of analogy. And this analogy may have been suggested by some C which, while being analogous to A and/or B, lies 'outside of' the two in the sense of being – in general – much simpler than either A or B.

CHAPTER 5

Concluding remarks

In this book, and in particular in Chapter 2, I have tried to clarify what von Humboldt and Whitney may have meant when they claimed everything in language to be based on analogy. I am just as convinced as they were that – in Hofstadter's (2001:537) colourful wording – analogy is "the lifeblood of human thinking". If A and T stand for analogy and thinking, respectively, then we have the implication 'if T, then A': thinking is basically analogical. On the other hand, there is a potentially infinite number of artificial or unnatural analogies which no one has endorsed or will endorse. Hence, we do *not* have the inverse implication 'if A, then T'.

Let us add a few caveats. Such expressions as 'human thinking' or 'human mind' are often used in an all-encompassing and therefore vacuous way. Let us consider the Euclidean geometry. It was the product of systematizing thinking by Euclid, and hence of one aspect of the human (i.e. Euclid's) mind, but this aspect of the human mind was not its subject matter. The geometrical figures that it dealt with had been perceived and conceptualized in a certain way by Euclid and (practically) everybody else, but these processes of perceiving and conceptualizing (qua another aspect of the human mind) were not its subject matter either. These all-important distinctions are likely to be lost as soon as we simply think of the Euclidean geometry as an exemplification (or emanation) of the human mind.

It is widely assumed that the study of language has no value unless it is completely embedded in the study of the human mind. As suggested in Section 1.7, this view is something of an oversimplification. But it is also threatened by vacuity. Consider the study of architecture around the world, on a par with the (typological) study of the world's languages. You are immediately struck by the formal diversity, but you will also notice certain uniformities, and these will presumably become more obvious, the more you devote time and energy to your study. Sooner or later you will move from describing the buildings to explaining why they are such as they are in fact. Your explanations will be couched in functional terms, and the functions which you will refer to are bound to be

socially shared, in spite of the fact that some buildings are more clearly prod-
ucts of individual creation than others. Would you say that your study has no
value unless it is considered as part of the study of the human mind? This would
be an odd thing to say, unless you extend the meaning of 'human mind' to
encompass the social world as well. But then it would be a redundant thing
to say.

In Section 1.8 I postulated a continuous cline that ranges from mechanical
to creative analogy. A prima facie similar distinction has been postulated by
Sampson (1980), who argues that phonology/morphology/syntax is 'mechanical' or 'predictable' whereas semantics (or rather semantics-cum-pragmatics)
is creative, and therefore 'non-mechanical' and 'non-predictable'; and he is
quite explicit (e.g. on p. 95–96) that the same creativity is characteristic of human rationality in general. What makes Sampson's argument interesting, is his
insistence that the creativity (of semantics/pragmatics, for instance) has an ontological basis: it is not just a result of our (temporary) ignorance, but reflects
the things as they really are. He bolsters his position by quoting (p. 10) Popper
to the effect that "to predict that an idea will be invented tomorrow would be to
invent it today". Hence, the notion of predicting creative behavior comes close
to entailing a contradiction. – Nevertheless, some additional distinctions need
to be made here. Let us review the 'possibility space' that we are dealing with.

First, I agree with Sampson (1980) that description of *structure* (but also
at least some part of semantic structure) is formalizable. But this does not
mean that structural descriptions are eo ipso 'mechanical'; and it should be
self-evident that formalization, as such, does not equal prediction. A formal description of English syntax, for instance, does not predict what a given speaker
or a group of speakers will say, and when. It would be a category mistake to
think differently:

> If we confine our attention to language instead of the actual speech acts that
> embody a use of language, there is, quite literally, nothing happening. There is
> nothing corresponding to the events (situations, states of affairs, conditions)
> that occur (obtain) in the actual world... If linguists are explaining anything,
> what they are explaining does not seem to be part of our spatiotemporal
> world... [To think otherwise] is the result of (or can be understood as) a mis-
> guided devotion to a certain model of explanation (the deductive-nomological
> model)...   (Dretske 1974: 24)

The same point, with many elaborations and ramifications, was made by
Michael Kac, Jon Ringen, and myself from the early 70s onwards (for documentation and discussion, cf. Itkonen 2003b, especially Appendix 1). It dawned

upon me only afterwards that what we were doing was explicate the great Paninian tradition.

To be sure, it has sometimes been claimed that "a grammar predicts sentences"; but this is a misuse of the term 'prediction'. It is just as misleading to equate 'formalized' with 'mechanical'. Assuming that it makes any sense to regard formal logic as 'mechanical', it is certainly not mechanical in the same sense as Newtonian mechanics is.

Second, structural descriptions (regarded as descriptions of institutional facts) can of course be provided with *psychological* interpretation, i.e. they may be regarded as hypotheses about how the corresponding structures are stored in the mind. This is what I mean by *static analogy*. Structural descriptions so interpreted are 'predictive' in exactly the same way as other psychological descriptions about comparable phenomena are.

Third, if – instead of just describing some (e.g. syntactic) structure – we devise a computer program meant to simulate the *process* of producing and/or comprehending the (syntactic) structure in question (cf. Appendix), then we have constructed an abstract machine, and therefore we are entitled to call our description 'mechanical' (in addition to the obvious fact that it is a 'formalization' of the relevant data). This is what I mean by *dynamic analogy*. Again, the description is 'predictive' to the same extent as other comparable descriptions are. More precisely, since acts of linguistic production and/or comprehension occur in space and time, it is not a category mistake to think that our mechanical (analogy-based) description of these processes could make genuine predictions. The most that can be said, however, is that we can predict (at a rather abstract level) *how* something will be produced or understood, if it will be produced or understood, but not *that* something will actually be produced or understood.

Fourth, if – instead of giving an abstract characterization of how sentences are produced or understood – we confine our attention either to actual speech acts or to such collective acts as linguistic changes, then the question of predictability becomes central. Because of their ineluctable *creativity*, however, it is impossible to predict the precise outcome of either individual speech acts or of collective linguistic changes. We must be satisfied with post hoc explanations (largely but not exclusively subsumable under dynamic analogy). On this issue I agree with Sampson (1980). Of course, we can outline more and more stringent constraints on possible speech acts or linguistics changes. But this is a far cry from genuine prediction.

Fifth, if we concentrate on sub-acts of integral speech acts and thus on subsentential units, and if we furthermore resort to the notion of *conditional probability*, then we can of course make perfectly good predictions. For instance, it is highly probable (but not certain) that if the definite article *the* has been uttered, a noun related to it will soon follow. – All these different options have been discussed at great length in Itkonen (1983a).

After this general survey of analogy, there would seem to remain one more question to be asked and answered. Why should there be analogy, rather than lack of analogy, in the first place? I doubt whether this question can be answered in an informative or non-circular way. The existence of analogy in mythologies and/or cosmologies seems to indicate that analogy coincides with the need for order (as opposed to chaos). This entails that, as suggested by Anttila (1989 [1972]:103), we must postulate "an innate faculty of analogizing". Far from being domain-specific, this faculty underlies the human mind in its entirety, as shown by the results of Chapter 3. And, as suggested by Peirce (cf. p. 21), we are perhaps so successful in creating order because we are surreptitiously aided in this by the non-chaotic character of the 'nature itself'.

Appendix

This appendix contains three parts:

1. the PROLOG program which solves the problems introduced in Section 2.5, B;
2. a technical explanation of the program;
3. a more informal summing-up.

1. The program

(1) transform(A1,B1,C1):-nl,s(A1,A),nl,s(B1,B),nl,s(C1,C),nl,
transf(A,B,C,[]).

(2) transf(A,B,[C|CT],D):-C=[W1,[X,H]],
member([W1,[X,H]],D),
transf(A,B,CT,D).

(3) transf(A,B,[C|CT],D):-C=[W2,[X,H]],
not member([W1,[X,H]],A),
append(D,C,D1),
transf(A,B,CT,D1).

(4) transf(A,[B|BT],C,D):-B=[W1,[X,H1]],
member(B,A),
member([W2,[X,H1]],C),
continue(A,BT,C,D,[W2,[X,H1]]).

(5) transf(A,[B|BT],C,D):-B=[W1,[X,H2]],
member([W1,[X,H1]],A),
member([W2,[X,H1]],C),
continue(A,BT,C,D,[W2,[X,H2]]).

(6) transf(A,[B|BT],C,D):-B=[W1,[X,H]],
not member([W1,[X,_]],A),
append(D,B,D1),
transf(A,BT,C,D1).

(7) transf(A,[B|BT],C,D):-B=[W1,[X,H]],
     member([W1,[X,_]],A),
     not member([W2,[X,_]],C),
     transf(A,BT,C,D).

(8) transf(A,[B|BT],C,D):-B=[W2,[X,H]],
     member([W1,[X,H]],A),
     member([W1,[X,H]],C),
     continue(A,BT,C,D,B).

(9) transf(A,[],C,D):-nl,tidy(D,E),nl.

(10) transf(A,B,[],D):-nl,tidy(D,E),nl.

(11) s(A,Y):-sen([],X,_,A,[],1),write(X),Y=X.

(12) sen(X,X3,_,A,B,H):-
     q(loc,A,C),[W|_]=A,append(X,[W,[q,H]],X1),
     aux(C,D),[W1|_]=C,append(X1,[W1,[aux,H]],X2),
     sen(X2,X3,_,D,B,H).

(13) sen(X,X2,subj,A,B,H):-
     np(X,X1,subj,ag,A,C,H),
     vp(X1,X2,subj,_,C,B,H).

(14) sen(X,X2,obj,A,B,H):-
     np(X,X1,obj,C,A,D,H),
     vp(X1,X2,obj,C,D,B,H).

(15) sen(X,X3,Y,A,B,H):-
     cop(A,C),[W|_]=A,append(X,[W,[cop,H]],X1),
     np(X1,X2,Y,_,C,D,H),
     advp(X2,X3,loc,D,B,H).

(16) sen(X,X2,A,B,C,H):-
     last(B,Y),adv(_,[Y|F],F),
     sen(X,X1,A,B,D,H),
     append(X1,[Y,[adv,H]],X2).

(17) sen(X,X3,A,B,C,H):-
     q(M,B,D),aux(D,E),append(E,blank,E1),
     [W|_]=B,append(X,[W,[q,H]],X1),
     [W1|_]=D,append(X1,[W1,[aux,H]],X2),
     sen(X2,X3,A,E1,C,H).

(18)   np(X,X1,W,A,B,C,H):-
　　　　det(B,D),
　　　　n(A,D,C),[Y,Z|_]=B,append(X,[[Y,Z],[W,H]],X1).

(19)   np(X,X1,C,ag,A,B,H):-
　　　　pn(A,B),[Y|_]=A,append(X,[Y,[C,H]],X1).

(20)   np(X,X3,W,ag,B,C,H):-
　　　　det(B,D),n(ag,D,E),[Y,Z|_]=B,append(X,[[Y,Z],[W,H]],X1),
　　　　relp(E,F),[W1|_]=E,append(X1,[W1,[relp,H+1]],X2),
　　　　vp(X2,X3,subj,_,F,C,H+1).

(21)   vp(X,X1,subj,_,B,C,H):-
　　　　v(intr,nc,B,C),[Y|_]=B,append(X,[Y,[v,H]],X1).

(22)   vp(X,X1,subj,pa,A,B,H):-
　　　　v(intr,pa,A,C),[W|_]=A,append(X,[W,[v,H]],X2),
　　　　advp(X2,X1,loc,C,B,H).

(23)   vp(X,X2,subj,A,B,C,H):-
　　　　v(tr,A,B,D),
　　　　verbhelp(B,D,Y1,Y2,H),
　　　　append(X,Y1,X0),append(X0,Y2,X1),
　　　　np(X1,X2,obj,A,D,C,H).

(24)   vp(X,X2,subj,A,B,C,H):-
　　　　v(vc,_,B,E),[W|_]=B,append(X,[W,[vc,H]],X1),
　　　　iv(X1,X2,subj,A,E,C,H).

(25)   vp(X,X2,A,B,C,D,H):-
　　　　cop(C,E),append(X,[is,[cop,H]],X1),
　　　　ap(E,D),adjhelp(E,D,Y,H),append(X1,Y,X2).

(26)   vp(X,X3,A,B,C,D,H):-
　　　　cop(C,E),append(X,[is,[cop,H]],X1),
　　　　ap(E,F),adjhelp(E,F,Y,H),append(X1,Y,X2),
　　　　iv(X2,X3,A,B,F,D,H).

(27)   vp(X,X2,_,_,A,B,H):-
　　　　cop(A,E),append(X,[is,[cop,H]],X1),
　　　　advp(X1,X2,loc,E,B,H).

(28)   vp(X,X3,subj,A,B,C,H):-
　　　　v(tr,sc,B,D),[W|_]=B,append(X,[W,[vs,H]],X1),
　　　　comp(D,E),[W1|_]=D,append(X1,[W1,[comp,H]],X2),
　　　　sen(X2,X3,F,E,C,H+1).

(29) iv(X,X2,subj,A,[to|B],C,H):-
        append(X,[to,[pr,H]],X1),vp(X1,X2,subj,A,B,C,H).

(30) iv(X,X2,obj,A,[to|B],C,H):-
        append(X,[to,[pr,H]],X1),v(tr,A,B,C),
        verbhelp(B,C,Y1,Y2,H),
        append(X1,Y1,X0),append(X0,Y2,X2).

(31) advp(X,X1,A,B,C,H):-
        adv(A,B,C),[W|_]=B,append(X,[W,[adv,H]],X1).

(32) advp(X,X2,A,B,C,H):-
        prep(A,B,D),[W|_]=B,append(X,[W,[prep,H]],X1),
        np(X1,X2,A,A,D,C,H).

(33) ap(A,B):-
        adj(A,B).

(34) ap([too|A],B):-
        adj(A,B).

(35) pn([john|A],A).

(36) pn([bill|A],A).

(37) pn([we|A],A).

(38) n(nag,[apple|A],A).

(39) n(nag,[question|A],A).

(40) n(nag,[bus|A],A).

(41) n(ag,[teacher|A],A).

(42) n(ag,[man|A],A).

(43) n(loc,[corner|A],A).

(44) n(loc,[room|A],A).

(45) n(loc,[house|A],A).

(46) v(intr,nc,[eat|B],B).

(47) v(intr,nc,[talk|B],B).

(48) v(intr,nc,[sleep|B],B).

(49) v(tr,nag,[eat|A],A).

(50) v(tr,ag,[talk,to|A],A).

(51) v(tr,nag,[discuss|A],A).

(52) v(tr,_,[get,off|A],A).

(53)   v(vc,A,[want|B],B).

(54)   v(vc,A,[have|B],B).

(55)   v(tr,sc,[say|B],B).

(56)   v(intr,pa,[went|B],B).

(57)   adj([stubborn|A],A).

(58)   adj([rotten|A],A).

(59)   adj([easy|A],A).

(60)   adj([hot|A],A).

(61)   adj([tired|A],A).

(62)   adj([difficult|A],A).

(63)   adj([tall|A],A).

(64)   aux([did|A],A).

(65)   cop([is|A],A).

(66)   comp([that|A],A).

(67)   relp([who|A],A).

(68)   q(loc,[where|A],A).

(69)   q(pe,[who|A],A).

(70)   det([the|A],A).

(71)   det([an|A],A).

(72)   adv(loc,[there|A],A).

(73)   adv(_,[blank|A],A).

(74)   prep(loc,[in|A],A).

(75)   verbhelp(B,D,Y1,Y2,H):-[A|D]=B,Y1=[A,[v,H]],
            Y2=[blank,[prep,H]].

(76)   verbhelp(B,D,Y1,Y2,H):-[A,C|D]=B,Y1=[A,[v,H]],
            Y2=[C,[prep,H]].

(77)   adjhelp(B,D,Y,H):-[A|D]=B,Y=[A,[ap,H]].

(78)   adjhelp(B,D,Y,H):-[too,A|D]=B,Y=[[too,A],[ap,H]].

(79)   append([],A,[A]).

(80)   append([A|B],C,[A|D]):-append(B,C,D).

(81)   member(X,[X|_]).

(82)   member(X,[Y|Z]):-member(X,Z).

(83)   first(A,X):-[X|_]=A.

(84)   last([A|AT],B):-last(AT,B).

(85)   last([A],A).

(86)   tidy([],B):-s(B,_),nl,nl,write(B),nl.

(87)   tidy([A|B],C):-first(A,blank),tidy(B,C).

(88)   tidy([A|B],C):-add(A,C,C1),tidy(B,C1).

(89)   add([[A,B],[X,H]],C,C2):-append(C,A,C1),append(C1,B,C2).

(90)   add([A,[X,H]],C,C1):-append(C,A,C1).

(91)   continue(A,B,[C|CT],D,[W,[X,H]]):-first(C,W),
      append(D,[W,[X,H]],D1),
      transf(A,B,CT,D1).

(92)   continue(A,B,C,D,W):-append(D,W,D1),
      transf(A,B,C,D1).

2.   Explaining the program

Analogical reasoning as applied to linguistic and other material is formalized in the form of a computer program in PROLOG. The program consists of two parts, the analogical reasoning component (clauses 2–10) and the parsing component (clauses 11–78). In addition to inspecting the grammatical correctness of the various sentences that are given as input to the program, the parsing component detects the semantical structure of the sentences. This information, in turn, is relied upon by the analogical reasoning rules. It is appropriate, therefore, to have an overview of the parser before going into the core of the program, the analogical reasoning rules.

Clauses 12–17 form the highest level of the phrase structure rule hierarchy. The program has two rules (clauses 13 and 14) of the form S → NP+VP. The reason for this is the need to differentiate the sentence types exemplified by (S1) and (S2):

    (S1)   The apple is too rotten to eat
    (S2)   The man is too stubborn to eat

Clause 13 accounts for sentences that begin with an NP that refers to an *agent*, and clause 14 for sentences beginning with an NP which refers to a *patient*. Because the linear structures of (S1) and (S2) are identical, we need to encode semantic information into the lexicon. In clauses 38–45 nouns are classified by their agentive (ag) or non-agentive (nag) nature. Proper names (PN) are automatically treated as agentive (clause 18). Transitive verbs, on the other hand, are classified according to the type of object they require. These differences have to be passed on, first to the NP and the VP, and then to the nature of the whole sentence, hence the need for two separate clauses.[1]

Clause 12 applies to questions that concern a whole proposition. In the present stage of the program, only questions regarding the location where something took place are possible, but it would be very easy to account for questions concerning time, habit, etc. Basically, this could be done by adding the relevant pronouns to the lexicon. Clause 15 recognizes questions of the type 'Is the man in the room?' Clause 16 allows for the specification of a whole sentence by an adverb (e.g. 'John slept *there*'). Clause 17 applies to questions of the form 'Where did John say that Bill went?'.

Clauses 18 and 19 recognize NPs of the types NP → Det+N and NP → PN. From these clauses it can also be seen that the phrase structure rules build new strings on the basis of grammatical sentences. These strings contain (in addition to the words of the original sentences) the role of each element in the sentence, and hierarchy numbers for the elements to keep track of embeddings. NPs with a relative clause are, in turn, recognized by clause 20, with the relative clause getting an hierarchy number one greater than the noun it specifies.

Clauses 21 and 22 recognize intransitive VPs; clause 22 accounts for verbs (such as *go*) that require an adverb in a complete sentence. Clause 23 (together with clauses 75 and 76) applies to transitive verbs. It is noteworthy that, for verbs such as *eat*, clause 75 adds a dummy preposition, *blank*, between the verb and the object to indicate the transitivity of the verb.[2] This clause also takes care of selection restrictions (in the present shape of the program, whether the verb requires an agentive or non-agentive object). Clause 24 recognizes verbs that require a verb to follow them (*have* as in 'I have to do this'; *want*). The rest of the sentence is accounted for by clause 29. Sentences predicating an adjective of the subject are handled by clause 25. Clause 26 (together with clauses 29 and 30) applies to the VPs in sentences such as (S1) and (S2) above. Copular sentences ending with an adverbial phrase (such as 'John is in the room') are taken care of by clause 27. Finally, clause 28 accounts for verbs which require a subordinate clause to follow (in this program, *say*). This also raises the hierarchy number of the rest of the sentence.

Clauses 2–10 perform the proportional analogical reasoning. In other words, they create a new sentence, D, using the material from sentences A, B and C, so that the analogy

$$\frac{A}{B} = \frac{C}{D}$$

is valid. We will hereafter use the letters A, B, C and D to denote the sentences (in the respective positions) of our example analogies.

Sentence D is formed by going through sentences B and C one element at a time and inspecting the relations of each element to the structure of sentence A (plus the part of sentence D that is ready). Analogical reasoning is actually performed on two levels: on the one hand, on the level of sentence structure (the rules as a whole and their mutual order), and, on the other hand, on the level of individual elements which don't have *exactly* matching roles in different sentences of the analogy (the rule expressed by clause 5).

As sentence C is examined element by element, it may happen that the element under consideration is already included in D (this can happen, e.g. when the word order is changed during the analogy). In this case this element of C can be neglected and the next one examined. In the program, this task is performed by clause 2.

Clause 3 applies when there is no element in A with a role matching that which the element under consideration has in C. When this happens, this element of C is added to D, and the program proceeds to the next element in C. This kind of situation arises, for example, in the following analogy:

$$\frac{\text{John ate the apple}}{\text{John ate}} = \frac{\text{John wants to talk to Bill}}{X},$$

X = John wants to talk

A (and B) do not include the verb *want*, but it clearly has to be a member of X.

Clause 4 checks whether or not the element in B that is under inspection is also a member of A. If it is, the program checks whether or not there is a member of C with a matching role. If there is, this element of C is added to D and the next element of B is taken into consideration. Sometimes the hierarchy number of the element will change during the transition from A to B. This possibility is accounted for by clause 5. The same change will then have to take place from C to D. In other words, this rule performs the following proportional analogy on the word level (W1, W2: words; R: role; H: hierarchy number):

$$\frac{\text{W1,R,H1}}{\text{W1,R,H2}} = \frac{\text{W2,R,H1}}{X}, \quad X = \text{W2,R,H2}$$

This rule would apply, for example, to every word in sentence A of the following analogy:

$$\frac{\text{Bill ate the apple}}{\text{John said that Bill ate the apple}} = \frac{\text{Bill talked}}{X},$$

X = John said that Bill talked

When sentence B contains elements that are not included in A (as the words *John* and *said* in the previous example analogy), the same additions should clearly take place on the other side of the equation. Here, clause 6 does the work.

Clause 7 checks whether or not B and A have a common element with a role such that no element with this role can be found in C. If this is the case, this element is not added to D. This kind of a situation would arise in this analogy:

$$\frac{\text{John wants to eat the apple}}{\text{John wants to eat}} = \frac{\text{John talks to Bill}}{X},$$

X = John talks

The verb *want* should clearly not be included in X.

Clause 8 applies when A has an element with the same role as the element of B that is being considered, but the word is not the same. Then, if C also has this element (completely identical with the element in A), this element of B is added to D. In other words:

$$\frac{W1,R,H}{W2,R,H} = \frac{W1,R,H}{X}, \quad X = W2,R,H$$

When all the elements of either sentence B or sentence C have been checked, the analogy has been completed. Clauses 9 and 10 apply in this situation. Sentence D can now be cleaned of the information concerning the roles of the words and of the possible blank elements that have been included. This is accomplished by clauses 86–90.

In order to have an idea of how the program performs the analogical reasoning, let us examine step by step the functioning of the program in solving the analogies in the three "anti-analogical" examples of Section 2.5, B. The first analogy has the sentences (19), (20), and (21) functioning as the input strings A, B and C (respectively) to the parsing component.[3] The parsing component now does its work, giving us the following:

A1:   John (subj,1) ate (v,1) blank (prep,1) an apple (obj,1)

B1:   John (subj,1) ate (v,1)

C1:   John (subj,1) is (cop,1) too stubborn (ap,1) to (pr,1)
        talk (v,1) to (prep,1) Bill (obj,1)

These strings function as input for the analogical reasoning component. The first rule to take effect is that expressed by clause 4: the first element of B1 is also included in A1, and C1 has a member with an equivalent role (that is: subj, 1). Therefore, this element of C1 has to be made the first element of D, and the following strings are given as input to the rules:

A2: John (subj,1) ate (v,1) blank (prep,1) an apple (obj,1)
B2: ate (v,1)
C2: is (cop,1) too stubborn (ap,1) to (pr,1) talk (v,1) to (prep,1) Bill (obj,1)
D2: John (subj,1)

Next, clause 3 notices that the first element of C2 is such that no element with that role (that is: cop,1) can be found in A. Therefore, that element will be added to D2, and we get:

A3: John (subj,1) ate (v,1) blank (prep,1) an apple (obj,1)
B3: ate (v,1)
C3: too stubborn (ap,1) to (pr,1) talk (v,1) to (prep,1) Bill (obj,1)
D3: John (subj,1) is (cop,1)

The next two steps are handled by clause 3 in a similar fashion (and for the same reason, of course), after which we have the following strings:

A4: John (subj,1) ate (v,1) blank (prep,1) an apple (obj,1)
B4: ate (v,1)
C4: talk (v,1) to (prep,1) Bill (obj,1)
D4: John (subj,1) is (cop,1) too stubborn (ap,1) to (pr,1)

Clause 5 now notices that the first element of B4 is also a member of A4, and that an element with a matching role can be found in C4. This element has to be added to D4, thus giving:

A5: John (subj,1) ate (v,1) blank (prep,1) an apple (obj,1)
B5: ø [empty string]
C5: to (prep,1) Bill (obj,1)
D5: John (subj,1) is (cop,1) too stubborn (ap,1) to (pr,1) talk (v,1)

Finally, clause 9 notices that B5 is an empty string, which means that the analogy has been completed. D5 can now be cleaned of the information concerning the roles of the elements, and the following proportional analogy has been shown to be valid:

$$\frac{\text{John ate an apple}}{\text{John ate}} = \frac{\text{John is too stubborn to talk to Bill}}{X},$$

X = John is too stubborn to talk

In the second analogy, i.e. the sentences (31)–(33) of Section 2.5, B, the parsing component gives the following strings:

A6: John (subj,1) slept (v,1)
B6: Where (q,1) did (aux,1) john (subj,1) sleep (v,1)
C6: John (subj,1) said (vs,1) that (comp,1) we (subj,2) have (vc,2) to (pr,2)
get (v,2) off (prep,2) the bus (obj,2)

The first two steps are handled by clause 6; there are no elements with roles $(q,1)$ and $(aux,1)$ in A6. Therefore, those elements are placed in the beginning of D:

A7: John (subj,1) slept (v,1)
B7: john (subj,1) sleep (v,1)
C7: John (subj,1) said (vs,1) that (comp,1) we (subj,2) have (vc,2) to (pr,2)
get (v,2) off (prep,2) the bus (obj,2)
D7: Where (q,1) did (aux,1)

Next, clause 4 adds the next element of C7 to D:

A8: John (subj,1) slept (v,1)
B8: sleep (v,1)
C8: said (vs,1) that (comp,1) we (subj,2) have (vc,2) to (pr,2)
get (v,2) off (prep,2) the bus (obj,2)
D8: Where (q,1) did (aux,1) John (subj,1)

The rest of the analogy is performed by clause 3: since no element of C8 has a role which matches that found in B8, C8 is moved, element by element, to D, and we have the follwing strings:

A9: John (subj,1) slept (v,1)
B9: sleep (v,1)
C9: ∅
D9: Where (q,1) did (aux,1) John (subj,1) say (vs,1) that (comp,1) we (subj,2) have (vc,2) to (pr,2) get (v,2) off (prep,2) the bus (obj,2)

Clause 10 now detects the empty string in C9 and the program proceeds to clean D9 of semantic information. In other words, the program has solved the following analogy:

$$\frac{\text{John slept}}{\text{Where did John sleep?}} = \frac{\text{John said that we have to get off the bus}}{\text{X}}$$

X = Where did John say that we have to get off the bus?

In the analogy complementary to the previous one, i.e. sentences (34)–(36), the analogical reasoning has the following starting point:

> A10: John (subj,1) said (vs,1) that (comp,1) Bill (subj,2) was (v,2) there (adv,2)
>
> B10: Where (q,1) did (aux,1) John (subj,1) say (vs,1) that (comp,1) Bill (subj,2) was (v,2) blank (adv,2)
>
> C10: John (subj,1) said (vs,1) that (comp,1) we (subj,2) have (vc,2) to (pr,2)
> get (v,2) off (prep,2) the bus (obj,2) there (adv,2)

After clause 6 has applied twice, we have:

> A11: John (subj,1) said (vs,1) that (comp,1) Bill (subj,2) was (v,2) there (adv,2)
>
> B11: John (subj,1) say (vs,1) that (comp,1) Bill (subj,2) was (v,2) blank (adv,2)
>
> C11: John (subj,1) said (vs,1) that (comp,1) we (subj,2) have (vc,2) to (pr,2) get (v,2) off (prep,2) the bus (obj,2) there (adv,2)
>
> D11: Where (q,1) did (aux,1)

The next four steps are handled by clause 4: the first four elements of B11 are also members of A11, and C11 has elements with a matching role. Therefore, they are the elements that have to be placed in the beginning of D (in the same order as in B11), after which we have:

> A12: John (subj,1) said (vs,1) that (comp,1) Bill (subj,2) was (v,2) there (adv,2)
>
> B12: was (v,2) blank (adv,2)
>
> C12: have (vc,2) to (pr,2) get (v,2) off (prep,2) the bus (obj,2) there (adv,2)
>
> D12: Where (q,1) did (aux,1) John (subj,1) say (vs,1) that (comp,1) we (subj,2)

After the next five steps, each one of which is handled by either clause 3 or clause 4, we have:

A13: John (subj,1) said (vs,1) that (comp,1) Bill (subj,2) was (v,2) there (adv,2)

B13: blank (adv,2)

C13: there (adv,2)

D13: Where (q,1) did (aux,1) John (subj,1) say (vs,1) that (comp,1) we (subj,2) have (vc,2) to (pr,2) get (v,2) off (prep,2) the bus (obj,2)

Finally, clause 8 notices that the element *there* (*adv,2*) has changed to *blank* (*adv,2*) in the transition from A to B, and that C13 also has the element *there* (*adv,2*). Hence, *blank* (*adv,2*) has to be added to D:

A14: John (subj,1) said (vs,1) that (comp,1) Bill (subj,2) was (v,2) there (adv,2)

B14: ø

C14: there (adv,2)

D14: Where (q,1) did (aux,1) John (subj,1) say (vs,1) that (comp,1) we (subj,2) have (vc,2) to (pr,2) get (v,2) off (prep,2) the bus (obj,2) blank (adv,2)

Now, clause 9 notices that the analogy has been completed. D can now be cleaned of the semantic information and the blank element, and the program has solved the following analogy:

$$\frac{\text{John said that Bill was there}}{\text{Where did John say that Bill was?}} = \frac{\text{John said that we have to get off the bus there}}{X}$$

X = Where did John say that we have to get off the bus?

Finally, the alleged problem for analogy concerning sentences (39)–(41) can be dissolved with e.g. the following analogy:

$$\frac{\text{John is in the house}}{\text{Is John in the house?}} = \frac{\text{The man who is tall is in the room}}{X,}$$

The parsing component gives us the following strings:

A15: John (subj,1) is (cop,1) in (prep,1) the house (loc,1)

B15: Is (cop,1) John (subj,1) in (prep,1) the house (loc,1)

C15: The man (subj,1) who (relp,2) is (cop,2) tall (ap,2) is (cop,1) in (prep,1) the room (loc,1)

The first two steps are performed by clause 4:

A16: John (subj,1) is (cop,1) in (prep,1) the house (loc,1)
B16: in (prep,1) the house (loc,1)
C16: who (relp,2) is (cop,2) tall (ap,2) is (cop,1) in (prep,1) the room (loc,1)
D16: Is (cop,1) the man (subj,1)

Next, clause 3 notices that the first element of C16 has such a role that no elements with that role can be found in A16. For this reason, that element (of C16) has to be added to D16. The same goes for the next two elements after that, and we have:

A17: John (subj,1) is (cop,1) in (prep,1) the house (loc,1)
B17: in (prep,1) the house (loc,1)
C17: is (cop,1) in (prep,1) the room (loc,1)
D17: Is (cop,1) the man (subj,1) who (relp,2) is (cop,2) tall (ap,2)

At this point, clause 2 notices that the first element of C8 is already included in D (as the first element), and the program can proceed to the next element in C:

A18: John (subj,1) is (cop,1) in (prep,1) the house (loc,1)
B18: in (prep,1) the house (loc,1)
C18: in (prep,1) the room (loc,1)
D18: Is (cop,1) the man (subj,1) who (relp,2) is (cop,2) tall (ap,2)

After this, clause 4 adds the remaining part of C (that is, C18) to D, for reasons which should by now be familiar. Next, clause 9 notices that the analogy has been completed, and we get the correct solution to the above analogy:

X = Is the man who is tall in the room?

3.   Summing-up

The input to the program is constituted by the sentences A, B, and C, and the output is whatever sentence replaces X. The input is closely modelled after Chomsky's (1986) original examples, in two senses. First, the input consists of *sentences*, and not of physical stimuli. Second, the input sentences, e.g. the sentences (19), (20), and (21) in the first analogy, are *known to be correct*. Therefore it is a fair assumption that sentences as simple as (23) and (25) are also known to be correct. In other words, if Chomsky has the right to assume that (19) and (20) are known to be correct (whereas e.g. *John ate to* is known to be incorrect), then we have the right to assume that (23) and (25) are known to be correct whereas (24) is known to be incorrect. The same principle applies more generally. If the (in)correctness of some complex expression is known, then the (in)correctness of any simpler expressions (which may be wholly or partly contained in the complex expression) is also known.

We are not engaged in making a language-learning algorithm. Therefore we take not just the correctness, but also the structures of A, B, and C as given; and from this, we compute (the structure of) whatever sentence replaces X. This is in keeping with the standard notion of analogy. E.g. the structure of water flow is simply taken as given, and the analogical inference consists in transferring this structure to the phenomenon of heat (cf. 1.6). Similarly, when the analogical equation *dog* : *dogs* = *cat* : *X* has to be solved in morphology, it is simply taken for granted that the structures (and the meanings) of the words involved are known. It would be unreasonable to claim that one cannot solve this (morphological) equation unless one has first shown how the sounds and the meanings involved in the words *dog, dogs*, and *cat* have emerged. Now, a comparable claim made within syntax would be just as unreasonable.

Analogy is defined as structural similarity, and the required structure is provided by the grammar component of the program. That is, this is the structure needed to explicate our intuitive notion of analogy. It is *not* the structure needed to explicate our intuitive notion of 'grammatical sentence of English', which is to say that we are not engaged in describing the Chomsky-type grammatical competence. Therefore, the grammar component of our program must not be evaluated by comparing it to existing competence grammars. Rather, it must be evaluated according to how well or how badly it contributes to achieving the overall goal of our program, which is – to repeat – the explication of the intuitive notion of analogy. (It is a well-known truth within the philosophy of science that theoretical concepts are justified in this indirect way.) Measured by this standard, our grammar component seems to perform quite well: it produces the analogies we want it to produce and refrains from producing any of the analogies we do not want it to produce. It might even be said that, from the psychological point of view, such grammatical notions are superfluous which do not show up in the description of the processes of sentence production and understanding.

It might seem that it is quite enough to have produced a program that explicitly shows the (analogical) relations of similarity between sentences, i.e. the relations that in standard grammatical descriptions remain merely implicit. However, since we wish to simulate the production of *new* sentences, which happens by replacing the X in an analogical equation, we must ensure that we *infer* the information about the new sentence from what we already know (i.e.

$$R = \frac{\triangle\triangle}{\triangle} \Rightarrow R' = \frac{\bigcirc}{X} \text{, and } X = \bigcirc$$

Figure A1. Solving a geometrical analogy

the three other sentences in the equation and their structural descriptions), instead of circularly *relying upon* this very information from the beginning. Indeed, we do proceed in this non-circular way. Although the grammar, taken as a whole, contains the (structural) information about the new sentences, in each particular grammar *application* (combined with an application of the analogy component) the information about the new sentence is not present as such in the starting point, but is deduced from it. Our analogical program handles in this non-circular way cases which, according to Chomsky, *cannot* be handled by analogy.

Our examples have been about syntax (supplemented by some semantic information). It would be quite easy, however, to produce morphological analogies by the same program. For instance, the rule of English plural-formation is expressed straightforwardly by analogies of the following form:

$$\frac{N_i}{N_i\text{-}s} = \frac{N_j}{X}, \quad X = N_j\text{-}s$$

Because we consider analogy as a pervasive capacity of the (human) mind, it is vitally important that the program applies without any modifications to non-linguistic material as well. Consider the example from Kedar-Cabelli (1988: 73–75) that is reproduced here in Figure A1.

R = 'remove the small triangle from inside the large triangle' and R' = 'remove the small object from inside the large object'. The (analogical) generalization consists in moving from R to R', and this process is performed by our program when the relevant information has been presented in the correct form. The following formulation is one possibility:

$$\frac{\begin{array}{c}\text{triangle (figure,1) contain (state,1)}\\\text{triangle (figure,2)}\end{array}}{\begin{array}{c}\text{circle (figure,1) contain (state,1)}\\\text{circle (figure,2)}\end{array}} = \frac{\text{triangle (figure,1)}}{X}$$

There still remain a few residual points to be clarified. We are concerned with the production of new sentences, rather than with language-acquisition. It is clear, however, that these two aspects cannot be kept neatly apart. When the pairs of sentences constituting the analogy are of equal complexity, we seem to have to do with the production of new sentences:

$$\frac{\text{John ate an apple}}{\text{John ate}} = \frac{\text{John drank milk}}{\text{John drank}}$$

But when the sentence pair on the right-hand side of the analogy is more complex than the one on the left-hand side, the process in question might also be viewed as being part of language-acquisition:

$$\frac{\text{John ate an apple}}{\text{John ate}} = \frac{\text{John is too stubborn to talk to Bill}}{\text{John is too stubborn to talk}}$$

This ambiguity of interpretation is only natural. Although it is advisable to distinguish, in principle, between acquiring a competence and putting it into use, it is impossible in practice to draw a hard-and-fast line between the two.

Although we are ostensibly dealing with production, i.e. solving the X in an equation, the discussion of our example (29) shows that the program may also be interpreted as explicating the process of understanding as well. This too is only natural because producing A normally entails the ability to understand A, just as understanding A normally entails the ability to produce A.

Finally, there remains the question of psychological reality (cf. 1.7). In the work on artificial intelligence it has been customary to distinguish between 'specification' and 'implementation' as two distinct desiderata of psychological research. Descriptions aiming at specification intend to replicate merely the content of certain mental processes: starting from a given input they produce the desired output, but the manner of doing so remains irrelevant. By contrast, descriptions aiming at implementation intend also to replicate the actual way in which mental processes derive the output from the input. It is clear that descriptions of the former type make a weaker claim to psychological reality than those of the latter type.

The analytical distinctions involved here may be summed up in the following way. Descriptions of linguistic structure, e.g. those executed within the generative tradition, intend to answer a question *What?* Descriptions of (psycho)linguistic processes intend to answer a question *How?*, or more precisely *What-and-How?* Processual descriptions aiming at specification intend to answer the question *How, in the abstract?* Processual descriptions aiming at implementation intend to answer the question *How, as a matter of fact?* (cf. Itkonen 1983a: 287–298; and here the end of 3.3).

It is well known that none of the current computer languages qualifies as a faithful reflection of mental representations and/or processes. Therefore implementation, in the sense defined above, is not yet a realistic goal for artificial-intelligence work. This applies also to our program, which is written in PROLOG. Yet it is also clear that computer programs have played and continue to play an indispensable role in furthering our understanding of mental processes. If we want to be explicit in the description of human cognition, there is simply no alternative to using computer programs.

Of course, our program applies to a small number of the syntactic (-cum-semantic) structures of English. However, there seem to be no principled obstacles to enlarging this number indefinitely.

Notes

Chapter 1

1. In the context of tool-making, the validity of the principle 'function determines form' can be taken for granted. In the evolutionary context, by contrast, it is subject to a few caveats. The sense in which 'explanation-by-function' must be taken is illustrated by the following passage:

> In North America the black bear was seen by Hearne swimming for hours with widely open mouth, thus catching, like a whale, insects in the water. Even in so extreme a case like this, if the supply of insects were constant, and if better adapted competitors did not already exist in the country, I can see no difficulty in a race of bears being rendered, by natural selection, more and more aquatic in their structure and habits, till a creature was produced as monstrous as a whale.
>
> (Darwin (1998 [1859]: 141–142)

It must also be remembered that, in the evolutionary theory, there is nothing fixed about functions: "an organ originally constructed for one purpose...may be converted into one for a wholly different purpose" (op. cit.: 146).

2. By mistake, the authors actually speak of "two triangles" and "two squares".

3. The so-called critical linguistics considers the reificatory capacity of language/thought as a distortion of reality; see e.g. Kress and Hodge (1979: 20–26). Without this capacity, however, it would take hours to formulate any claims about the nature of culture, for instance; and science, of course, would become impossible.

4. Referring to a source from 1840, Koestler mentions (p. 122) the possibility that the following account may not be genuine. In his view, however, it "has an authentic ring".

5. But notice that reliable quantifiction of non-physical concepts has turned out to be quite difficult; and the existence of conflicting intuitions about the nature of many-valued implication clearly argues against the Platonist interpretation of many-valued logic.

6. Because there is a conceptual connection between analogy and generalization, it is not quite easy to understand a position which wants to have one without the other. Such a position has been endorsed by generative linguistics. The central desideratum of generative descriptions has always been *significant generalization*. For instance, in the heyday of classical transformational grammar it was assumed that postulating a deep structure common to several surface structures was the right way to make significant generalizations about the latter. More recent examples can be added. Thus, analogy is central to generative linguistics.

And yet, generative linguistics has always been anxious to deny the very existence of analogy and continues even today to do so; cf. 2.2.

7. Of course, 'square root' is not (directly) observable.

8. To be sure, abduction *can* produce also observational laws; but this is not the typical case.

9. Incidentally, this formulation – that there may be two or more (theoretical) analyses of *one* and the *same* data – shows that there must be a distinction between 'observable' and 'theoretical', even if the viability of any such distinction has been denied by thinkers as dissimilar as Popper and Kuhn. Indeed, the 'theory-laden' nature of observation and/or experimentation has become an article of faith in popularized philosophy of science. It has been debunked e.g. by Hacking (1983:Ch. 9–10), with the aid of several examples taken from the history of science.

10. Newton-Smith (1981:210–212) assumes that even 'refined' common sense is capable of inductive generalizations only, whereas science is characterized by the abductive leap to the (supposedly) best explanation. It seems fair to say that Newton-Smith has an uncommonly low opinion of common sense.

11. The qualification '*primary* source' implies that it is by no means the case that all metaphors can be traced back to image-schemata. This is true of e.g. 'Time is money'. Just like other institutional (and normative) entities, money – although the source of the metaphor – just cannot be reduced to our bodily experiences; hence it is not a primary source.

12. Incidentally, Heidegger's philosophy is to a large extent based on deliberate German-language puns of this kind. Thus, for him, existence – when it is not just 'being there' (*da sein*) – has much to do with (human) *hands*: it is either being 'in front of hands' (*vorhanden sein*) or 'to(wards) hands' (*zuhanden sein*).

13. This is emphatically confirmed by Gentner et al. (2001b), and is evident already from the title of their article: 'Metaphor is like analogy'.

14. It might be retorted that the X-bar syntax postulates an identical structure for the four lexical categories and even for the sentence resulting from the projection of these categories. But the results of X-bar-type projections are compositional, i.e. they are not blends; and, second, nobody has ever claimed that the *meanings* of lexical units and/or phrases – like those of *drinks* and *beer*, or those of *Bill* and *drinks-beer* – are structurally the same. It may also be added that the X-bar syntax seems to be a case of aprioristic *over*-use of analogy, or analogy running amuck (cf. 2.5, B).

15. The idea of non-psychological or 'autonomous' research was later both explicated and put into practice in Kac (1992).

16. Within psychological research, in turn, the non-axiomatic human mind must of course be described as 'axiomatically', i.e. as economically and elegantly, as possible.

17. This view was confirmed in discussion by Paul Kiparsky in Los Angeles, June 1982.

18. In the same context Hockett also mentions the following significant fact that has been overlooked much too often:

> Sooner or later, the child produces utterances he has not previously heard from someone else. At first these newly coined utterances will be rejected by those about

him … But by the time the child has achieved linguistic adulthood, his speech no longer contains *errors* [although, as mentioned just before, "*lapses* there may still be"]; for he has become an authority on the language, a person whose ways of speaking *determine* what is and what is not an error.

Over the years, I have had reason to insist on this change of perspective again and again.

19. It is a different matter that the *correct* morpho-syntactic structure can be seen as a result of linguistic changes each of which is *rationally* explainable. Similarly, if the correct morpho-syntactic structure stands in an iconic relation to its referent, this can be seen as a *rational* solution to the problem of representation.

20. Interestingly, generativism insists on viewing the whole (= sentence) as analogous to its parts (= phrases). This is a good example of an excessive use of analogy (cf. Note 14).

Chapter 2

1. Katz (1981:43–44, Notes 30 and 44) points out that a few such passages of Chomsky's 1955 dissertation as contradict his later views have been either altered in the 1975 version or expurgated from it. For some reason, this passage is not among them.

2. Thus, it turns out that, the appearances notwithstanding, Chomsky's way of practicing linguistics has not changed in the least since those early days when he made the following comment: "I am interested in explaining intuition. If you cannot accept this as the purpose of linguistic study, I am lost" (Chomsky 1964a: 168). Notice that what is being criticized here is not autonomous linguistics as such – in this respect I disagree with Derwing (1980) – but autonomous linguistics masquerading as psychological research (cf. 1.7). The method- ologically unique status of 'competence' has been perfectly captured by Kiparsky's (1975) claim that transformational grammar qua psychological theory cannot be falsified even in principle, but can only be verified or shown to be true:

> Psychological experiments involving production and perception are unfortunately going to constitute evidence in one direction only – a positive result will confirm the psychological reality of the tested grammatical rule, but a negative one will not disconfirm it. This is an unfortunate but normal situation in many sciences. When we dig and find a skull we conclude that the place was inhabited, but when we fail to turn up anything we don't know for sure that the place was uninhabited.
>
> (p. 203)

3. This example, which is one of those employed by Chomsky, was much discussed in the electronic mail-box LINGUIST LIST in 1998. Notice, incidentally, that it *is* possible to assign to the last sentence a (secondary) interpretation which makes it acceptable. Just imagine an artist saying the following: "If I see a house red, I paint it red."

4. The Arab grammarians realized perfectly well that this is a metaphorical way of speaking. In reality, the relation between verbs and nouns is a conventional one, and any causation that occurs here is due to speakers who choose to follow the convention when they speak.

5. It is remarkable that this theoretical analysis was felt to be necessary although it changes the meaning of the original construction: 'the servant-boy' → 'a servant-boy'.

6. The situation is complicated by the fact that, in addition to a typical intransitive sentence like *qāma Zaydun* ('Zayd stood up'), there also exists an explicitly topical construction with an inverse word order, viz. *Zaydun qāma* ('As for Zayd, he stood up'); cf. Itkonen (1991: 136–139).

7. Maybe Chomsky would like to argue that (24) *should* be a correct sentence; that it is not, would then speak against analogy. But this is like arguing that analogy fails because *bit* and *but*, although formally similar, belong to different word-classes.

8. Languages with free word order are here partial exceptions but even they conform to the regularity exhibited by the following examples.

9. The sentence *My wife was planning a party* has been offered as a putative counter-example. But notice that before you utter this sentences you do 'see' both your wife and the party, even if you do not see them in the same 'mental space'.

10. Even their universal validity may well be questioned; cf. e.g. Jelinek and Demers (1994), Sasse (2001), Itkonen (2001).

11. In Tamil there are four 'genders' in the singular (= masculine, feminine, honorific, nonrational) and two in the plural (= rational vs. nonrational).

12. In this respect, Western linguistics has returned to its roots. While Plato does not unam-biguously decide for the *phusei* or language-as-picture view in his *Kratylos*, he nevertheless envisages it as an option to be taken seriously; and he reaches the conclusion that although language may not be *phusei*, at least it *should* be. See Itkonen (1991: 166–174, esp. p. 171).

13. In the domain of typology and universals research, many important analogies remain to be explored. For instance, an analogy between a set of the infant's preverbal concepts and a set of ubiquitous linguistic structures could explain why the latter are such as they are in fact.

Chapter 3

1. Sometimes 'cognitive' and 'neurological' are treated as synonymous, which is nonsense. Claiming that 'cognitive' and 'neurological' are non-synonymous, and that the former should be reduced to the latter, may not be nonsense, but it is certainly far from clear how, exactly, this type of reduction should be carried out. – Around 1900 Wilhelm Wundt defended the view, rediscovered by Searle (1992), that there is only consciousness and physi-ology, but no mental unconscious. Paul disagreed in the fourth edition (= 1909) of his book and postulated the unconscious on the analogy of the conscious:

> Nach Wundt existiert nichts Geistiges ausserhalb des Bewusstseins; was aufhört, bewusst zu sein, hinterlässt nur eine physische Nachwirkung. Durch diese müsste demnach der unleugbare Zusammenhang zwischen früheren und späteren Be-wusstseinsakten vermittelt sein; ... Es bleibt also doch nichts übrig, wenn man überhaupt einen Zusammenhang zwischen früheren und späteren Bewusst-

seinsvorgängen erkennen will, als auf [unbewusstem] psychischem Gebiete zu bleiben und sich die Vermittlung nach *Analogie der Bewusstseinsvorgänge* zu denken.   (Paul 1975 [1880]:25; emphasis added)
(According to Wundt, there is nothing mental outside of consciousness; whatever ceases to be conscious leaves only a physical trace. It is supposed to mediate the undeniable connection between earlier and later acts of consciousness.... If a connection is admitted to exist between earlier and later acts consciousness, the only viable option is to remain in the domain of the [unconscious] mental and conceive of the mediation *on the analogy of acts of consciousness.*)

Writing in 1915, Freud was more explicit on the analogy between the conscious and the unconscious:

All these conscious acts ... fall into demonstrable connection if we interpolate between them the unconscious acts which we have inferred. ... But here we encounter the objection that these latent recollections can no longer be described as psychical, but that they correspond to residues of somatic processes ... [T]his objection is based on the equation ... of what is conscious with what is mental. This equation is either a *petitio principii* ...; or else it is a matter of convention, of nomenclature. ... [A]ll the categories which we employ to describe conscious mental acts, such as ideas, purposes, resolutions and so on, can be applied to [the latent states of mental life]. ... [T]hat other people, too, possess a consciousness is an inference which we draw by analogy ... Psychoanalysis demands nothing more than that we should apply this process of inference to ourselves also ....
                                                                                (Freud 1984: 168–171)

2. Of course, in a more careful formulation 'emitting' too should be couched in conceptualist terminology.

3. Hintikka (1973) presents a version of logic which, from the formal point of view, is an exact imitation of Lorenzen's and Lorenz's dialogical or game-theoretical logic. Hintikka admits this, but he thinks (p. 80–81, also 108–109) that there is nevertheless an "absolutely crucial" difference between the two versions, based on the fact that Lorenzen's and Lorenz's games are purely formal, 'indoor' games concerned with logical truth only, whereas his own 'outdoor' games are played in constant reference to the external reality. This is a curious misunderstanding. In the dialogical conception, the definition of logical truth is *based on* the definition of empirical truth; and empirical truth is defined by finding out whether or not certain objects of the external reality possess certain properties and relations.

Chapter 4

1. This idea of 'plenitude', created by Plato and further developed by Aristotle, assumes a hierarchy constituted by *continuous* gradations. Thus, Lovejoy (1936:57) notes that in the history of Western philosophy Aristotle has "encouraged two diametrically opposed sorts of conscious or unconscious logic", namely "the habit of thinking in discrete, well-defined class-concepts and that of thinking in terms of continuity, of infinitely delicate shadings-off of everything into something else". In linguistic writings of cognitivist and/or functional orientation, it has become customary to picture Aristotle as the arch-foe of 'family resemblances' and 'prototypes'. Now we see that this picture is false. It is a curious fact that those who most vociferously claim to have renounced any type of black-and-white thinking apply precisely this type of thinking to how they write history (and to much else, besides).

2. What seems curious in retrospect, is that Galileo failed to see the analogy between the motion of a cannon-ball and the motion of a planet. The reason for this oversight was his adherence to the traditional view that the (inertial) motion of the planets had to be circular.

3. Both Hobbes and Hume failed to see the merely metaphorical nature of their commitment to the Newtonian ideal because in reality they both remained securely within the confines of philosophy. They formulated general statements about the human rationality, but they did not care to test those statements by trying to find out whether they were confirmed or disconfirmed, during a definite time-interval, by the *real, observable* actions of a definite group of persons; for discussion, cf. Itkonen (1983a: 6.2.3).

4. There is a meta-analogy between Hegel (1807) and Zlatev (2001) insofar as the latter too postulates three analogous historical developments, namely those of the mankind (= phylogeny), men (= ontogeny), and robots (= robotogeny).

5. As such, this analogy had of course been invented much earlier; cf. e.g. Hobbes (1968 [1651]: 81): "why may we not say, that all *Automata* (Engines that move themselves by springs and wheeles as doth a watch) have an artificiall life?"

6. It may be added that, as reported by Hodges (1983: Ch. 3), Turing himself tried already in 1937 to construct actual 'logic-machines' similar to those defined by Shannon (1938).

7. It is revealing that Kuhn (1970: 75) mentions Koestler only in a short and disparaging note.

8. Once again, no distinction is made between material and structural similarity.

9. Gardner (1985: 220) offers an instructive analogy (sic) from the field of linguistics: "The point is not whether syntax can be looked at separately – of course, any component can be examined in isolation. The question is, rather, what is to be gained or lost by adhering rigorously to such a research program."

10. As several commentators have pointed out, the title of Popper's book, in the English translation, refers to the very notion whose existence Popper vehemently denies: the logic of scientific discovery.

Appendix

1. Actually, the program *could* run with just one rule of this form. However, this would require a more complex coding of semantic information that would be far more difficult to handle (mostly due to the way PROLOG executes the programs). Including two separate clauses of this form is a way of keeping the program *as a whole* as simple as possible.

2. If this seems *ad hoc* to someone, we can assure the reader that the same thing can be accomplished by making a distinction between superordinate and subordinate categorizations (in the case of the verb 'eat' these would amount to *verb* and *transitive verb*, respectively). This would result in taking *four* parameters into account in the analogical reasoning process, and would therefore increase the size of the program unnecessarily. It is clear, however, that this would not affect the main point of this program.

3. The input format to the program is the following: transform([john,eat,an,apple], [john,eat],[john, is,too,stubborn,to,talk,to,bill]). In other words, the words are entered in lower case, separated by commas, and in the form in which they occur in the lexicon. For clarity of presentation, we have presented the strings in a form closer to the sentential form.

References

Anderson, John R. (1978). *The architecture of cognition*. Cambridge, MA: Harvard University Press.

Anderson, John M. (1992). *Linguistic representation: Structural analogy and stratification*. Berlin: Mouton de Gruyter.

Anderson, Stephen R. (1992). *A-morphous morphology*. Cambridge: Cambridge University Press.

Anttila, Raimo (1977a). *Analogy*. The Hague: Mouton de Gruyter.

Anttila, Raimo (1977b). Dynamic fields and linguistic structure: A proposal for a Gestalt linguistics. *Die Sprache, 23*(1), 1–10.

Anttila, Raimo (1989 [1972]). *Historical and comparative linguistics*. Amsterdam: Benjamins.

Anttila, Raimo (1991). Field theory of meaning and semantic change. *L.A.U.D. Series A. Paper No. 301*. University of Duisburg.

Aristotle (1941). *The basic works of Aristotle*. Edited and with an introduction by Richard McKeon. New York: Random House.

Asher, R. E. (1985). *Tamil*. London: Croom Helm.

Bailey, Charles-James N. (1973). *Variation and linguistic theory*. Arlington: Center for Applied Linguistics.

Baker, Mark C. (1995). *The polysynthesis parameter*. Oxford: Oxford University Press.

Baker, G. P. & P. M. S. Hacker (1984). *Language, sense, and nonsense*. Oxford: Blackwell.

Bates, Elisabeth & Brian MacWhinney (1989). Functionalism and the competition model. In Brian MacWhinney & Elizabeth Bates (Eds.), *The crosslinguistic study of sentence processing* (pp. 3–73). Cambridge: Cambridge University Press.

Bauer, Laurie (1992). *Introducing linguistic morphology*. Edinburgh: Edinburgh University Press.

Becker, Thomas (1990). *Analogie und morphologische Theorie*. München: Wilhelm Fink Verlag.

Berger, Peter L. & Thomas Luckmann (1966). *The social construction of reality*. Garden City, NY: Doubleday.

Berwick, Robert & Amy Weinberg (1984). *The grammatical basis of linguistic performance*. Cambridge, MA: MIT Press.

Bickerton, Derek (1973). On the nature of a creole continuum. *Language, 49*, 641–649.

Black, Max (1962). *Models and metaphors*. Ithaca: Cornell University Press.

Blackmore, Susan (1999). *The meme machine*. Oxford: Oxford University Press.

Bloom, Paul, Mary A. Peterson, Lynn Nadel, & Merril F. Garrett (Eds.). (1996). *Language and space*. Cambridge, MA: The MIT Press.

Bloomfield, Leonard (1933). *Language*. New York: Holt.

Boas, Franz (1964 [1911]). Linguistics and ethnology. In Dell Hymes (Ed.), *Language in culture and society: A reader in linguistics and anthropology* (pp. 15–26). New York: Harper & Row.

Boden, Margaret (1990). *The creative mind*. London: Weidenfeld & Nicolson.

Bohas, G., D. E. Guillaume, & D. E. Kouloughli (1990). *The Arabic linguistic tradition*. London: Routledge.

Böhme, Gernot (Ed.). (1976). *Protophysik*. Frankfurt a/M: Suhrkamp.

Bolinger, Dwight (1961). Syntactic blends and other matters. *Language, 37,* 366–381.

Bolinger, Dwight (1968). *Aspects of language*. New York: Harcourt.

Bolinger, Dwight (1975). Meaning and form: Some fallacies of asemantic grammar. In Koerner (Ed.), 3–35.

Botha, Rudolf P. (1971). *Methodological aspects of transformational generative phonology*. The Hague: Mouton.

Boudon, Raymond (1974). *The logic of sociological explanation*. Penguin Books.

Butts, Robert E. & James Robert Brown (Eds.). (1989). *Constructivism and science: Essays in recent German philosophy*. Dordrecht: Kluwer.

Bybee, Joan (1985). *Morphology*. Amsterdam: Benjamins.

Carnie, Andrew & Eithne Guilfoyle (2000). Introduction. In Andrew Carnie & Eithne Guilfoyle (Eds.), *The syntax of verb initial languages* (pp. 3–11). Oxford: Oxford University Press.

Chomsky, Noam (1957). *Syntactic structures*. The Hague: Mouton.

Chomsky, Noam (1964a [1958]). A transformational approach to syntax. In Fodor & Katz (Eds.), 211–245.

Chomsky, Noam (1964b). Current issues in linguistic theory. In Fodor & Katz (Eds.), 501–618.

Chomsky, Noam (1965). *Aspects of the theory of syntax*. Cambridge, MA: The MIT Press.

Chomsky, Noam (1966). *Topics in the theory of generative grammar*. The Hague: Mouton.

Chomsky, Noam (1967). Recent contributions to the theory of innate ideas. *Synthese, 17,* 2–11.

Chomsky, Noam (1968). *Language and mind*. New York: Harcourt.

Chomsky, Noam (1972). *Problems of knowledge and freedom*. London: Fontana/Collins.

Chomsky, Noam (1975a [1955]). *The logical structure of linguistic theory*. New York: The Plenum Press.

Chomsky, Noam (1975b). *Reflections on language*. New York: Pantheon.

Chomsky, Noam (1980). *Rules and representations*. New York: Columbia University Press.

Chomsky, Noam (1986). *Knowledge of language*. New York: Praeger.

Chomsky, Noam (1992). *A minimalist program for linguistic theory*. MIT Working Papers in Linguistics.

Clark, Herbert (1996). *Using language*. Cambridge: Cambridge University Press.

Clark, Ronald W. (1973). *Einstein: The life and times*. New York: World Publishing Company.

Cohen, David & Jessica R. Wirth (Eds.). (1975). *Testing linguistic hypotheses*. Washington: Hemisphere Publishing Corporation.

Cohen, Jonathan L. (1981). Can human irrationality be experimentally demonstrated? *The Behavioral and Brain Sciences, 4,* 317–370.

Cohen, Jonathan L. (1986). *The dialogue of reason: An analysis of analytical philosophy.* Oxford: Clarendon Press.

Crain, Stephen & Mineharu Nakayama (1987). Structure dependence in grammar formation. *Language, 63*, 522–543.

Croft, William (1990). *Typology and universals.* Cambridge: Cambridge University Press.

Croft, William (1991). *Syntactic categories and grammatical relations.* Chicago: The University of Chicago Press.

Croft, William (1998). Linguistic evidence and mental representations. *Cognitive Linguistics, 9*(2), 151–173.

Croft, William (2000). *Explaining language change: An evolutionary approach.* London: Longman.

Croft, William (2003). *Typology and universals* (2nd ed.). Cambridge: Cambridge University Press.

Darwin, Charles (1998 [1859]). The *origin of species.* Chatham, Kent: Wordsworth.

Davies, Martin (1994). *Musical meaning and expression.* Ithaca: Cornell University Press.

Dawkins, Richard (1976). *The selfish gene.* Oxford: Oxford University Press.

Deane, Paul (1991). Limits to attention: A cognitive account of island phenomena. *Cognitive Linguistics, 2*(1), 1–61.

DeLancey, Scott (1997). What an innatist argument should look like. *SKY Journal of Linguistics, 10*, 7–24.

DeLancey, Scott (2000). The universal basis of case. *Logos and Language, 1*(2), 1–15.

Dennet, Daniel C. (1991). *Consciousness explained.* Boston: Little & Brown.

Derbyshire, Desmond C. & Geoffrey K. Pullum (Eds.). (1990). *Handbook of Amazonian languages,* Vol. 2. Berlin/New York: Mouton de Gruyter.

Derwing, Bruce (1973). *Transformational grammar as a theory of language acquisition.* Cambridge: Cambridge University Press.

Derwing, Bruce (1980). Against autonomous linguistics. In Perry (Ed.), 163–189.

Derwing, Bruce L. & Peter R. Harris (1975). What is a generative grammar? In Koerner (Ed.), 297–314.

Dickinson, Anthony (1988). Intentionality in animal conditioning. In Weiskrantz (Ed.), 305–325.

Douglas, Mary (1986). *How institutions think.* Syracuse, NY: Syracuse University Press.

Dretske, Fred. I. (1974). Explanation in linguistics. In David Cohen (Ed.), *Explaining linguistic phenomena* (pp. 21–41). Washington, DC: Hemisphere Publishing Corporation.

Dunbar, Robin (1998). Theory of mind and the evolution of language. In Hurford et al. (Eds.), 92–110.

Emmorey, Karen (1996). The confluence of space and language in signed languages. In Bloom et al. (Eds.), 171–209.

Engberg-Pedersen, Elisabeth (1996). Iconicity and arbitrariness. In Elisabeth Engberg-Pedersen, Michael Fortescue, Peter Harder, Lars Helftoft, & Lisbeth Falster Jakobsen (Eds.), *Content, expression and structure* (pp. 453–468). Amsterdam: Benjamins.

Evans, Jonathan St. B. T. (1982). *The psychology of deductive reasoning.* London: Routledge.

Everett, Dan & Barbara Kern (1997). *Wari'.* London: Routledge.

Fauconnier, Gilles (1997). *Mappings in thought and language.* Cambridge: Cambridge University Press.

Fauconnier, Gilles (2001). Conceptual blending and analogy. In Gentner et al. (Eds.), 255–285.

Fauconnier, Gilles & Mark Turner (1996). Blending as a central process of grammar. In Adele Goldberg (Ed.), *Conceptual structure, discourse, and language* (pp. 113–130). Stanford: CSLI.

Fodor, Jerry (1975). *The language of thought.* New York: Crowell.

Fodor, Jerry (1983). *The modularity of mind.* Cambridge, MA: The MIT Press.

Fodor, Jerry & Jerrold Katz (Eds.). (1964). *The structure of linguistic theory.* Englewood Cliffs, NJ: Prentice-Hall.

Fodor, Jerry & Ernest Lepore (1992). *Holism: A shopper's guide.* Oxford: Blackwell.

Foley, William A. (1986). *The Papuan languages of New Guinea.* Cambridge: Cambridge University Press.

Foley, William A. (1997). Polysynthesis and complex verb formation: The case of applicatives in Yimas. In Alex Alsina, Joan Bresnan, & Peter Sells (Eds.), *Complex predicates* (pp. 355–395). Stanford: CSLI.

Follesdal, Dagfinn & Risto Hilpinen (1971). Deontic logic: An introduction. In Hilpinen (Ed.), 1–35.

Fortescue, Michael (1984). *West Greenlandic.* London: Croom Helm.

Freud, Sigmund (1984 [1915]). The unconscious. In *On metapsychology: The theory of psychoanalysis* (pp. 167–210). The Pelican Freud Library, Vol. 11. Penguin Books.

Freudenthal, Hans (1960). *Lincos: Design of a language for cosmic intercourse.* Amsterdam: North-Holland.

Fung Yu-lan (1953). *A history of Chinese philosophy,* Vol. II. London: Allen & Unwin.

Gabelentz, Georg von der (1891). Die *Sprachwissenschaft: ihre Aufgaben, Methoden und bisherigen Ergebnisse.* Leipzig: T.O. Weigel Nachfolger.

Gardner, Howard (1985). *The mind's new science.* New York: Basic Books.

Gentner, Dedre (1989). The mechanisms of analogical learning. In Vosniadou & Ortony (Eds.), 199–241.

Gentner, Dedre, Keith J. Holyoak, & Boicho N. Kokinov (Eds.). (2001a). *The analogical mind.* Cambridge, MA: The MIT Press.

Gentner, Dedre, Brian Bowdle, Philip Wolff, & Consuelo Boronat (2001b). Metaphor is like analogy. In Gentner et al. (Eds.), 199–253.

Gibbs, Raymond & Teenie Matlock (1999). Psycholinguistics and mental representations. *Cognitive Linguistics, 10*(3), 263–269.

Givón, Talmy (1979). *On understanding grammar.* New York: Academic Press.

Givón, Talmy (1990). *Syntax,* Vol. II. Amsterdam: Benjamins.

Givón, Talmy (1995). *Functionalism and grammar.* Amsterdam: Benjamins.

Givón, Talmy (2002). *Bio-linguistics.* Amsterdam: Benjamins.

Goldberg, Adele (1995). *Constructions.* Chicago: University of Chicago Press.

Goldstein, E. Bruce (1989). *Sensation and perception* (3rd ed.). Pacific Grove: Brooks/Cole.

Greimas, A. J. (1983). *Du sens II.* Paris: Seuil.

Grmek, Mirko Drazen, Robert S. Cohen, & Guido Cimino (Eds.). (1981). *On scientific discovery.* Dordrecht: Reidel.

Hacking, Ian (1983). *Representing and intervening.* Cambridge: Cambridge University Press.

Haiman, John (Ed.). (1985). *Iconicity in syntax.* Amsterdam: Benjamins.

Haiman, John (1998). *Talk is cheap.* Oxford: Oxford University Press.

Haley, Michael C. (1999). Metaphor, mind, and space: What Peirce can offer Lakoff. In Michael Shapiro (Ed.), *The Peirce seminar papers,* Vol. IV (pp. 417–440). New York: Berghahn Books.

Hallpike, C. R. (1979). *The foundations of primitive thought.* Oxford: Clarendon Press.

Hampshire, Stuart (1996). Introduction. In Benedict de Spinoza, *Ethics* (pp. vii–xvi). Penguin Books.

Hanson, N. R. (1965). *Patterns of discovery.* London: Cambridge University Press.

Harris, Zellig (1966 [1946]). From morpheme to utterance. In Joos (Ed.), 142–153.

Harris, Zellig (1961 [1949]). *Structural linguistics* (5th ed.). Chicago: The University of Chicago Press.

Harris, Alice & Lyle Campbell (1995). *Historical syntax in cross-linguistic perspective.* Cambridge: Cambridge University Press.

Haspelmath, Martin (1999). Optimality and diachronic adaptation. *Zeitschrift für Sprachwissenschaft, 18,* 180–205.

Haspelmath, Martin, Ekkehard König, Wulf Oesterreicher, & Wolfgang Raible (Eds.). (2001). *Language typology and language universals,* Vol. 1/1. Berlin: de Gruyter.

Haukioja, Jussi (2000). Grammaticality, response-dependency, and the ontology of linguistic objects. *Nordic Journal of Linguistics, 23,* 3–25.

Hegel, G. F. W. (1975 [1807]). *Phänomenologie des Geistes.* Frankfurt a/M: Suhrkamp.

Heine, Bernd (1997). *Foundations of cognitive grammar.* Chicago: The University of Chicago Press.

Heine, Bernd, Ulrike Claudi, & Friederieke Hünnemeyer (1991). *Grammaticalization: A conceptual framework.* Chicago: The University of Chicago Press.

Helman, David (Ed.). (1988). *Analogical reasoning.* Dordrecht: Kluwer.

Hempel, Carl G. (1965). *Aspects of scientific explanation.* New York: The Free press.

Henle, M. (1962). On the relation between logic and thinking. *Psychological Review, 69,* 366–378.

Herrnstein, R. J. & E. G. Boring (Eds.). (1965). *A source book in the history of psychology.* Cambridge, MA: Harvard University Press.

Hesse, Mary (1963). *Models and analogies in science.* London: Sheed & Ward.

Hilpinen, Risto (Ed.). (1971). *Deontic logic: Introductory and systematic readings.* Dordrecht: Reidel.

Hintikka, Jaakko (1973). *Logic, language-games, and information.* Oxford: Clarendon Press.

Hjelmslev, Louis (1963 [1943]). *Prolegomena to a theory of language* (2nd ed.). Madison: University of Wisconsin Press.

Hobbes, Thomas (1968 [1651]). *Leviathan.* Penguin Books.

Hockett, Charles F. (1966 [1948]). A note on 'structure'. In Joos (Ed.), 279–280.

Hockett, Charles F. (1966 [1954]). Two models of grammatical description. In Joos (Ed.), 386–399.

Hockett, Charles F. 1966. *The state of the art.* The Hague: Mouton.

Hodges, Andrew (1983). *Alan Turing: The enigma.* New York: Simon and Schuster.

Hoekstra, Teun & Jan Kooij (1988). The innateness hypothesis. In John A. Hawkins (Ed.), *Explaining language universals* (pp. 31–55). Oxford: Blackwell.

Hofstadter, Douglas (1995). *Fluid concepts and creative analogies.* Penguin Books.

Hofstadter, Douglas (2001). Epilogue: analogy as the core of cognition. In Gentner et al. (Eds.), 499–538.

Holland, John, Keith Holyoak, Richard Nisbett, & Paul Thagard (1986). *Induction: Processes of inference, learning, and discovery*. Cambridge, MA: The MIT Press.

Holyoak, Keith & Paul Thagard (1995). *Mental leaps: Analogy in creative thought*. Cambridge, MA: The MIT Press.

Holyoak, Keith, Dedre Gentner & Boicho N. Kokinov (2001). Introduction. In Gentner et al. (Eds.), 1–19.

Hookway, Christopher (1985). *Peirce*. London: Routledge

Hopper, Paul (1998). The paradigm at the end of the universe. In Anna Giacalone Ramat & Paul Hopper (Eds.), *The limits of grammaticalization* (pp. 147–158). Amsterdam: Benjamins.

Hopper, Paul & Elisabeth Traugott (1993). *Grammaticalization*. Cambridge: Cambridge University Press.

Householder, Fred W. (1971). *Linguistic speculations*. Cambridge: Cambridge University Press.

Householder, Fred W. (1977). Innateness and improvisability. In Robert J. Di Pietro & Edward L. Blansitt (Eds.), *The third LACUS forum* (pp. 479–485). Columbia, SC: Hornbeam Press.

Howard, Jonathan (1982). *Darwin*. Oxford: Oxford University Press.

Hudson, Richard (1999). Review of Ray Jackendoff. *The architecture of the language faculty*. *Cognitive linguistics, 10*(3), 255–261.

Hume, David (1962 [1739]). *A treatise of human nature, Book I*. Glasgow: Fontana/Collins.

Hume, David (1972 [1739–1740]). *A treatise of human nature, Book II*. Glasgow: Fontana/Collins.

Hurford, James R., Michael Studdert-Kennedy, & Chris Knight (Eds.). (1998). *Approaches to the evolution of language*. Cambridge: Cambridge University Press.

Inhelder, Barbara & Jean Piaget (1958). *The growth of logical thinking from childhood to adolescence*. New York: Basic Books.

Itkonen, Esa (1968). Zur Charakterisierung der Glossematik. *Neuphilologische Mitteilungen LXIX*(3), 452–471.

Itkonen, Esa (1970). An epistemological approach to linguistic semantics. *Ajatus: The Yearbook of the Philosophical Society of Finland, 32*, 96–142.

Itkonen, Esa (1974). *Linguistics and metascience*. Studia Philosophica Turkuensia 2.

Itkonen, Esa (1975). Transformational grammar and the philosophy of science. In Koerner (Ed.), 381–445.

Itkonen, Esa (1978). *Grammatical theory and metascience: A critical inquiry into the philosophical and methodological foundations of 'autonomous' linguistics*. Amsterdam: Benjamins.

Itkonen, Esa (1980). Qualitative vs. quantitative analysis in linguistics. In Perry (Ed.), 334–366.

Itkonen, Esa (1981). Review article on Lass (1980). *Language, 57*, 688–697.

Itkonen, Esa (1982a). Short-term and long-term teleology in linguistic change. In J. Peter Maher, Allan R. Bomhard, & E. F. K. Koerner (Eds.), *Papers from the 3rd international conference on historical linguistics* (pp. 85–118). Amsterdam: Benjamins.

Itkonen, Esa (1982b). Change of language as a prototype for change of linguistics. In Anders Ahlqvist (Ed.), *Papers from the 5th international conference on historical linguistics* (pp. 142–148). Amsterdam: Benjamins.

Itkonen, Esa (1983a). *Causality in linguistic theory: A critical inquiry into the methodological and philosophical foundations of 'non-autonomous' linguistics.* London: Croom Helm.

Itkonen, Esa (1983b). Review of Katz (1981). *Lingua, 60,* 238–244.

Itkonen, Esa (1984). On the 'rationalist' conception of linguistic change. *Diachronica, 1,* 203–216.

Itkonen, Esa (1988). Is there a difference between Hegel's dialectical method and the explicative method of analytical philosophy? In Hans Heinz Holz & Juha Manninen (Eds.), *Vom Werden des Wissens – Philosophie, Wissenschaft, Dialektik* (pp. 245–250). Köln: Pahl-Rugenstein.

Itkonen, Esa (1991). *Universal history of linguistics: India, China, Arabia, Europe.* Amsterdam: Benjamins.

Itkonen, Esa (1994). Iconicity, analogy, and universal grammar. *Journal of Pragmatics, 22,* 37–53.

Itkonen, Esa (1996). Concerning the generative paradigm. *Journal of Pragmatics, 25,* 471–501.

Itkonen, Esa (1997). The social ontology of linguistic meaning. *SKY Journal of Linguistics, 10,* 49–80.

Itkonen, Esa (2000). Tolkaappiyam: The basic work of the ancient Tamil language and culture. *SKY Journal of Linguistics, 13,* 75–99.

Itkonen, Esa (2001). Concerning the universality of the noun vs. verb distinction. *SKY Journal of Linguistics, 14,* 75–86.

Itkonen, Esa (2003a). *Methods of formalization beside and inside both autonomous and non-autonomous linguistics.* University of Turku: Publications in General Linguistics 6.

Itkonen, Esa (2003b). *What is language? A study in the philosophy of linguistics.* University of Turku: Publications in General Linguistics 8.

Itkonen, Esa (2004). Typological explanation and iconicity. *Logos and Language, V*(1), 21–33.

Itkonen, Esa & Jussi Haukioja (1997). A rehabilitation of analogy in syntax (and elsewhere). In András Kertész (Ed.), *Metalinguistik im Wandel* (pp. 131–177). Frankfurt a/M: Peter Lang.

Jackendoff, Ray (1983). *Semantics and cognition.* Cambridge, MA: The MIT Press.

Jackendoff, Ray (1987). *Consciousness and the computational mind.* Cambridge, MA: The MIT Press.

Jackendoff, Ray (1992). *Languages of the mind.* Cambridge, MA: The MIT Press.

Jackendoff, Ray (1994). *Patterns in the mind.* New York: Basic Books.

Jackendoff, Ray (1996). The architecture of the linguistic-spatial interface. In Bloom et al. (Eds.), 1–30.

James, William (1948 [1892]). *Psychology.* New York: Holt.

Jelinek, Eloise & Richard Demers (1994). Predicates and pronominal arguments in Straits Salish. *Language, 70,* 697–763.

Jespersen, Otto (1922). *Language: Its nature, development, and origin.* Oxford: Oxford University Press.

Jespersen, Otto (1965 [1924]). *Philosophy of grammar.* London: Allen & Unwin.

Joas, Hans (1996). *Die Kreativität des Handelns.* Frankfurt a/M: Suhrkamp.

Johnson, Mark (1987). *The body in the mind.* Chicago: The University of Chicago Press.

Johnson-Laird, P. N. (1983). *Mental models.* Cambridge: Cambridge University Press.

Johnson-Laird, P. N. (1996). Space to think. In Bloom et al. (Eds.), 437–462.

Johnson-Laird, P. N. & Ruth M. J. Byrne (1991). *Deduction.* Hillsdale, NJ: Lawrence Erlbaum.

Joos, Martin (Ed.). (1966). *Readings* in *linguistics* (4th ed.). Chicago: The University of Chicago Press.

Kac, Michael B. (1974). Autonomous linguistics and psycholinguistics. *Minnesota Working Papers in Linguistics and Philosophy of Language, 2,* 42–47.

Kac, Michael B. (1992). *Grammars and grammaticality.* Amsterdam: Benjamins.

Kamlah, Wilhelm & Paul Lorenzen (1967). *Logische Propädeutik.* Mannheim: Bibliographisches Institut.

Kant, Immanuel (1956 [1787]). *Kritik der reinen Vernunft.* Hamburg: Felix Meiner.

Katz, Jerrold (1981). *Language and other abstract objects.* Oxford: Blackwell.

Kedar-Cabelli, Smadar (1988). Analogy – from a unified perspective. In Helman (Ed.), 65–103.

Kennedy, John M. (1993). *Drawing and the blind: Pictures to touch.* New Haven: Yale University Press.

Kenny, Anthony (1973). *Wittgenstein.* Penguin Books.

Kiparsky, Paul (1974). Remarks on analogical change. In John M. Anderson & Charles Jones (Eds.), *Historical linguistics II* (pp. 257–275). Amsterdam: North-Holland.

Kiparsky, Paul (1975). What are phonological theories about? In Cohen & Wirth (Eds.), 187–209.

Kiparsky, Paul (1992). Analogy. In William Bright (Ed.), *International encyclopedia of linguistics,* Vol. 1 (pp. 56–61). Oxford: Oxford University Press.

Kiparsky, Paul (1993). Paninian linguistics. In R. E. Asher (Ed.), *The encyclopedia of language and linguistics,* Vol. 1(6) (pp. 2918–2923). Oxford: Pergamon Press.

Kirby, Simon (1999). *Function, selection, and innateness: The emergence of language universals.* Oxford: Oxford University Press.

Klima, Edward S. & Ursula Bellugi (1976). Poetry and song in a language without sound. *Cognition, 4,* 45–97.

Kneale, William & Martha Kneale (1975 [1962]). *The development of logic.* Oxford: Oxford University Press.

Koerner, E. F. K. (Ed.). (1975). *The transformational-generative paradigm and modern linguistic theory.* Amsterdam: Benjamins.

Koestler, Arthur (1964 [1959]). *The sleepwalkers.* Penguin Books.

Koestler, Arthur (1967 [1964]). *The act of creation.* New York: Dell.

Kosslyn, Stephen (1980). *Image and mind.* Cambridge, MA: Harvard University Press.

Koyré, Alexandre (1971 [1933]). *Mystiques, spirituels, alchimistes du XVIe siècle allmand.* Paris: Gallimard.

Kress, Gunther & Robert Hodge (1979). *Language as ideology.* London: Routledge.

Kuhn, Thomas S. (1970). *The structure of scientific revolutions* (2nd ed.). Chicago: University of Chicago Press.

Lakoff, George (1987). *Women, fire, and dangerous things*. Chicago: University of Chicago Press.

Lamb, D. & S. M. Easton (1984). *Multiple discovery*. Trowbridge: Avebury.

Langacker, Ronald (1991a). *Foundations of cognitive grammar*, Vol. II: *Descriptive applications*. Stanford, CA: Stanford University Press.

Langacker, Ronald (1991b). *Concept, image, and symbol*. Berlin: Mouton de Gruyter.

Langer, Suzanne (1942). *Philosophy in a new key*. Cambridge, MA: Harvard University Press.

Langhade, Jacques (1985). Grammaire, logique, études linguistiques chez Al-Fārābī. In Cornelis Versteegh, Konrad Koerner, & Hans-J. Niederehe (Eds.), *The history of linguistics in the Near East* (pp. 129–141). Amsterdam: Benjamins.

Lapidge, Michael (1978). Stoic cosmology. In John M. Rist (Ed.), *Stoic philosophy* (pp. 161–185). Cambridge: Cambridge University Press.

Lass, Roger (1980). *On explaining language change*. Cambridge: Cambridge University Press.

Lass, Roger (1997). *Historical linguistics and language change*. Cambridge: Cambridge University Press.

Laudan, Larry (1981). *Science and hypothesis*. Dordrecht: Reidel.

Lavie, René Joseph (2003). *Le locuteur analogique ou la grammaire mise à sa place*. Université de Paris 10 Nanterre, Thèse doctorale.

Lees, Robert (1960). Multiply ambiguous adjectival constructions in English. *Language, 36*, 207–221.

Lepage, Yves (2003). *De l'analogie rendant compte de la commutation en linguistique*. Université de Grenoble, Mémoire d'habilitation à diriger les recherches. http://www.slt.atr.co.jp/~lepage/pdf/dhdryl.pdf.gz

Levelt, Willem J. M. (1989). *Speaking: From intention to articulation*. Cambridge, MA: The MIT Press.

Levinson, Stephen C. (2003). *Space in language and in cognition: Explorations in cognitive diversity*. Cambridge: Cambridge University.

Lévi-Strauss, Claude (1966). *The savage mind*. Chicago: University of Chicago Press.

Lightfoot, David (1982). *The language lottery*. Cambridge, MA: The MIT Press.

Linell, Per (1979). *Psychological reality in phonology*. London: Cambridge University Press.

Lloyd, G. E. R. (1966). *Polarity and analogy: Two types of argumentation in early Greek thought*. Cambridge: Cambridge University Press.

Locke, John L. (1998). Social sound-making as a precursor of language. In Hurford et al. (Eds.), 190–201.

Lorenz, Kuno (1989). Rules versus theorems. In Butts & Brown (Eds.), 59–76.

Lorenzen, Paul (1969). *Methodisches Denken*. Frankfurt a/M: Suhrkamp.

Lorenzen, Paul & Kuno Lorenz (1978). *Dialogische Logik*. Darmstadt: Wissenschaftliche Buchgesellschaft.

Lovejoy, Arthur O. (1936). *The great chain of being*. Cambridge, MA: Harvard University Press.

Lukács, Georg (1973 [1948]). *Der junge Hegel*. Frankfurt a/M: Suhrkamp.

Manktelow, K. I. & D. E. Over (1990). *Inference and understanding*. London: Routledge.

Marr, David (1982). *Vision*. San Fransisco: Freeman.

Matthews, Peter H. (1972). *Inflectional morphology*. Cambridge: Cambridge University Press.

McGinn, Colin (1989). *Mental content*. Oxford: Blackwell.

Meier, R. P. (1987). Elicited imitation of verb agreement in American Sign Language: Iconically or morphologically determined? *Journal of Memory and Language, 26*, 362–376.

Meillet, Antoine (1958 [1912]). L'évolution des formes grammaticales. In Antoine Meillet, *Linguistique historique and linguistique générale* (pp. 130–148). Paris: Champion.

Minsky, Marvin (1967). *Computation*. Cambridge, MA: The MIT Press.

Mithun, Marianne (1988). The grammaticization of coordination. In John Haiman & Sandra A. Thompson (Eds.), *Clause combining in grammar and discourse* (pp. 331–359). Amsterdam: Benjamins.

Mithun, Marianne (1991). The role of motivation in the emergence of grammatical categories: The grammaticization of subjects. In Elisabeth Traugott & Bernd Heine (Eds.), *Approaches to Grammaticalization*, Vol. II. (pp. 159–184). Amsterdam: Benjamins.

Moessel, Ernst (1926). *Die Proportion in Antike und Mittelalter*. München: Beck.

Münxelhaus, Barbara (1976). *Pythagoras musicus*. Bonn / Bad Godesberg: Verlag für systematische Musikwissenschaft.

Nagel, Ernest (1961). *The structure of science*. New York: Harcourt.

Needham, Rodney (1967). Right and left in Nyoro symbolic classification. *Africa, 37*(4), 423–451.

Neisser, Ulric (1976). *Cognition and reality*. San Fransisco: Freeman.

Neuendorff, Hartmut (1973). *Der Begriff des Interesses*. Frankfurt a/M: Suhrkamp.

Newton-Smith, W. H. (1981). *The rationality of science*. London: Routledge.

Nuyts, Jan (1992). *Aspects of a cognitive-pragmatic theory of language*. Amsterdam: Benjamins.

Nuyts, Jan (2001). *Epistemic modality, language, and conceptualization*. Amsterdam: Benjamins.

Ouhalla, Jamal (1994). *Introducing transformational grammar*. London: Edward Arnold.

Owens, Jonathan (1988). *The foundations of grammar: An introduction to medieval Arabic grammatical theory*. Amsterdam: Benjamins.

Palmer, Gary (1996). *Towards a theory of cultural linguistics*. Austin: University of Texas Press.

Pandit, G. L. (1983). *The structure and growth of scientific knowledge*. Dordrecht: Reidel.

Paul, Hermann (1975 [1880]). *Prinzipien der Sprachgeschichte*. Tübingen: Niemeyer.

Payne, Doris L. & Thomas Payne (1990). Yagua. In Derbyshire & Pullum (Eds.), 249–474.

Pera, Marcello (1981). Inductive method and scientific discovery. In Grmek et al. (Eds.), 141–165.

Perrot, D. V. (1957). *Swahili*. Hodder & Stoughton.

Perry, Thomas A. (Ed.). (1980). *Evidence and argumentation in linguistics*. Berlin: de Gruyter.

Pinker, Stephen (1994). *The language instinct*. New York: Morrow.

Pintzuk, Susan, George Tsoulas, & Anthony Warner (2000). Syntactic change: Theory and method. In Susan Pintzuk, George Tsoulas, & Anthony Warner (Eds.), *Diachronic syntax* (pp. 1–22). Oxford: Oxford University Press.

Plato (1963). *The collected dialogues*. Edited by Edith Hamilton & Huntington Cairns. Princeton, NJ: Princeton University Press.

Polya, G. (1973 [1945]). *How to solve it*. Princeton, NJ: Princeton University Press.

Popper, Karl (1957). *The poverty of historicism.* London: Routledge.

Popper, Karl (1965 [1934]). *The logic of scientific discovery.* New York: Harper & Row.

Popper, Karl (1972). *Objective knowledge.* Oxford: Clarendon Press.

Postal, Paul M. (1968). Epilogue. In Roderick A. Jacobs & Peter S Rosenbaum, *English transformational grammar* (pp. 267–289). Waltham, MA: Blaisdell.

Prosch, Harry (1964). *The genesis of twentieth century philosophy.* New York: Doubleday.

Przywara, Erich (1995). *Analogia entis.* Milano: Vita e Pensiero, Pubblicazioni dell'Università Cattolica.

Pylyshyn, Zenon (1984). *Cognition and computation.* Cambridge, MA: The MIT Press.

Raible, Wolfgang (2001). Linguistics and genetics: Systematic parallels. In Haspelmath et al. (Eds.), 103–122.

Rice, Keren (2000). *Morpheme order and semantic scope.* Cambridge: Cambridge University Press.

Ringen, Jon D. (1975). Linguistic facts. In Cohen & Wirth (Eds.), 1–41. Reprinted in Perry (Ed.), 97–132.

Rubinstein, Robert A., Charles Laughlin, Jr., & John McManus (1984). *Science as cognitive process: Toward an empirical philosophy of science.* Philadelphia: University of Pennsylvania Press.

Sacks, Oliver (1990). *Seeing voices: A journey into the world of the deaf.* Berkeley: University of the California Press.

Sampson, Geoffrey (1980). *Making sense.* Oxford: Oxford University Press.

Sandra, Dominiek (1998). What linguists can and can't tell you about the human mind: A reply to Croft. *Cognitive Linguistics, 9*(4), 361–378.

Sandra, Dominiek & Sally Rice (1995). Network analyses of prepositional meaning: Mirroring whose mind – the linguist's or the language user's? *Cognitive Linguistics, 6*(1), 89–130.

Sapir, Edward (1921). *Language.* New York: Harcourt, Brace & World.

Sasse, Hans-Jürgen (1988). Der Irokesische Sprachtyp. *Zeitschrift für Sprachwissenschaft, 7*, 173–213.

Sasse, Hans-Jürgen (2001). Scales between nouniness and verbiness. In Haspelmath et al. (Eds.), 495–509.

Saussure, Ferdinand de (1962 [1916]). *Cours de linguistique générale.* Paris: Payot.

Schaller, Susan (1991). *A man without words.* New York: Summit Books.

Searle, John (1992). *The rediscovery of the mind.* Cambridge, MA: The MIT Press.

Seung, T. K. (1982). *Structuralism and hermeneutics.* New York: Columbia University Press.

Shannon, Claude E. (1938). A symbolic analysis of switching and relay circuits. *Transactions of the American Institute of Electrical Engineers, 57*, 1–11.

Shelley, Cameron (2003). *Multiple analogies in science and philosophy.* Amsterdam: Benjamins.

Simon, Herbert A. (1979 [1976]). From substantive to procedural rationality. In Frank Hahn & Martin Hollis (Eds.), *Philosophy and economic theory* (pp. 65–86). Oxford: Oxford University Press.

Sinha, Chris & Tania Kuteva (1995). Distributed spatial semantics. *Nordic Journal of Linguistics, 18*, 167–199.

Skousen, Royal (1989). *Analogical modeling of language.* Dordrecht: Kluwer.

Skousen, Royal, Deryle Lonsdale, & Dilworth B. Parkinson (Eds.). (2002). *Analogical modeling: An exemplar-based approach to language*. Amsterdam: Benjamins.

Slagle, Uhlan V. (1975). On the nature of language and mind. In Koerner (Ed.), 329–347.

Spelke, Elisabeth S. (1988). The origins of physical knowledge. In Weiskrantz (Ed.), 168–184.

Staal, Frits (1989). *Rules without meaning*. New York: Peter Lang.

Stegmüller, Wolfgang (1974). *Probleme und Resultate der Wissenschaftstheorie und Analytischen Philosophie*, Vol. I: *Wissenschaftliche Erklärung und Begründung* (2nd ed.). Berlin: Springer.

Steinberg, Danny D. (1970). Psychological aspects of Chomsky's competence – performance distinction. *Working Papers in Linguistics*, 2(2), 180–192. Honolulu: University of Hawaii, Department of Linguistics.

Stokoe, William C. (1978 [1960]). *Sign language structure*. Silver Spring, MD: Linstok Press.

Suppes, Patrick (1981). The limits of rationality. *Grazer Philosophische Studien*, 12(13), 85–101.

Talmy, Leonard (2000). *Towards a cognitive semantics*, Vol. I. Cambridge, MA: The MIT Press.

Thomas, Downing (1995). *Music and the origins of language*. Cambridge: Cambridge University Press.

Tomlin, Russell (1986). *Basic word order*. London: Croom Helm.

Toulmin, Stephen (1974). *Human understanding: The collective use and evolution of concepts*. Princeton, NJ: Princeton University Press.

Trubetzkoy, N. S. (1958 [1939]). *Grundzüge der Phonologie*. Göttingen: Vandenhoeck & Ruprecht.

Tuggy, David (1999). Linguistic evidence for polysemy in the mind: A response to William Croft and Dominiek Sandra. *Cognitive linguistics*, 10(4), 343–368.

Turing, Alan (1965 [1936]). On computable numbers, with an application to the Entscheidungsproblem. In Martin Davis (Ed.), *The undecidable* (pp. 115–151). New York: Raven Press.

Tye, Michael (1993). *The imagery debate*. Cambridge, MA: The MIT Press.

van der Zee, Emile & Urpo Nikanne (2000). Introducing cognitive interfaces and constraints on linking cognitive information. In Emile van der Zee & Urpo Nikanne (Eds.), *Cognitive interfaces* (pp. 1–17). Oxford: Oxford University Press.

Varro, Marcus Terentius (1938). *De lingua Latina I–II. Varro on the Latin language*. With an English translation by Roland G. Kent. London: Heinemann.

Vennemann, Theo (1972). Analogy in generative grammar: The origin of word order. In Luigi Heilman (Ed.), *Proceedings of the 11th international congress of linguists*, Vol. 2 (pp. 79–83). Bologna: Il Mulino.

von Wright, Georg Henrik (1951). Deontic logic. *Mind*, 60, 1–15.

von Wright, Georg Henrik (1963). *Varieties of goodness*. London: Routledge.

Vosniadou, Stella & Andrew Ortony (Eds.). (1989). *Similarity and analogical reasoning*. Cambridge: Cambridge University Press.

Wallin, Nils (1991). *Biomusicology*. Stuyvesant, NY: Pendragon Press.

Wason, P. C. & Philip Johnson-Laird (1972). *Psychology of reasoning*. Cambridge, MA: Harvard University Press.

Weiskrantz, L. (Ed.). (1988). *Thought without language*. Oxford: Clarendon Press.

Whitney, William Dwight (1979 [1875]). *The life and growth of language.* New York: Dover.

Wilcox, Sherman (2001). William C. Stokoe (July 21, 1919 – April 4, 2000). *Semiotica,* *133*(1/4), 1–14.

Winograd, Terry (1983). *Language as a cognitive process.* Vol. I: *Syntax.* Reading, MA: Addison-Wesley.

Wittgenstein, Ludwig (1958 [1953]). *Philosophical investigations.* Oxford: Blackwell.

Zaehner, R. C. (1962). *Hinduism.* Oxford: Oxford University Press.

Zinov'ev, A. A. (1963). *Philosophical problems of many-valued logic.* Dordrecht: Reidel.

Zlatev, Jordan (1997). *Situated embodiment.* Department of Linguistics, Stockholm University.

Zlatev, Jordan (2001). The epigenesis of meaning in human beings, and possibly in robots. *Minds and Machines, 11*(2), 155–195.

Zukav, Gary (1980 [1979]). *The dancing wu li masters: An overview of the new physics.* Fontana Paperbacks.

Zvelebil, Kamil (1973). *The smile of Murugan: On Tamil literature of South India.* Leiden: E.J. Brill.

Name index

Subject index

In the series *Human Cognitive Processing* the following titles have been published thus far or are scheduled for publication: